Church Watch

CHURCH WATCH

Christianity in the Countryside

Leslie J. Francis

First published in Great Britain 1996
Society for Promoting Christian Knowledge
Holy Trinity Church
Marylebone Road
London NW1 4DU

British Library Cataloguing-in-Publication Data
A catalogue record of this book is available from
the British Library

ISBN 0-281-04951-3

Typeset by Datix International Limited, Bungay, Suffolk
Printed in Great Britain by
The Cromwell Press, Melksham, Wiltshire

CONTENTS

PREFACE

BISHOP PETER NOTT described my previous book, *Rural Anglicanism*, published in 1985, as a 'doom-laden document' which did 'a great deal of harm to the morale of the country church'. Bishop Eric Wild wrote that 'this is not only an irritating book, it is a bad and ignorant book'. Archbishop Robert Runcie described it as a 'timely and devastating study' which is 'scrupulously researched . . . and buttressed by vivid case studies as well as statistics'. For some reason, my study caused controversy as well as interest.

Church Watch: Christianity in the Countryside re-examines the evidence ten years later, and does so over a wider canvas. Last time I studied only the Church of England; this time I am exploring the Roman Catholic Church, the Free Churches and some sects as well. Last time I studied only one diocese; this time I am concentrating on ten different geographical areas in very different parts of England. Last time I tried to blend three research perspectives; this time I am focusing on one method in depth. Once again my aim is to see the rural churches as they really are, and I know already that some of my reviewers would have preferred me to look in another direction.

The most controversial part of *Rural Anglicanism* was the two chapters based on the social science method of participant observation. A team of ordinands, whom I had specially trained for the purpose, visited every Anglican church within one rural deanery and attended every service held in those churches on the third Sunday in May.

An unexpected consequence of the book was the invitation from a number of theological colleges, ministry training courses and rural pastoral studies units to repeat the process in different places and with different groups of students. The exercise was recognized to be a valuable learning experience as well as a valid research exercise. In this way the *church watch* project was born.

vi

This book draws on the findings of ten detailed church watch weekends. The complete details of four church watch weekends are presented in chapters 10 through 13, which describe church life in the four different types of countryside: urban shadow, accessible, less accessible and remote or marginal. The other six church watch weekends are employed selectively in chapters 3 through 9, which describe the seven types of community: hamlets, small villages, medium villages, large villages, suburban villages, market towns and resorts.

Each church watch experience involved the same painstaking process. Each was based on the area defined by one Anglican rural deanery, but included all the denominations active within that deanery. Well in advance of the weekend I obtained both current and historic Ordnance Survey maps in order to locate the redundant churches and closed chapels as well as the places of worship in current use. Then I personally visited each site in order to check the accuracy of the information. On the Friday and Saturday of the church watch weekend, I trained the team of visitors in the techniques of participant observation and sent them out to visit every place of worship and church or chapel building, whether redundant or still in use. On the Saturday evening and throughout the Sunday the team of visitors set out to attend every service in church, chapel or makeshift worship centre.

The size of the task varied from deanery to deanery. In marginal deanery there were nineteen services on the church watch weekend. In urban shadow deanery there were forty-nine active churches and seventy-three services on the church watch weekend. Some of the team of visitors attended three services each on the Sunday.

After the services had been attended I studied the observation schedules completed by the visitors and listened to their personal tales. I have also tried to attend as many services as possible in these deaneries myself, both on the church watch weekends and on subsequent Sundays. The accounts given have been carefully checked for accuracy, authenticity and fairness. It is not surprising, therefore, that the study has taken eight years to complete, alongside a full research agenda concerned with other aspects of church-related research.

The strength of participant observation as a method of research is that it offers to hold up a mirror to the rural church.

As a method it is neither critical nor judgemental. My hope is that those who hold responsibility for shaping the future of the rural church will have the confidence to look into this mirror and the insight to deal creatively with what they see. The data provided by participant observation remain partial. They need to be set alongside data provided by other objective methods of social research and interpreted within informed theological perspectives.

None of this research would have been possible without the encouragement, interest and active participation of the theological colleges, ministry training courses and pastoral studies units, with their staff and students. I owe them all a great debt of gratitude. I am also grateful to the clergy and lay people who have welcomed us into their services.

My personal gratitude is also extended to the parishioners of Great Bradley, Little Wratting, North Cerney and Bagendon who originally shaped my concern for rural ministry when I served as their non-stipendiary parish priest; to Anne Rees and Diane Drayson who have helped shape the manuscript; and to the Principal and Governors of Trinity College, Carmarthen, who have actively fostered the development of research in empirical theology.

Leslie J. Francis
Trinity College, Carmarthen
and University of Wales, Lampeter

I

INTRODUCTION

Overview

THIS BOOK SETS out to observe the rural church in all its variety. It looks at the variety of different denominations present in a variety of different rural contexts. The method employed is the social science perspective of participant observation. This is a slow and painstaking way of assembling detail. As a consequence the fieldwork has taken eight years to complete. What is provided is a collage of snapshots of rural churches taken during the late 1980s and the early 1990s. Throughout, the emphasis is on *displaying* the strengths and weaknesses of rural chapels and rural churches, rather than on *judging* their performance. My interest in displaying such detail arises from one basic concern. I believe that plans and policies devised for the future of the rural church need to be grounded in a realistic and objective awareness of how things really are in the present. The data provided by this study have clear implications for discussions concerned with such issues as ministry, maintenance, mission, buildings, liturgy, worship, church music, preaching, clergy training, lay leadership, Sunday schools, children's work, baptism policy, folk religion and secularization.

Defining 'Rural'

Lewis Carroll's Humpty Dumpty had a way with words: Humpty Dumpty made words mean precisely what he wanted them to mean. Alice found that this made conversation difficult at times.[1]

Certainly, Humpty Dumpty could have a field day with the word 'rural'.

What is obvious from the literature is that there is no generally agreed consensus about what defines the word 'rural'. What is equally obvious from extended familiarity with rural areas is that the word is properly used in different senses in different contexts. For example, rural commuter areas of Sussex differ fundamentally from rural industrial areas of County Durham and rural farming communities of the Welsh border.

However, when the church comes to discuss its concern with its life, witness and mission in rural areas, it is helpful to have at least some level of agreement as to what is within the area of discussion. Alice would find this useful, even if Humpty Dumpty might resist the limitations imposed by agreeing to a working definition.

Since Anthony Russell has done much to set the church's agenda on rural debate, I propose in this study to follow his example of opting for a definition based on community size. Anthony Russell argued that for the purpose of his study:

> the rural population may be defined as those who live in market towns and villages up to 10,000, of which there are approximately 13,000 such settlements in England and Wales, in which very nearly 20% of the population live.[2]

The areas and communities selected for study in the present book also come within this definition.

The analytic framework indicated by the chapter structure of the present book sets out to examine the churches' presence in areas of less than 10,000 inhabitants by means of two different systems. The first system, employed in chapters 3 through 9, is based on my own distinction between different *types of communities*; the second system, employed in chapters 10 through 13, is based on Anthony Russell's distinction between different *types of countryside*. Both systems are somewhat arbitrary and the choice of just these two systems does not imply that together they are able to make all the distinctions necessary for a thorough analysis of the rural church. Any single study is inevitably limited in the focus and scope which it is possible to concentrate into one volume. It is for other researchers to demonstrate the limitations of these two systems by illustrating the power of other competing analytic systems.

Types of Countryside

Anthony Russell has attempted to distinguish between different types of countryside. In some of his earlier statements[3] he identified three types of English countryside 'on a continuum moving out from urban areas'. Subsequently, he has refined his position to distinguish between 'four countrysides in England which form concentric rings around the principal metropolitan areas'.

In his two publications, *The Country Parish*[4] and *Christian Unity in the Village*,[5] Anthony Russell defined these four country-sides as *urban shadow countryside, accessible countryside, less accessible countryside* and *remote or marginal countryside*:

> *Urban shadow countryside* can be found in the immediate vicinity of urban areas. In this countryside, commuters tend to be predominant, and the villages often have the feel of a discontinuous suburb. The farming community, though present, is not particularly evident, and, because of the proximity of an urban centre, the facilities and services in the village are often minimal.
>
> *Accessible countryside* frequently has better facilities as the urban centre is at a great distance. Commuters and the retired live in considerable numbers in these villages, but the farming community and the local resident group are more evident. By definition, communications to the nearest metropolitan centres, either by rail or by car, are good.
>
> *Less accessible countryside* (sometimes defined as that area beyond a travelling distance of one hour from a metropolitan centre) is characterized, in some areas, by de-population. Commuters are less evident, though there are significant numbers of retired people in such villages. The farming and local resident community is much more evident than in the previous two types, but services and facilities are seriously affected by the spiral of decline in village life.
>
> In *remote or marginal countryside*, the local resident community and the farmers form a majority of the year-round population, although there are some retired people. Second homes and occasional holiday residents play an important role in many

areas. Services and facilities in the remoter countryside have been seriously contracted in recent decades.

This definition has also become incorporated into the General Synod's Green Paper, *A Rural Strategy for the Church of England: A Proposal for an Archbishops' Commission on Rural Areas.*[6]

As yet there has been little attempt to set Anthony Russell's definitions to work empirically. The Second Hereford Rural Consultation attempted to do so in 1986 and found difficulties:

> But the experience of the Consultation also suggests that the mixture of different kinds of 'rural' is highly complex and that the idea of 'concentric rings around the principal metropolitan areas' does not ring true outside commuter country.[7]

The Second Hereford Rural Consultation took evidence from the Rural Dean of Abbeydore on the Welsh border. He tested out the four categories of countryside on his own deanery. He reports that:

> It needs to be stressed that there is really no such thing as rural life if by that phrase we mean a stereotype or amalgam of assorted averages. Even the comment about four countrysides is open to misunderstanding. I tried fitting the parishes in the deanery into them and ended up very confused. I agree that there needs to be some sort of key of understanding to which people can refer, but its approximate quality and the fact that categories are not necessarily mutually exclusive needs to be stressed very strongly.

A similar point was made by Andrew Bowden in his study *Ministry in the Countryside.*[8] Bowden argued that:

> As everyone knows, two villages which are geographically only a mile apart can be sociologically very different. This is why Russell's division of villages in 'urban shadow', 'accessible', 'less accessible' and 'remote or marginal' (depending on how far they are from a large conurbation), while conceptually very helpful, is ultimately inadequate.

In spite of such difficulties, I have found Anthony Russell's definitions of considerable practical value. They work in general terms and for whole areas, more satisfactorily than in specific terms and for individual places. For this reason, when I use Anthony Russell's theory to provide the analytic framework for chapters 10 through 13, I base my study on whole deanery units, rather than on specific parishes. These four chapters look in turn at one example each of a rural deanery in the urban shadow countryside, the accessible countryside, the less accessible countryside and the remote or marginal countryside. In other words, each of these four chapters presents the overview of a *whole* church watch weekend. While one deanery is insufficient to form the basis for generalization, it does, however, enable a great deal of descriptive detail to be conveyed.

Types of Communities

In my earlier study, *Rural Anglicanism*,[9] I suggested that, from the churches' point of view, the size of the rural community is crucial in determining the nature of the life of the local church. My statistical analyses suggested that church life does not grow in a linear fashion according to population size, but in a stepwise series of progressions.

I attempted to account for this phenomenon in terms of a simple theory of thresholds and saturation points. I suggested that the size of the community actually helps to determine what the local church is able to offer, and what the local church actually offers helps to determine the number of people with whom it makes regular contact. On this account, the population figure needs to pass beyond certain thresholds before the rural church is able to develop certain new aspects of church life. On the other hand, worshipping communities reach saturation points through which they are unable to grow unless they can develop certain new aspects of church life.

In order to illustrate this theory of thresholds and saturation points, I compared the statistical performance of units with populations between 600 and 1,500 with units of populations between 1,500 and 2,500. The fact of the matter is that often very little difference is found in the number of people who come to church in parishes of 700 or 1,400, but once the population figure of 1,500 is reached new possibilities for growth emerge. In my earlier book I argued as follows:

The problem, then, is to understand why it is that there is a failure for church contact to grow in relationship to population growth between the 600 and the 1,500 mark. It seems to be the case that benefices below a population of 1,500 are restricted in the range of facilities which the church can offer. There are insufficient church members to allow the church to develop the full kind of life that facilitates growth. For example, the number and range of services is restricted; there may be insufficient people to support a church choir, house groups, youth groups, and so on. At the same time, the narrow range of facilities actually provided by the church becomes easily saturated and unable to expand to draw in new people. Benefices of this size seem to be caught between the need to stimulate fresh church involvement and the lack of a sufficiently large pool of committed parishioners to make the work successful.[10]

Developing this theory further in the present study, I now distinguish between seven different kinds of unit in which the dynamics and potential of church life may look rather different. I describe these units as *hamlets, small villages, medium villages, large villages, suburban villages, market towns* and *resorts*.

It is this analytic framework which I adopt for chapters 3 through 9. Each of these chapters is able to look in depth at a few examples of church life within one of these specific kinds of communities. In other words, each of these seven chapters presents a detailed picture of a few communities drawn from *several* church watch weekends. Again, the number of examples chosen is insufficient to form the basis for generalization; it does, however, enable a great deal of descriptive detail to be conveyed.

Types of Research

My aim in this book is to profile the rural church against two different analyses of how rural areas may differ one from another. The first analysis is based on my own distinction between seven types of communities. The second analysis is based on Anthony Russell's distinction between four types of countryside.

There are a number of different tools available to the social scientist by which the data needed for such analyses could be generated. In my previous book, *Rural Anglicanism*, I employed three of these tools: historical statistics, questionnaire surveys and participant observation. Each of these tools has its own peculiar strengths and weaknesses. The problem of combining all three tools in one study is that none of the tools can be exploited to its full potential in view of restrictions imposed by space and time. The present study, therefore, is based on the use of one technique: participant observation. Participant observation was selected as the most useful tool for the particular task in hand. In chapter 2 I describe and justify the selection of this technique. I am also planning a further book about different aspects of the rural church based on the use of questionnaire survey techniques. It is important to use the right tool for the right job. It is equally important not to overclaim for what can be achieved by any one tool, or to criticize a method for not achieving what it does not claim to achieve.

The real strength of participant observation is that it facilitates a thorough and in-depth portrait of the rural church and enables detail to be captured which would elude the other research methods. In the present study such detail includes the mapping of redundant churches and closed chapels as well as those buildings which are still in regular active use. Such detail also includes the whole spectrum of weekend services provided within a defined geographical area, whether those services take place in well-defined church buildings, in public halls, in the doctor's surgery or in private homes. Only patient and detailed familiarity with an area generates insight into such issues.

The data presented in this book are derived from the in-depth study of ten Anglican rural deaneries. The unit of a rural deanery was selected simply as a device of defining a geographical area. Once selected, the geographical area was carefully charted on the Ordnance Survey map and every building currently used for worship was located on this map. These buildings included not only churches and chapels, but the kingdom hall, the school in which the Christian Fellowship meets, the doctor's surgery where the Catholic Mass is celebrated on Saturday evening, and the private home in which the Society of Friends hold their meeting. Old Ordnance Survey maps were then put alongside the current edition in order to pinpoint closed churches and chapels.

In each case the deanery has been studied as the result of an invitation from a theological college, ministry training course or rural pastoral studies unit. Groups of between ten and fifty-five ordinands have worked together to visit every place of worship and to attend every service within the deanery on a given weekend.

The ordinands have benefited in two ways from this experience. First, they have been trained in a specific research method and have experienced for themselves how research in empirical theology may contribute towards understanding and developing the church's ministry and mission in rural areas. As a consequence they should be better equipped to evaluate published research on church-related topics. Second, they have experienced in a disciplined way what it is like to be a visitor in a strange church and to attend an unfamiliar form of worship. As a consequence they should be better equipped to develop the resources of their future churches and services to respond to the needs of visitors and to local people on the fringes of church life.

The data from these ten deaneries are used in two different ways in this book. Chapters 3 through 9 set out to profile the rural church within the seven types of community. Each of these chapters presents a small sample of in-depth studies of individual communities. These communities are selected in view of their size or location from a variety of church watch programmes conducted in a range of deaneries and at different times of year. By way of contrast, chapters 10 through 13 set out to profile the rural church within the four types of countryside. Each of these chapters reports the *overall* findings from one church watch programme conducted throughout a whole deanery, selected to illustrate the particular characteristics of one type of countryside. For example, in the chapter on urban shadow countryside, information from seventy-three different services is brought together in overview. In this kind of chapter it is not possible to illustrate any one service in detail.

Each of these presentations in its own way holds up a mirror to the rural church and reflects back specific aspects of church life. No claim is being made that the mirror has been held up in all the right places or that the situation is not constantly changing. As in all scientific research, the challenge is now there for other researchers to replicate and to refine these studies. My conviction remains, however, that the future of the rural church will be more secure if based on research rather than on rhetoric.

2
LOOK
AND SEE

With Closed Eyes

THE REGULAR TRIP to the supermarket becomes a matter of habit. I stick to the same store because I know where things are. My trolley follows a well-worn path between the rows of shelves like a well-conditioned rat in an experimenter's maze. My journey is rewarded when I find the products I want in the places where I expect to find them.

Some areas of the shop I no longer bother to explore. Having once learnt that the products on these shelves are of no interest to me, my trolley gives them a wide berth. I am into focused shopping.

A while ago, I rushed into my local supermarket shortly before closing to buy the jar of coffee which I had forgotten on the previous shopping trip. I homed in on the familiar shelf to find it taken over by tins of soup. Feelings of disorientation gave way to frustration: why should the manager decide to relocate the stock?

At that moment my attitude to the store had changed. I was no longer an old friend in a familiar environment. I had become a stranger in an alien land. It was like being new to the town all over again and I had to begin again the process of learning how to find my way around. First, I searched frantically, all to no avail. The newly arranged store was not prepared to give up its secrets so easily. Then, I began to look for clues and for signs; surely there must be a hidden rationale or plan in the manager's new design for the store? If only I could identify this plan, then surely coffee would be easy to discover. Again I failed. Eventually the patient assistant led me back to the main entrance and pointed out to me the new large plan giving the key to the reordered superstore. Coffee was right there by the entrance, third shelf on the left. Had I been a stranger to the town that plan would have been the first thing to catch my eye when I walked into the shop. Because I thought I knew my way around, I was blind to the obvious. Having had my eyes opened I looked at the whole store with a new interest. I walked each row of shelves as if for the first time. I saw a range of products to which previously I had been blind. And having seen, there were some I decided to taste.

Perhaps from time to time we all need some special stimulus to open our eyes to see what is really around us.

An Eye-Opener

What is true of shops is also true of churches. The church which we know best is the church we are least likely to perceive accurately. Those responsible for taking services are perhaps even more likely to be blind to their own church than are the regular members of the congregation. It is all too easy to adopt the habit of seeing the church and its worship through the limited perspective of those actually involved in leading it. The choir trainer may forget how difficult a new complex hymn tune may appear to the unmusical worshipper. The preacher may forget how difficult it is to concentrate on abstract argument without illustration, anecdote or visual aid. The person familiar with the structure of the liturgy may forget the difficulties encountered by the uninitiated.

From time to time those of us involved in the church's ministry need to experience and to see things from the other point of view. It is all too easy for clergy to avoid doing this. After being ordained for a few years, I found myself looking forward to holiday periods precisely as an opportunity to become a member of someone else's congregation. Sometimes the experience was exhilarating; sometimes it was depressing; always it was challenging and educational. Deliberately I would try to go to two or three different kinds of service on my Sundays off.

One of the first sermons I remember hearing on one of my holiday visits to a strange church was preached by a clergyman who had himself just returned from his annual holiday. I do not go to church when I am on holiday, he told his congregation, because that is too much like a busman's holiday; but absence makes the heart grow fonder and I look forward to coming back here refreshed. I began to wonder if he would be conducting his service in the same way that Sunday if he had dared to expose himself to the ministry of other churches during his holiday.

Two particular holiday experiences helped to focus my interest in becoming sensitive to the hidden messages given by churches and by ministers to the visiting worshipper. Both experiences were sharpened because I came to them as an alien in a foreign culture. The first took place in the Armenian Orthodox cathedral in New York City; the second on the Isle of Skye.

Sunday morning in New York City could have offered me a range of churches in which to worship. I opted for the Armenian Orthodox cathedral partly because it was within easy walking distance of the YMCA where I was staying and partly because the opportunity to share in Armenian worship is not something which would regularly come my way. I was, of course, expecting to feel somewhat out of place, but I had little idea just how out of place I should really feel. The Armenian Orthodox cathedral clearly exists in New York City to serve the needs of its committed members, a cultural minority in a cosmopolitan city. It is not there as a witnessing church intent on drawing strangers, foreigners and visitors into its life, worship and ministry.

When I arrived the service was just about to begin. The vast interior of the cathedral was sparsely populated with a distinctive congregation. I was made to feel like an intruder from the moment of my arrival. My nationality, my appearance, my dress, my native language, all identified me immediately as an outsider. People stare at outsiders; they do not offer them friendship. No welcome was offered; no book was placed in my hand. I was left to find my own way to a seat. When, at last, I got hold of a service-book, I found it impossible to find my way around it. During the service the regular worshippers stood and sat and stared at my ineptitude. At one point in the service, the principal celebrant and ministers greeted the members of the congregation with a kind of hand clasp; but the visitors were excluded.

After the first hour and a half of the service, I had to leave to catch my Greyhound coach for a 200-mile trip to the conference I was attending. My curiosity had been satisfied, but my spiritual hunger had been left unfed. I had been made to feel very much the stranger that I was, an alien intruder within their worshipping community. How I longed for there to have been a door-keeper to have made me welcome. How I longed for a guide to help me follow the service. How I longed for a sympathetic group of people to have made me feel at home. How I longed for the celebrant and ministers to offer the newcomer a sign of welcome and a little friendly guidance. But then I began to wonder if the visitor would really have fared much better in my own church.

Sunday in the rural isolation of the Isle of Skye provides a stark contrast to the crowded city streets of New York, yet as a visiting worshipper on the Isle of Skye I found myself recognizing many of the experiences and feelings I had previously encountered in the Armenian Orthodox cathedral. This time I had made my choice between the Church of Scotland, the Free Church of Scotland, the Episcopalian Church of Scotland, the Free Presbyterian Church of Scotland and one or two other variants on the same basic theme. Being on holiday, I wanted to experience a different form of worship in a different culture; but once again I was not fully prepared for the extent of the difference. It would, perhaps, be unfair to reveal the choice which I made.

Before getting out of the car, I noticed that the men and women, boys and girls going into the church all carried a black book. I had a Bible with me in the car and, although it had a blue cover, I decided to take it into the service with me. This was, in a sense, my first mistake. I did not realize that the churches in Scotland had their own special version of the Bible.

Just inside the entrance lobby of the church I was confronted by a table. On the table there were two piles of books and a plate for money. I placed my offering on the plate and picked up a book from the first pile. The title was in Gaelic, so I exchanged it for a book from the second pile. The title proclaimed simply *Holy Bible*. I do not need this, I thought, I have brought my own. This was, in a sense, my second mistake. Since there was no one to ask about the books I needed, I walked into the church itself, wondering where I would find a hymn-book.

I always feel slightly shy of walking into a strange church. I like to slip quietly into a seat near the back. In this church the door was at the back so an unobtrusive entry should have been easy, especially since I had left it quite late and the service was about to begin. However, the regular congregation had already filled the seats at the back and I found it necessary to walk conspicuously past them to the first empty seat towards the front. This was, in a sense, my third mistake. As a holiday-maker I suddenly felt very aware of my damp anorak, in front of a suit-wearing congregation.

In the pew I was relieved to find a hymn-book; I read its preface as I waited for the service to begin. The minister announced the first hymn as 'paraphrase 17'. As a well-trained Anglican I prepared myself to stand. It is so difficult being a visitor in the front row of a strange church, since you cannot copy the behaviour of those in front of you. In Scotland, apparently, they sit to sing. I thumbed through my hymn-book in vain to find paraphrase 17. When I looked round, I saw other people singing from the back pages of their Bible. Only then did it dawn on me that my blue-covered Bible was useless in a Presbyterian congregation where black-covered Bibles included paraphrases at the back; but no one offered me a more suitable text. I felt very conspicuous and excluded. As the service proceeded, paraphrase 17 was followed by other paraphrases and by metrical psalms also taken from the Bible. The hymn-book found in my pew was not used once. I began to dread the invitations to sing.

Like my Sunday morning in New York, once again I had been made to feel very much the stranger that I was, an alien intruder within this worshipping community. How I longed for there to have been a door-keeper to have made me welcome. How I longed for a guide to have shown me how to use the book. How I longed for a sympathetic group of people to have absorbed me into an inconspicuous place near the back. How I longed for the minister to have offered the new-comer a sign of welcome and a little advice on how to feel at home and how to find my way around a strange form of service.

After the service several people spoke to me. The minister shook my hand and asked me if I were on holiday on Skye. But already the welcome had arrived too late. For more than an hour I had felt excluded, isolated and alienated. I suspected that if I had attended that church as an unbeliever questing a faith, I would have gone home unconvinced and most unwilling to return. But then I began to wonder if the visitor would have fared better in my own church.

That same evening on the Isle of Skye I drove sixteen miles to attend a different church. The journey across the peninsula of the island took longer than I had anticipated. On this occasion I arrived not in time to see other people walking into the church, but to hear the strains of the first hymn already under way. I hesitated on the steps and nearly turned away, but there were two sidesmen standing in the entrance hall who beckoned me to come in. They assured me that it was quite acceptable to arrive late. One of them gave me a Bible. He opened up the back pages and said, 'Here are the paraphrases and the psalms we shall sing.' The other sidesman showed me to a seat near the back. Although the service had already begun, I felt able to slip in quite inconspicuously. As soon as I had sat down, the man sitting behind me leaned forward and found the place for me in my book. I sang the last verse or two of the paraphrase and I was happy.

After the opening paraphrase the minister asked us to stand and pray and in this gentle way he let us know both what we were doing next and the appropriate posture to adopt for doing it. He opened the prayers by bringing before God the assembled congregation. He made special mention of the visitors and holiday-makers in the congregation. He prayed that they might find refreshment in their holiday and that they might receive welcome and blessing from sharing in the worship of this church.

The contrast with the morning service could not have been greater. The fascinating thing, however, is that both churches started with the same potential. They both belonged to the same tradition in terms of their system of church government, their form of ministry, their use of Scripture, their form of service, their musical culture. It was not the tradition itself which had made me feel alienated during the morning service, but the assumptions which had been made about the essential compatibility between the tradition and the group of people who had assembled to worship together that morning. But then I began to wonder if my church was conscious of the assumptions it was making.

Observation Techniques

Wearing my professional hat as a social psychologist, rather than as a parish priest, I recognized that what I was doing in a fairly unsystematic way during my holiday was in fact drawing on a well-established research tradition in the social sciences. For example, I was aware of the range of ways in which observation techniques had been used in educational research to learn about pupil behaviour, teaching techniques, classroom decision-making processes and so on. Working on these models, it seemed to me that there was considerable potential in the techniques of systematic observation both to learn about the strengths and weaknesses of Christian churches today and to help train clergy and lay leaders to see the life of their worshipping community more accurately and more perceptively.

From the research point of view, properly used, observation techniques could help to build up a picture of where the church is weak and where the church is strong. They could help to identify good practice and to describe bad practice. They could help to bring to consciousness aspects of church life which were unconscious and to make explicit some of the assumptions and presuppositions implicit in worship and church community life. They could help to make more widely available insights which promote church growth and issue warnings about those aspects of church life which hinder growth.

From the training point of view, properly used, observation techniques could help ministers, lay leaders and local churches to see themselves as others see them. They could help promote sensitivity and insight, pastoral and liturgical skill, educational and catechetical techniques.

At one level, there was little new in what I had in mind. The idea of closely observing what was happening in different churches and at different church services had certainly occurred to others. Back in the 1840s Joseph Leech, under the name of 'The Churchgoer', was writing regular accounts of his unannounced visits to the city and rural churches in the *Bristol Times*.[1] Joseph Leech's perceptive and critical eye has provided a unique account of church life in the mid-nineteenth century. More recently, Gavin Stamp's contribution to *The Church in*

Crisis contained accounts of his visits to services during the 1980s.[2]

The problem with both Joseph Leech and Gavin Stamp is their essential selectivity. They were selective in the churches they visited, in the services they attended at these churches, and in what they chose to observe and to record on any given occasion. There is no guarantee, therefore, that another 're-searcher' working in the same area would have chosen to visit the same churches, to attend the same services or to record the same set of observations. In other words, their data are anecdotal rather than scientific.

In order to bring scientific rigour to the idea of applying observation techniques to the life of the church, two conditions need to be met. The first condition brings system to what is to be observed. This means that different individuals are trained to look out for the same things and to make the same kind of judgements about those things. The second condition brings system to where the observers go to make their observations. This means that the choice of churches visited or services attended is not haphazard, but designed to give a complete and fair view of the variety which is likely to be encountered in any given area.

System is brought to what is observed through the careful design and construction of an 'observation schedule'. The obser-vation schedule is a well-planned check-list of points to look out for and clear guidelines about how to record the observation of these points. The check-list helps to ensure that each observer covers precisely the same issues. The guidelines about how to record observations help to ensure that the observations of different people are recorded in comparable categories. Before being sent out to undertake their own fieldwork, observers need to be trained in how to use the check-list, how to interpret what they see and how to record their observations. This helps to ensure that different observers come back with the same account of what they have been sent out to observe.

System is brought to the places of observation through the careful design of a 'sampling frame'. The sampling frame is a well-thought-through account of how the churches and services are chosen to form the basis of the observations. One approach to the sampling question would be to draw up a list, say of all the services in a diocese on a given Sunday; and then to choose a sample of these services at random, perhaps choosing every tenth one on the list, or by putting all the services in a hat and pulling out the requisite number like raffle tickets. Another approach would be to choose a smaller geographical area, say a deanery, and to attend every service in that deanery on a given Sunday. Both methods help to ensure that the services attended are not a matter of arbitrary choice or of the observer's personal whim.

As a consequence of my own informal visiting of churches and attending church services at holiday times, I began to draw up two systematic check-lists. One I called the *church visitors' observation schedule*. The aim of this check-list is to systematize the things which I should look out for when first visiting an unfamiliar church building. The other I called the *churchgoers' observation schedule*. The aim of this check-list is to systematize the things I should be alert to when first attending services in a strange church.

As well as using these check-lists myself when away from home, I found that I had the opportunity to share them with groups of other people. The first really systematic attempt to set the list to work in a proper piece of research happened with a team of ordinands from Westcott House who collected data for the last two chapters of my book, *Rural Anglicanism*. The experience of projects like this has enabled me to revise and refine my observation schedules in order to make them more complete, more systematic, more useful and more objective.

The Church Visitors' Observation Schedule

The church visitors' observation schedule sets out to make explicit the implicit messages being conveyed by the church building itself to visitors about the life and ministry of the worshipping community in that place. The bulk of the schedule is concerned with objective descriptions of what is being pro- claimed by the building and what is not being said. Then a second part asks the visitors to make some subjective assessments about aspects of the church. The use of subjective judgements is, of course, more controversial than the objective descriptions.

The first objective question on the observation schedule is whether the church is locked or unlocked and, if locked, whether or not a key holder is named. Locked and unlocked churches proclaim quite different messages. The locked church, like the locked house, proclaims that it is there to serve the needs of the family on the inside, the needs of those who possess the key. The locked church proclaims that it is there to protect the treasures inside and to guard possessions and wealth against trespassers, intruders and robbers. The locked church proclaims that it is vulnerable in a hostile and alien world. The open church proclaims that it is there to serve the needs of the wider community, to be available to welcome visitors, to offer sanctuary and shelter to those who might need it. The open church proclaims that it is there as a place of peace for prayer, meditation and worship.

Locked churches proclaim different messages depending on whether they name the key holder or not. The locked church which also names a key holder makes it known that it recognizes that local residents and visitors may wish to go in. The locked church which names a key holder proclaims that it is probably locked for security reasons, recognizes the inconvenience or difficulty which this may cause, and yet shows some willingness to welcome and to receive those who wish to visit or to use the building for prayer. The locked church which names no key holder makes it plain that it is a private, rather than a public building. The locked church which names no key holder proclaims that it neither expects nor welcomes visitors; nor is it available to serve the needs of those who may wish for a holy place in which to meet with God.

Next there is a set of objective questions regarding the availability of information about the activities and people associated with the church. This set of questions begins by noting what is said about Sunday and weekday services. Some churches proclaim this information very boldly on notices outside, while others pin a notice in the porch or inside the church itself, even when the church is kept locked. The church which does not advertise service times is making it plain that it does not expect non-members to attend. Those who do not already know what is going on are not invited to find out. The observation schedule asks the observers not simply to note whether or not such information is available, but to record the pattern of Sunday services over the period of a month. This helps to document the wide range of patterns in different churches and in different places.

Alongside details of Sunday services and weekday activities, some churches make a special point of giving information about baptisms, weddings and so on. These churches acknowledge that there are specific times in life, like marriage or the birth of a child, when people who are not regular churchgoers nevertheless appreciate the ministry of the church and may not know how that ministry can be made available to them.

The church building can act as the 'shop-window' for the life of the church in a community, or it can help to shield that life from view. The church which publicly names its minister and key lay people proclaims that these people are available and accessible in the community. Churches which do not publicly name their leadership proclaim that they do not envisage that people will come seeking help or advice from them. The observation schedule invites the observers to note carefully who are named and how much information is given. The list of people includes not only the minister, but also the lay leaders. The information checked includes not only the names of these people, but also their addresses and telephone numbers.

The visitors' observation schedule also records where this key information about activities and personnel is made available, if at all. This helps to distinguish between what the church regards as important enough to display outside, what it displays in the ante-room or porch and what it displays in the church itself.

Following on from this, observers are asked to note carefully the range of notices available on the church notice-board or in the church. Both the content and presentation of notices give insight into what the church regards as important and the care it takes to communicate this to others.

In particular, observers are asked to be alert to four types of notices. First, they are prompted to look at what the church is specifically saying to visitors. Some churches make a specific point of welcoming visitors, while others do not appear to acknowledge that visitors exist. Second, they are asked to look for evidence of the church's work among children and young people. For example, is there a Sunday school, junior church or weekday club for children or young people? Are there signs of children's display work in the church; do young people have the opportunity to share their own work with the adult worshipping community? Third, they are asked to look specifically at what the church is saying about money. Is the church appealing for money to support its ministry, maintain its organ or to contribute to local or national charities? Is there a fabric appeal to maintain the church building? Fourth, in Anglican churches observers are asked to look out for the statutory table of fees for weddings, funerals, churchyard monuments and so on. They are also asked to note the year when this information was published. Some Anglican churches display the up-to-date fees; some display no fees; others display out-of-date information.

Next, observers are asked to note the range of books that is available for use in church, especially in terms of Bibles, hymn-books and service-books. This provides a clue to the type of services held and also indicates if there is material available to help the visitor's private meditation and prayer.

The final part of the visitors' observation schedule moves beyond the objective recording of what is available at the church. Observers are asked to look carefully at thirteen aspects of the church and to rate these aspects on a seven-point scale ranging from 'very good' through 'good', 'fair', 'poor' and 'bad' to 'very bad' and 'not apparent'. The thirteen aspects of the church are: the condition of the hymn-books, the condition of the service-books, the cleanliness of the church, the condition of kneelers, the flowers, the bookstalls, the display screen in the church, the notice-board in the porch or ante-chapel, the notice-board outside, the repair of the building outside, the churchyard, the parish magazine and the guidebook. It is aspects of the church like these which are important communicators of the ethos and life of the church.

The Churchgoers' Observation Schedule

The churchgoers' observation schedule sets out to help church-goers pay close attention to all that is happening in the service and to become more conscious of the features of the service which either promote or inhibit worship. Like the church visitors' observation schedule, the churchgoers' observation schedule is concerned both with objective descriptions and with subjective assessments.

To begin with, churchgoers are encouraged to note carefully what takes place when they first walk into the church to attend the service. In many ways, the kind of reception given to visitors is crucial for setting the atmosphere for their participation in the rest of the service. Churchgoers are, therefore, asked to note carefully if the minister or someone else welcomes them or speaks to them when they arrive, whether they are shown to a seat or left to find somewhere to sit for themselves. They are asked to note how they gain access to the books or service sheets they need in order to participate fully in the service. In some churches these are handed out at the door; in some they are ready in the pew; in some they are left out in an obvious place to be picked up; in others it is sometimes quite difficult for visitors to acquire what is needed. Simple matters like the availability of hymn-books or service-books can be so easily overlooked by regular worshippers who are at home in their church, but they can become the cause of difficulty or embarrassment to strangers who do not know their way around the church.

Next, churchgoers are asked to note the actual time when the service starts and to compare this with the advertised time. They are asked to note when the service ends and to calculate the duration of the service. They are also asked to time the sermon.

To help observers become more conscious of the congregation they are joining, they are asked to count the congregation, first as a simple breakdown of male and female worshippers and then as an estimate of those who are over twenty-one. Next they are asked to divide the congregation into seven age groups and to count the number of people in each age group: the under-sixes, the six- to ten-year-olds, the eleven- to fifteen-year-olds, the sixteen- to twenty-year-olds, the twenty-one- to forty-year-olds, the forty-one- to sixty-year-olds and the over-sixties. Inevitably, any attempt to guess individuals' ages is going to be arbitrary.

The next part of the churchgoers' observation schedule analyses how leadership is shared in the church. Churchgoers are asked to note the age and sex of all the people who are actively involved in some way in conducting the service or in preparing for it. This includes those who give out books, take the collection, read lessons, give out notices, lead intercessions, take part in the offertory procession, serve at the altar, make the coffee, ring the bells, play the organ, and so on. In some churches everything seems to be done by the minister; in some churches just one key lay person seems to be entrusted with all the jobs; in other churches the tasks and functions are shared much more widely.

In order to encourage churchgoers to listen carefully to what is being said in the sermon, they are asked to take sufficiently detailed notes to enable them to reconstruct the main thrust of it afterwards. The discipline of taking notes during a sermon not only helps listeners to recall what has been said, but also sensitizes them to listen to the finer points of sermon construction. Any difficulties listeners experience trying to grasp what others are saying should help them to overcome those difficulties in their own preaching.

The final part of the churchgoers' observation schedule moves beyond the objective recording of what has taken place to some subjective assessments about the church. This time churchgoers are asked to evaluate the sermon, the minister, the congregation and the service content by means of a semantic differential grid. They are offered a set of bipolar adjectival pairs, for example audible-inaudible, and asked to assess on a continuum how far these adjectives fairly describe the aspect of the service under review. The results form the semantic differential grid.

Facing Criticism

When I wrote *Rural Anglicanism*, I decided to base my study on one diocese and to research that diocese from three different methodological perspectives, using the techniques of historical analysis, questionnaire surveys and participant observation. Having become familiar with the role of observation techniques in social and educational research I was, perhaps naively, rather surprised by the very strong reaction on the part of some clergy and bishops against my attempt to bring that technique into the service of the Christian churches.

It was my training of ordinands as observers which particularly irritated some of my critics. Parts of the picture uncovered by my original survey were uncomfortable and depressing. Some of my critics attributed this to the unfair biases of the observers, rather than to the reality of the situation which they set out to describe. For example, two parish priests writing in their parish magazines were quick to be critical of the ordinands' observations. The Reverend Colin McCarter, writing from his rural Cotswold parishes, described the ordinands as 'inexperienced, possibly enthusiastic, fault-finding (not fact-finding) young men, who may some day be ordained'. The Reverend

Gordon Taylor, writing from his not so rural parish of St Giles in the Fields, central London, concluded: 'If that sort of thing is typical of the training given today in our theological colleges, they would be better closed down.'

The three bishops who joined the fray were the Bishop of Worcester, the former Bishop of Reading and the present Bishop of Norwich. Writing to *The Times*, the Bishop of Worcester lamented the chapters as 'a list of horror stories, the product of an ordinands' field day'. The Bishop of Reading, writing in the *Oxford Diocesan Magazine*, took a more savage line:

> they were recruited from Westcott House, an institution in Cambridge which purports to prepare men for the priesthood, and then sent out to visit a number of churches separately on a given Sunday, making reports on what they found. It tells us a great deal about these seminarians – they reveal themselves as censorious, imperceptive, humourless and unloving. But, never mind; given time and good training vicars they will be eventually licked into shape.

The Bishop of Norwich, publishing similar reviews in the Rural Theology Association's journal and the *Tablet* said that he:

> found the method of chapter 12 irritating. The personal impressions of ordinands who are largely from urban areas and trained for urban ministry are hardly the most reliable judges of the state of the rural church. Ordinands are notoriously difficult to please. . . . It was probably an interesting exercise for them, but such personal impressions are not to be taken seriously as genuine social research.

In the face of such episcopal disapproval, perhaps a wise researcher would have given up and reverted to the traditional and much less harmful research pursuits of the rural clergy. What prevented me from doing this was the great deal of encouragement which came from other rural dioceses. For example, the reviews in many rural diocesan newsletters actually said that the accounts rang true for them and helped them to recognize their own situations. Andrew Bowden in Gloucestershire wrote:

It documents accurately what a critical visitor would probably make of many of our services. It underlines the unintentional but total insensitivity to visitors characteristic of many village congregations.

John Armes in Carlisle said, 'There is plenty to help us see ourselves as others see us.' Norman Payne in Leicester reckoned that 'names are disguised to prevent recognition, but the rural deanery studied in detail could well have been Goscote' – a Leicester deanery.

The Bishop of Crediton in the diocese of Exeter reported that 'some of our rural deans have already read the report, and their judgement seems to be that much of it is relevant to our churches in Devon too'.

Canon Norman Crowder in Portsmouth argued that 'those who read these well-researched pages may not like all that they read, but they will surely recognize some of the rural parishes they have known'.

Stanley Prins in Newcastle found that 'the experience of the "visitors" to the churches researched seemed uncommonly familiar and uncomfortably true'.

Richard Burt in Ely believed that the study 'has important things to say about every rural diocese'. Similarly, Peter Coleman in *Theology* argued that 'these impressions could be matched in most of rural England'. Gwynne Edwards in the *Baptist Times* extended the relevance of the study by saying that 'the observations are devastatingly frank, and make challenging reading for many denominations'.

From this random sample of reviews I took encouragement that perhaps, after all, the observations of this group of ordinands, trained in the ideas of participant observation, were not too wide of the mark. But, if this is so, the urgent job now is to test what this group of observers found among just one denomination in one deanery over a fuller range of denominations and a wider range of geographical areas.

There is, after all, something both very salutary and very Christian in trying to see ourselves as others see us.

Part One
TYPES OF COMMUNITIES

The seven chapters in part one each look in depth at a few examples of church life within different kinds of rural communities. I describe these different kinds of rural communities as *hamlets*, *small villages*, *medium villages*, *large villages*, *suburban villages*, *market towns* and *resorts*. Each chapter presents a detailed picture of a few communities drawn from *several* church watch weekends. The names given to the communities and to the individuals are fictitious.

3
HAMLETS

Mole End

THE ORDNANCE SURVEY map pinpoints Mole End in the middle of nowhere, on a narrow lane winding across country between two small villages. It is marked on the map with one main building and a cross, denoting church or chapel without spire or tower. Before setting out to visit Mole End, John and Bill checked to see what they could learn about this religious building. It was mentioned neither in the diocesan directory nor in the local Methodist circuit plan.

When they arrived at Mole End, John and Bill found themselves at the centre of a large and prosperous estate. The impressive architecture and neatly tended grounds of Mole Hall dominated the view and looked particularly impressive in the warm light of a sunny mid-October afternoon. Around the hall there was a large complex of farm buildings and the cottages built to house the hall staff. John and Bill could see nothing remotely like a church or chapel. While they were looking around, they met one of the local inhabitants and asked. He showed no surprise that two young strangers should be looking for a church at Mole End and pointed over to the buildings in the farmyard. The church marked on the map was a private chapel attached to Mole Hall, a first-floor room above the estate office.

John and Bill walked up the stone steps to the chapel. They found the door locked, with no sign to indicate that it was ever used. Content that they had checked it out, and that nothing was likely to be happening there on the following Sunday, they continued their journey to the next village, Oatby. In the porch of Oatby church they found a huge notice inviting the congregation to share in the 'Annual Harvest Festival at Mole Hall on Sunday at 3.00 p.m.'. John and Bill were puzzled that the service had not been advertised at Mole Hall itself, but decided to respond to the invitation displayed in Oatby church.

On Sunday afternoon John and Bill arrived back in Mole End at 2.50 p.m. There were three cars parked in the yard which had not been there the previous day, but apart from that everything still looked very quiet. They walked up the steps into the chapel. At the top of the steps a Methodist minister, in a dark grey suit and preaching gown, gave them a mechanical handshake and a copy of *Hymns of Faith*. An Anglican minister, in cassock, surplice, hood and scarf, was also standing at the back of the chapel, but was not actively involved in the welcoming process; he was staring into the middle distance.

This upper room had not been designed originally to serve as a chapel, but had been converted at a later date. A slightly raised platform at one end of the room formed a sanctuary, where an altar had been placed against the far wall. The altar frontal had once been designed in gold braid on a white background; now it looked dull, worn and grubby. In the centre of the altar stood a brass cross and to either side an empty brass candle holder; candles were not provided. Today the step in front of the altar rail was laden with the harvest produce, clearly indicating that sacramental worship was neither intended nor expected.

Either side of the centre aisle there were eight rows of pews, providing accommodation for about sixty-four worshippers. Today the left-hand side of the church already looked comfortably occupied with twenty-seven people seated. On the right-hand side only the back two rows were occupied. John and Bill took the next row back. After this only one more family came into the service, a middle-aged man and woman, their two sons and their daughter-in-law. They came to occupy the two front rows on the right-hand side, the father carefully instructing the other four where to sit. John and Bill correctly identified them as the Mole-Smith family, the owners of Mole Hall; then they realized why the right-hand set of pews had been left empty and regretted taking a place there themselves, on 'the family's' side of the church.

When the owners of Mole Hall had settled down, the clergy began the service; although it was still only 2.57 p.m. they were obviously not expecting any further worshippers to arrive.

Looking round the congregation, John and Bill were conscious just how much this annual service was really a family occasion. The first row of pews on the left-hand side contained three generations: two teenage children, their parents and their grandmother. The next row also contained three generations: a couple in their twenties, father and grandfather. Behind them were a couple in their twenties with two young children. Behind them were a couple in their thirties, again with two children. Further back there were three couples in their sixties and a row of elderly women.

The form of service was a hymn sandwich, lasting three-quarters of an hour. The service was conducted by the Anglican minister, while the Methodist minister preached the sermon. Neither minister seemed to feel particularly at home in the chapel, nor did one of them welcome and introduce the other.

After the first hymn, 'Come, ye thankful people, come', the Anglican minister offered an opening prayer and invited the congregation to join in the Lord's Prayer; the traditional form of the Lord's Prayer was used. After the prayers, the minister nodded vigorously towards Mr Mole-Smith until he stood up to read the first lesson. The first lesson was Psalm 148, read from the Authorized Version of the Bible:

> Praise the Lord from the earth, ye dragons, and all deeps:
> Fire, and hail; snow, and vapours; stormy wind fulfilling his
> word.

The second hymn, 'All things bright and beautiful', was followed by the second lesson. This was the parable of the sower from Matthew 13, read by Mr Mole-Smith's elder son, again from the Authorized Version:

> And the disciples came, and said unto him, Why speakest thou
> unto them in parables? He answered and said unto them, Because
> it is given unto you to know the mysteries of the kingdom of
> heaven, but to them it is not given.

After the third hymn, 'To thee, O Lord, our hearts be raised', the Anglican minister asked someone to switch on the chapel lights so he could see to read the prayers. During the fourth hymn, 'We plough the fields, and scatter the good seed on the land', a collection was taken. Then the Methodist minister settled down to read his well-prepared sixteen-minute sermon. He chose as his theme the parable of the sower.

The preacher examined the four sorts of soil onto which the seed falls in the parable. The stony ground shows that there are some minds into which the Christian truth will never enter. Changing his metaphor, he likened preaching to people like this to water on a duck's back. It is a tragedy that some will never discover the Christian truth. The shallow soil shows that some people are quickly swayed by new ideas, but do not follow them through. Many begin the Christian way: it is sad that so few can make the running. They are like Pliable in *The Pilgrim's Progress*. The thorny soil shows that we cannot have two crops; we have to choose corn or thorn. Many lives are too full to listen properly to the Christian message, many are too self-centred and too self-possessed. It is a tragedy that many do not find Christ until it is too late. The clean deep soil shows the hearts which are open to the Christian message. And now the crowning harvest makes the loss insignificant.

The question, said the preacher, is whether the soil can be changed. Farmers know that soil can be changed; and human beings can be transformed as well. Christ is saviour as well as teacher, ploughman as well as sower. The message of the parable of the sower is, therefore, one of encouragement. The church today seems plunged into insignificance, but ultimately the good soil shall bring forth the good harvest.

The parable, said the preacher, is also a challenge and demands a decision from us, to decide what kind of soil we are. We must decide and then do three things. We must hear the Christian message. We must be receptive to the Christian message, even if it hurts. We must put the message into action. Sow your seeds. Do your work. The harvest then is certain.

The service then closed with the hymn 'For the beauty of the earth' and the Anglican minister said the grace. After the service, both ministers stood by the door to shake hands. John and Bill received their handshakes and went to stand outside in the courtyard. The other people obviously knew each other well as part of a close and closed community. No one tried to engage

John and Bill in conversation, so they took the initiative. 'We are visitors', they said to one of the younger families. 'Are services held here every week?' In reply they learnt that the chapel was used only once a year, for the estate's harvest festival. 'Is the chapel Church of England or Methodist?' Bill asked naively. No one seemed able to answer this question; the only answer that seemed to make sense was that it was Mr Mole-Smith's chapel and he invited whom he would to take the annual service in it.

Little Wold

Little Wold nestles sleepily on one of the byroads off the beaten track. It boasts a population of seventy-five people, lying halfway between Great Wold, an even smaller community, and Upper Wold. At the turn of the century there were three places of worship in Little Wold: the Anglican parish church, the Wesleyan chapel and the Primitive chapel. The Wesleyan chapel had fallen into disuse, possibly at the time of the union of the Methodist churches. Today it still stands at the crossroads in the village, a derelict and dilapidated ruin, witnessing to the passing significance of the rural gospel and to the inability of the trustees to negotiate an alternative future for their forebears' investment.

At the other end of the village stands the much smaller, yellow brick, Primitive chapel, proclaiming its foundation date of 1858. This building has a well-cared-for look about it, but no indication that it is still in business as a place of worship. There is no notice-board outside to indicate denomination, times of services or names and addresses of the minister or local contact people. To find out what this chapel has to offer, Peter engaged the family living next to the chapel in conversation. According to this family, services took place in the chapel most Sunday afternoons at 3.00 p.m.

Leaving the chapel, Peter went in search of the ancient parish church on the opposite side of the road. The parish church was set well back from the road and is approached by a narrow path, stretching between two cottages. The path was rather overgrown and the churchyard even more so. There was no notice-board on the path leading up to the church. The porch was very untidy; broken glass jars and crumbling guttering were strewn across the floor. The porch notice-board was empty, apart from a decaying notice 'on the rules of church membership', published in 1932 and sold for 2½d. The door was locked. Peter looked in all the likely places for the key, but he failed to find it. Walking round the church he peered in through some of the windows. Like the porch, the inside looked neglected and decaying.

By this stage Peter was beginning to wonder whether the ancient parish church was still in use or not. Looking over the churchyard hedge he saw two young children and their father playing ball in their garden: he called out to ask the man whether he knew anything about the church which adjoined his garden. The man welcomed a stranger with whom to talk, but he obviously knew little or nothing about the church so close to his own home. He went to fetch his wife and to ask her. She said that as far as she knew nothing happened there, and suggested that Peter should go to ask Mr Forrest a few doors away.

Mr Forrest was delighted to respond to enquiries about the church. According to Mr Forrest's account, the vicar had got five other churches and did not want this one as well. Mr Forrest said that the vicar called a meeting here a couple of years ago, said that no one came to the church, that the building needed repair and that we would have to close it. We were all so shocked that we let it happen. But now I have got up a support group to press for its reopening. We have always had a church in the village; we don't want to have to go across to Great Wold to get married or buried. So we have been raising money. We've got £800 already; not bad from coffee mornings, jumble sales and the like. We are having a meeting with the vicar next month. Of course, he is dead against it. He says we don't need a church here, but we say that we do.

Peter began to press Mr Forrest on his plans for the reopened church: 'What will you use the church for when you have got it reopened?' 'We've got people who want to be married and christened here. We don't see why they should have to go over to Great Wold.' 'Yes, I see. But will you want to use it on Sundays as well?' 'Yes, we'll have services here again, like we always used to.' 'And do you want to go to them every Sunday?' 'Well, not me personally. I've never been a great churchgoer, but I shall go to the harvest festival and weddings and the like. And I daresay the wife will go on Sundays.'

Closing a village church is rarely an easy matter. Peter left the village feeling sad for the vicar of Little Wold, suspecting that he was already struggling to keep open more churches than were really needed in the area. In his attempt to simplify the situation by proposing the closure of Little Wold church, the vicar had already made many enemies in the village. By pressing to reopen their church, the people of Little Wold were saying quite clearly that the Methodist chapel in the parish was not an adequate focus for their needs and that they would resist the invitation to see the Anglican church in Great Wold as an appropriate substitute for their own parish church.

The church for which the people of Little Wold were pressing, however, was one which would meet their requirements for weddings, baptisms and funerals and which would help them to celebrate the major religious festivals of rural life, like the harvest festival and the carol service. They were not queuing up to become regular committed Sunday worshippers. While the ageing Mr Forrest may well be campaigning for the reopening of his parish church, it seems very likely that the young father in the house next door would not notice whether the church was reopened or permanently closed.

Peter was left saddened by the ambiguous message currently being proclaimed by the decaying and uncared-for church building. Perhaps when an ancient parish church is abandoned, he thought, responsibility should be taken to make it quite plain to those who visit that the building is no longer in use for public worship and to indicate the whereabouts of the alternative church or churches to that community.

Recognizing that Little Wold was a community in which two of its three churches had already been closed, Peter was intrigued to discover the kind of support given by the community to the one remaining church. On Sunday afternoon he decided to attend the chapel service. He arrived at the chapel at 2.50 p.m. The door was still firmly locked and there were no signs of cars parked outside or of people walking along the village street towards the chapel. Peter sat in his car and waited. The time, 3.00 p.m., was announced on the car radio and still the chapel was locked. Peter decided to go and knock on the door of the house from which he had enquired about the chapel services on the previous day. Today, however, there was no one at home.

Peter drove away, still wondering what provisions were made for worship in Little Wold.

Wellington St Peter

It was 9.00 p.m. on a cold, but bright, mid-December Saturday when Christopher found the hamlet of Wellington St Peter. The signpost pointing to a lane off the main road read 'Wellington St Peter, 1 mile, access only'. Turning into this lane, Christopher was greeted by a forest of road signs: no through road, weight limit 2 tons, road narrows, bends for $\frac{1}{2}$ a mile. And the road most certainly did narrow. Tyre marks dug deep into the high banks on either side. Christopher prayed that no heavy farm vehicle would be coming too quickly in the opposite direction.

At the end of the lane, Christopher was greeted by the most beautiful vista. Driving past a row of picturesque thatched cottages, he came to the graceful Georgian manor-house, the stately Victorian Gothic vicarage and the tall majestic west tower of the church. The lane stopped at the church, petering out into a footpath down to the river's edge. Opposite the church, sheep were grazing in the undulating fields. All was bathed in the brilliant early morning December sun, still low in the sky.

According to the diocesan directory, the hamlet of Wellington St Peter has an adult population of forty-eight; the church has an electoral roll of twenty-six, over half the population. The parish is now part of a rural team ministry.

The first impression conveyed by the church building itself is one of picturesque decay and neglect. The churchyard gate stands half open, the woodwork rotten and hinges broken. The churchyard is overgrown and unkempt. Virginia creeper grows wild and unruly over the south-facing walls of the church and has begun to grow over the Gothic archway leading into the porch.

Looking into the church porch, Christopher found that it had been taken over by a dozen or so farmyard hens, sheltering from the cold. At his unexpected arrival, the hens panicked and rushed against the closed door leading into the church. Then they scuttled out into the open. A handwritten note in the porch gave the service pattern for December. No services take place on the first Sunday of the month; on the second and fourth Sundays there is an 8.30 a.m. Holy Communion service; on the third Sunday there is a 4.00 p.m. evensong. The special arrangement for celebrating Christmas was a carol service on Christmas Eve at 4.00 p.m. There were no other notices in the porch.

The church door was unlocked, so Christopher opened it. Immediately inside the door there hung a heavy red curtain, protection against the winter draughts. Trying to find a way through this curtain, Christopher failed to notice the steep step down into the nave. Inside, the church felt cold, damp and musty. It had been rebuilt in the 1860s, with high narrow windows which had been filled with stained glass. The bright December sun played through these windows, filling the inside with pools of iridescent light. But, somehow, this only seemed to accentuate the overall darkness and gloom of the building.

Hymn-books and prayer-books were thrown untidily into a lopsided and decaying bookcase by the door. Christopher picked up several copies of the Book of Common Prayer and *The English Hymnal*. Covers were tatty; pages were torn or missing; some were mouldy.

Christopher decided to return to Wellington St Peter the following morning in order to attend the 8.30 a.m. Holy Communion service. On the Sunday morning he arrived at 8.20 a.m. The church door was unlocked, but no one else seemed to be there. He picked up a copy of the Book of Common Prayer and sat in a pew towards the back. Then a man and woman in their early seventies arrived. The woman went straight into the vestry; the man went to the back to switch on the lights and the heaters. He spoke to Christopher: 'We will try to warm the place up a bit', he said. Shivering, Christopher thought that perhaps he had left it a little too late to generate much warmth for that morning's service.

Walking up into the chancel, the man tried to switch the lights on there as well. He flicked the switch but nothing happened. His wife came out from the vestry and they discussed the problem loudly. Without the lights, the chancel was very dark indeed.

The team vicar arrived at 8.25 a.m., carrying a large black suitcase. He was told about the problem concerning the lights. Then a woman in her forties came in and began to ring the bell unsteadily. The man who seemed in overall charge shouted her a word of encouragement to keep trying: 'It will come with a bit of practice', he said. Two more women in their sixties arrived and then a husband and wife in their mid-fifties.

The service began promptly at 8.30 a.m. The team vicar processed swiftly through the chancel and up the three steps into the sanctuary. He was wearing old English Advent vestments in a deep blue, which looked as if they might have been in the church since the days of its Tractarian restoration. He began the 1662 communion service in the traditional eastward position. The chancel was so dark that he had some problem in reading the service.

The vicar came down to the chancel step to read the epistle. As he walked down, he was staring angrily at the light fitments in the chancel which were refusing to work. At the beginning of the epistle, the church door was noisily opened and a woman in her fifties came in. Towards the end of the epistle, the door opened again; this time the new arrivals were a couple in their mid-thirties. During the reading of the gospel, attention was diverted to a dog barking outside and to the voice of a woman trying to pacify it. The dog was being tethered in the porch. The door opened and a woman in her fifties came in.

By the end of the gospel, there was now a congregation of eleven, equivalent to nearly one quarter of the adult population of the parish. This was no poor country congregation, but one that showed every sign of rural affluence.

There was no preaching ministry at this service. The gospel was followed by the creed and the creed by the collection. The collection was taken by the man who had been responsible for turning on the lights and heating. While the collection was being taken, the team vicar went back into the vestry to look for the alms dish.

The rest of the service followed the prayer-book order and concluded with the blessing at 8.59 a.m. After removing his chasuble, the team vicar came to the door to greet the members of the congregation as they left. He made a particular point of thanking the woman who had rung the bell and of welcoming Christopher, whom he thought he had seen somewhere before. No one else spoke to Christopher. Rather than return directly home, he decided to follow the footpath down to the river.

Somehow it felt less cold walking by the river on this crisp December morning than it had felt sitting in church.

Kegling Minor

James' first sight of St Mary's church at Kegling Minor was on a cold December afternoon. He had driven past the low thatched public house, the Wheatsheaf, and the cluster of houses which constitute the hamlet of Kegling Minor, before coming to the massive Georgian old rectory. Opposite the old rectory, a track led off to Rectory Farm and to the church. James had decided to leave the car outside the old rectory and walk up the track. At the bottom of the lane he passed the derelict old school, which had once been built by the rector of the parish. At the top of the lane he came to Kegling Minor church and the rectory farmhouse.

The nave and chancel of Kegling Minor church had been built by the Normans. The tower had been added in the thirteenth century and the porch in the sixteenth century. Today Kegling Minor church serves a community of about a hundred adults. Amazingly, it had been a parish all on its own, with the vast Georgian rectory, until the last rector died at a great age in 1953. Then the rectory was sold and the parish joined to the much larger village of Kegling Major.

James' first impressions of Kegling Minor church were of decay and neglect. The small community appeared unable or unwilling to maintain its medieval church. The churchyard gate was rotting on its hinges and stood half open; the churchyard wall had fallen in several places and the rubble remained where it fell. The path leading to the porch was uneven and overgrown. In the porch there hung three notices, none of which advertised times of services or information about pastoral care.

The first notice was the table of fees for weddings, funerals and churchyard monuments, as were applicable in 1967. The second notice was the table of kindred and affinity, 'Wherein whosoever are related are forbidden in scripture and our laws to marry together'. The third notice was a faded welcome to visitors which read:

Whosoever thou art that
enterest this church, leave

it not without one prayer to God
for thyself, for those who minister,
and for those who worship here.

An earlier visitor had written at the bottom of the notice the poignant message, 'But when I tried to enter it was locked', and signed the postscript with the date 8 April, 1964. Years later James, too, found the church door locked, but as a hardened church visitor he hunted persistently for the key. No, it was not under the mat; no, it was not on the ledge inside the porch. The key had been craftily concealed under the eaves outside the porch.

Letting himself into the church, James found no signs to contradict his first impressions of decay and neglect. Although it was the church's season of Advent, the altar still carried a green frontal, which hung damp, grubby and frayed. A heavy plastic sheet protected the altar from the offerings of the birds who clearly found their way into the church. On the back seat there was a pile of battered books, the Book of Common Prayer and *Hymns Ancient and Modern: Standard Edition* bound together as one volume. A heavy blue curtain separated off the space under the tower which was used as a vestry. Inside the vestry cupboards there were decaying sets of vestments and altar frontals.

Also in the vestry, James found the service register which revealed a pattern of two 11.00 a.m. matins and one late morning Communion service each month. The register also revealed that the monthly Communion service was attended by between two and ten communicants; no figures were entered for attendance at matins. James decided, therefore, to return at 11.00 a.m. on the second Sunday in December to witness the service of matins for himself.

As James returned on Sunday morning, at 10.50 a.m., he was welcomed by the solitary church bell. It was being rung by the sixty-year-old reader who had come to lead the service. James was the first member of the congregation to arrive; by 11.00 a.m. he had been joined by four elderly ladies and a couple in their thirties with two young children. The church felt very cold. James noticed that the regulars had all sat near one of the three Calor gas stoves and he began to wish that he had done so as well.

The reader was responsible for leading the whole service

himself. He read both lessons and played the harmonium to accompany the four hymns. In spite of the small size of the congregation, there was a real feeling of warmth in the service. Simple hymns had been chosen and they were sung with confidence. The congregation also joined in saying the psalms and canticles with confidence. They felt like a small group of people who were used to worshipping together.

The reader did not mount the pulpit for his sermon, but began preaching from the chancel step. He had no notes and talked in a direct and relaxed way. His theme was 'getting ready for Christmas'. Soon he was walking down the aisle and engaging the young children and their parents in conversation. He discussed how they had been preparing for Christmas at home and in school. He then began to build their enthusiasm for making a crib and decorating the church ready for the carol service. James guessed, rightly, that the reader was a primary school teacher by profession.

After the service, James fell into conversation with the reader and with the rest of the congregation. They were pleased and eager to welcome a stranger and seemed genuinely sad that James was only passing through. He learnt that the reader was responsible for taking the two services of matins each month and that the vicar came to take the monthly Communion service. The reader obviously regarded this as 'his church'. Twenty years ago he lived in the village; now he lives six or seven miles away but still comes back to take the services of matins and to help with the communion service. The best service of the year, he said, was the annual carol service on the Sunday before Christmas at 6.00 p.m. He invited James to return for the carol service and James decided to do so.

The Sunday before Christmas was a cold but fine evening. The lights had been left on in the yard at Rectory Farm to illuminate some space for parking cars. The churchyard gate had been propped open and the path leading to the church porch was lighted by hurricane-lamps. The church porch was a riot of evergreens. The inside of the church, too, had been transformed. For the first time James realized that there was no electricity in the church. Wooden candle holders had been strapped to the ends of each pew and other candles flickered wildly and dangerously on the window-sills and on the pew-ledges. A large corona of candles hung in the chancel. An old oil-lamp was placed on top of the harmonium. A Christmas tree had been placed at the back of the church and a large crib had been installed at the front. The crib had been made by the reader's class at school and transferred to the church when the school had broken up for Christmas.

By 5.55 p.m. all the pews in the tiny nave were packed, holding about sixty people. By 6.00 p.m. the congregation had crowded into the choir-stalls which could seat an extra dozen or so people, and some people were left standing by the tree at the back. The lighted candles and the human bodies made the church feel much warmer than it had done the previous Sunday.

The carol service itself was a straightforward sequence of eight carols and seven lessons, following one after another without commentary. The reader began the service by welcoming the worshippers, introducing the visiting organist and thanking those who had decorated the church and set up the candle holders. He apologized for the fact that there were two different editions of the *Bethlehem Carol Sheet* in use that night and that the carols had different numbers in each edition. James was sitting too far away from a candle to read his carol sheet anyway, so he was not bothered by that information.

Just as in the carol service from King's College chapel, the carol service in Kegling Minor began with a solo voice singing the first verse of 'Once in royal David's city'; the voice that of a young mother who had been in matins the previous week. She was followed by her oldest daughter reading the traditional verses from the third chapter of Genesis, in the Authorized Version, as 'God announces in the Garden of Eden that the seed of woman shall bruise the serpent's head'.

The range of ages, voices and accents reading the other six lessons seemed to indicate that the whole of the local community was involved. The second lesson, in which 'the prophet Micah foretells the glory of little Bethlehem', was read with all the force of a retired sergeant-major, from a pocket-sized copy of the Authorized Version. The third lesson, in which 'the Angel Gabriel salutes the blessed Virgin Mary', was read by a tiny but forceful lady in her seventies, who had typed her lesson on a sheet of paper and carried her own torch to help her see to read it. The fourth lesson, 'St Luke tells of the birth of Jesus', was read from a modern translation by a teenage boy with a public school accent. The fifth lesson, 'the shepherds go to the manger', was also read from a modern translation, but in a rich local accent by a middle-aged man. The sixth lesson, in which 'the wise men are led by a star to Jesus', came across in a rich Scottish brogue, read by a very smartly dressed woman in her fifties. She seemed to experience great difficulty in seeing her text in the dim lighting, since by this time some of the candles had already burnt right down and gone out. The final reading, from St John's Gospel, was read with great care and feeling by the reader himself:

> In the beginning was the Word,
> and the Word was with God,
> and the Word was God.

All the carols were well-known ones, sung lustily by the whole congregation. While some people were hunting for the words in the two different editions of the *Bethlehem Carol Sheet*, others simply lifted up their voices and sang. 'Once in royal David's city' was followed by 'O little town of Bethlehem', 'Hark! The herald-angels sing', 'Silent night! Holy night!', 'Away in a manger', 'While shepherds watched their flocks by night' and 'We three kings of Orient are'. The final carol was 'Oh come, all ye faithful', the service ending with the rather premature Christmas day greeting:

> Yea, Lord, we greet thee,
> born this happy morning;
> Jesu, to thee be glory given;
> Word of the Father,
> now in flesh appearing.

During the service two incidents distracted attention from the smooth flow of lessons and carols and brought considerable amusement to some of the congregation. From the beginning of the service, it was obvious that a bird had decided to join the worshippers. For most of the time the bird was silent and out of sight. Occasionally, however, it fluttered round the church and joined in the singing. The bird's *pièce de résistance* was when it came to rest on the oil-lamp over the harmonium and began to singe its tail feathers in the heat. The second distraction came right at the end of the service from the candles placed in front of the Christmas crib. They had been set amid greenery in a base of Oasis. When the first candle had burnt right down, Oasis, it was found, burns brilliantly and with a pungent smell.

The whole service lasted just three-quarters of an hour. The reader stood in the porch to greet people as they left; he seemed to know everyone and to have a word for each of them. He recognized James and wished him a happy Christmas. Outside, neighbours were talking with each other in the light of the hurricane-lamps which still illuminated the church path. James felt that he had been privileged to share in a Christmas celebration which meant so much to the local community.

Upper Butterscotch

Upper Butterscotch is a farm and a row of cottages in the middle of nowhere. The Ordnance Survey map showed a cross at Upper Butterscotch, so Patrick went to explore it on Friday afternoon. The first time, driving down the lane, Patrick saw nothing that resembled a church or chapel; the second time his attention was caught by a decaying shed-like building, hidden from the road by trees and hedgerows. The grounds all around the building were overgrown and unkempt, but a shabby notice by the door still proclaimed that a service was held every Sunday at 2.30 p.m. The space left to name the preacher for next week was left ominously blank. The notice-board conveyed no other information.

Patrick's first impression was that the chapel was probably no longer used. He was able to trace the circuit minister's telephone number from a local vicar and telephoned to ask if there was really a service this Sunday. He learnt from the minister that there was in fact a service held once a month in the chapel at 2.30 p.m. and it so happened that Patrick had chosen to visit on the right weekend. Patrick could not help thinking that the old chapel notice-board was somewhat misleading and he was glad that he had thought to check before turning up to a service.

When Patrick returned on Sunday afternoon at 2.20 p.m., the space for the preacher's name had been filled, 'Mrs A. Jones, BA', but as yet there were no other cars outside. A few minutes later the preacher arrived in a new Metro. Then a Land-Rover arrived with one elderly man who unlocked the chapel and let the preacher in. A large battered Ford brought a husband, wife, three young daughters between the ages of five and ten, and grandmother. Grandmother got out first, spotted Patrick and came across to talk to him. She welcomed him to the chapel and introduced him to her son, daughter-in-law and granddaughters all by their Christian names. She seemed to assume that somehow Patrick knew her name. She was the chapel organist. Then another family of mother, father, three children under the age of ten and grandfather arrived.

Outside, the chapel looked shabby and derelict; inside, it was clean and newly painted. There were bright colourful posters on the front wall. The two families clearly knew each other very well. The children began playing together and their parents were in no hurry to settle down into a pew. They made Patrick welcome and introduced him to the preacher as a visitor.

The preacher began the service by saying, 'I am not using the pulpit today because we are all friends here and I feel a long way away from you up there.' Instead, she dragged the Calor gas stove into the centre and used it as a desk for her books and notes.

The first hymn was one of praise, 'Praise to the living God'. The organist peddled the harmonium with amazing vigour and gave a good positive lead. The small congregation sang lustily, while the youngest child crawled under the pews to stare up at Patrick. The hymn-book Patrick had been given was a very battered copy, with a number of pages missing. Unfortunately the missing pages included the opening hymn.

The preacher had prepared the service well. The opening prayers of adoration and confession were simple and direct, intelligible to children but not patronizing to adults. For the first reading from Scripture she selected some verses from Psalm 18: 'I love you, O Lord my strength'. This theme was picked up in the second hymn, 'O love of God, how strong and true'.

During the second hymn there were sounds of footsteps outside. The chapel door creaked open and a young woman in her early twenties walked in, followed by eight children around the age of eleven. After the hymn, the preacher welcomed the newcomers: 'When I usually come here there are five or six grown-ups. Today we already have one visitor and now we have this great invasion of visitors. How exciting. I am going to scrap the service I had planned and do something different. How do we all get to know each other? How do you get to know new people when they come to your school?' For the next five minutes the preacher orchestrated a question-and-answer session involving the resident young members of the congregation and the young visitors. We learnt that the visitors were from a church youth club on holiday in the area. Then the preacher went on to develop the theme of how we get to know Jesus, by actually meeting him, talking with him, asking him into our lives as our own personal friend. 'The only way to really get to know Jesus is to ask him into your life and to say "I would like you, Jesus, to be my friend." And it will hit you one day that Jesus is always with you.'

The preacher then returned to the service she had planned, but by this time the visitors were nicely integrated into the community. The hymn, 'O Lord of every living thing', was followed by a reading from the Acts of the Apostles about St Barnabas and another hymn, 'O grant us light that we may know'.

For her main address, which lasted sixteen minutes, the preacher spoke about St Barnabas. She identified five features of Barnabas' character: he was generous, welcoming to people, accepting of others, humble and open to the influence of God's Spirit. She applied each of these qualities to the life of Methodism today. Are we generous with our money and with our time for the circuit? I am the youngest local preacher by about fifty years in the circuit, why are not more people coming forward? Are we welcoming to visitors? Do we accept others from different traditions, or are we still suspicious of the priests who wear robes or the charismatics who hold up their hands? Are we humble and unselfish? Are we open to God's Spirit?

The service closed with the Lord's Prayer, the hymn 'O master, let me walk with thee' and the grace. After the service people stayed and talked. The speaker spoke with Patrick about the loyalty of the members of this small chapel. She explained that there are just seven members now, but that all of them were there for the afternoon service. The preacher's analysis was that it was the organist who was the key person in keeping the chapel going. The other members were all related to her. 'It's become a kind of family sanctuary', the preacher said, 'but when she goes, the others will be happy enough to join up with the village chapel.'

4
SMALL
VILLAGES

Castle Wold

THE BRIGHT EARLY morning June sun shone invitingly as
Tony drove through the undulating countryside to arrive ten
minutes early for the 8.30 a.m. Holy Communion service at
Castle Wold. Way before he arrived at the centre of the long
straggling village, he was impressed by the stark outline of the
medieval parish church on the prominent hillock at the far end
of the community. But this medieval shrine was not his destina-
tion. In the early years of the present century a more convenient
church had been built closer to the centre of the village.

The gate into the churchyard was open and seemed to be
inviting visitors. A bold handwritten notice, pinned behind a
glass panel, confirmed that the service for the second Sunday in
the month was the 8.30 a.m. Holy Communion. Each Sunday
there is just one service at Castle Wold; this week it was their
turn for the vicar's first service of the day.

The churchyard grass had been very recently cut. The smell
of the newly mown grass began to tease Tony's hay fever
allergy. A new churchyard path had been recently laid in crazy
paving and led the visitor along the full length of the south side
of the church to the west entrance at the base of the tower.
Tony opened the door. The darkness of the interior was a stark
contrast to the brightness of the June exterior. The door led
into a windowless antechamber under the tower. As he peered
inside, the light let in by the west door enabled Tony to see
another door leading from the antechamber into the church

itself. He tried to reach this door before the west door slammed shut. He failed in the race and stood for a moment bewildered in the darkness.

Suddenly the inside door was swung open, as if in answer to prayer, and the vicar was standing there to welcome him.

'Hello, who are you?' the vicar enquired starkly as he grasped Tony's hand with vigour. 'A visitor', Tony replied timidly. 'What's your name?' 'Tony Walsh.' 'Are you staying in the village?' 'No.' 'Where are you staying, then?'

Tony thought quickly and named the neighbouring market town, adding, 'But I thought I would start my day early and come out to a village church.'

'Good of you to come', said the vicar and gave Tony a service-book. The service-book was an abridgement of the Book of Common Prayer, containing just the communion service and the collects and readings. 'We use the Book of Common Prayer here', said the vicar, and then after a short pause added enigmatically, 'well, after a fashion.'

Inside, the new church in Castle Wold was built to a very strange design. Instead of the usual pattern of a central open nave, perhaps with an aisle to either side, the early twentieth-century architect had constructed a powerful central arcade. This had the effect of splitting the nave right down the middle, joining very awkwardly with a central chancel arch. Tony decided to sit on the left-hand side of the nave and resigned himself to feeling cut off from the people on the right-hand side. The back two pews were already occupied so he sat in the third pew from the back. No one came to sit in front of him, so he enjoyed a front row position. No sooner had Tony knelt down to prepare himself for the service, than the vicar came and took him by the shoulder. He wanted to make an introduction with the person sitting behind him. 'Mrs Smith, this is Mr Walsh. He is staying in the town and decided to come and join us this morning.' Mrs Smith smiled at Tony, with an uncomfortable embarrassment, and allowed him to return to his prayers.

The service began a minute early. Wearing cassock and surplice, the vicar walked the short distance from the vestry to the sanctuary at a brisk speed and started straight into the Lord's Prayer. The Lord's Prayer began as an almost inaudible whisper and finished as a shout. The volume dropped slightly for the collect for purity.

After the summary of the law, taken from the 1928 prayer-book but not included in the text given to the congregation, the vicar read both readings himself. The opening reading from the first epistle of St John included some lovely tongue-twisting phrases which exercised the vicar's delight in dramatic reading to the full. The passage reached its climax with a feast of pronouns: 'And he that keepeth his commandments dwelleth in him, and he in him: and hereby we know that he abideth in us, by the Spirit which he hath given us.'

The creed provided the first real opportunity for the congregation to participate, and they did so with conviction. The three ladies sitting behind Tony followed the vicar's distinctive pace and emphases with the pattern of familiarity, as did the voices on the other side of the church. Tony could see four people standing on that side of the church and tried to speculate as to how many were being concealed from his sight by the central arcade.

Much to Tony's surprise, no collection was taken. At the offertory a lady in her mid-sixties went to the back, collected the offertory plate and marched it briskly to the altar. Tony suddenly realized that he must have failed to notice the plate when he came in. At the altar the vicar received the plate, then gave it back to the lady who returned it, with the collection still on it, to the back of the church. Tony felt rather relieved that he could make amends for his financial oversight on his way out.

The prayer for 'the whole state of Christ's church' had been subtly rewritten by the vicar. Odd words had been changed and new material was interpolated. At intervals the congregation were invited to participate by contributing the response 'hear our prayer' after the bidding 'Lord, in thy mercy'. Tony began to understand what was meant by the vicar's enigmatic words of welcome: 'We use the Book of Common Prayer here – well, after a fashion.'

The other main departure from the Book of Common Prayer came after the distribution of communion. No post-communion prayer was used after the Lord's Prayer; the progression moved directly to the Gloria. Like the opening Lord's Prayer, the vicar treated the Gloria like a virtuoso performance. On this occasion the effect was achieved not by variations in volume so much as by variations in pitch. The Gloria emerged as a singsong solo. The Gloria was followed by the blessing and after the blessing the service was concluded by a neatly constructed post-communion prayer, which reflected neither the linguistic structure nor the eucharistic theology of the Book of Common Prayer.

After the service, the vicar came to the back of the church to talk with the members of the congregation and to encourage them to talk with each other. He took great care not to let the visitor feel left out of this and led one of the men in his mid-seventies, who had been sitting at the other side of the church, over to meet Tony. 'Mr Peters, this is Mr Walsh. He is staying in the town and has come out to join our service.' Tony was astonished that his name had been remembered. After making a few friendly enquiries, Mr Peters asked Tony if he had visited the old church on the hill yet. Then he launched into the tale of how the new church had been built at the turn of the century at Canon Rose's own expense. According to the tale, Canon Rose, already well on in years, had fallen and broken his leg one Sunday morning while negotiating the steep hill to the church. He resolved that, when healed, he would build a new church nearer to the vicarage and to the centre of the village; and the old church was left to fall into disrepair. Tony silently contemplated how the influence and authority of the country parson had changed in such a comparatively short time.

Mr Peters continued to tell how the parish was currently busy fund-raising to bring the old church back into use. 'Such a beautiful old building cannot be allowed to deteriorate and to fall down.' Already Castle Wold had raised enough money for a new roof. Gently Tony began to ask Mr Peters about their plans for the restored church. Mr Peters spoke enthusiastically about the restoration of Sunday services and the ideal situation of the building for local weddings. Looking round at the congregation and the vicar assembled together in Castle Wold for their early service on the second Sunday of the month, Tony wondered if they really needed a second church. Now that they had all come out from behind the columns, Tony saw that there had been a congregation of ten: seven women and three men. One of the ladies looked to be in her mid-forties; the rest of the congregation and the vicar were all clearly over sixty. Perhaps the ageing

Canon Rose had been correct in identifying the idea that the future needs of the church in Castle Wold, now a community of 230 inhabitants, would be best served by a smaller new church in the village centre.

Tony was surprised just how little information the church was displaying about itself. The only notice-board inside or outside was the one by the gate. This gave details of the monthly pattern of services, but nothing else. Nowhere could Tony discover the vicar's name or address. There was no information about arrangements for weddings or baptisms. The table of fees was nowhere displayed. There was no sign of a parish magazine or church guidebook. There was no sign of a ministry among children and young people, or indication of any weekday meetings or activities for children, young people or adults. Pinned to the inside of the door there was a card of greeting from the cathedral sent to mark the patronal festival, an out-of-date public liability insurance certificate, the quota assessment for the previous year and the flower rota. The beauty of the flowers and the care with which they had been arranged prompted Tony to look up the name of the lady who had been responsible for them this week and found it to be Mrs Smith. He said a silent thank you to Mrs Smith, assuming that this was the same lady to whom he had been introduced before the service.

Thorswell

Thorswell is a small village of 200 inhabitants. Once it had a parson and a parsonage all to itself; now it is part of a four-parish benefice. The total population of all four parishes is 990 and their combined electoral rolls total 158. Thorswell's electoral roll carries forty-one names. There are no other churches or chapels in any of these four villages.

This benefice of four parishes is served by a young rural priest in his early thirties. His aim has been to organize a pattern of services throughout the benefice to allow for as much stability as possible. All four parishes wanted to retain a regular Sunday morning service. However, the parishes did not provide lay leadership to help take these services and their parish priest is unable to squeeze more than three consecutive services into one morning.

According to the parish priest, one solution would have been to offer each church an early morning, a mid-morning and a late morning service once a month and allow each church to forgo its morning service once a month. The problem with such a pattern is that it is very difficult for the parishioners to remember when the service is going to take place from one Sunday to the next. This kind of arrangement is found particularly disruptive by fringe church members and becomes an additional disincentive for churchgoing. This benefice of four parishes, therefore, opted for a different solution. One parish settled for the regular 11.00 a.m. service; two of the parishes decided to share the 9.30 a.m. service, alternating with evensong every other week; the fourth parish favoured a service every week at 8.30 a.m. At least this seemed an easier pattern for the villagers to remember.

Thorswell is the church which settled for the weekly 8.30 a.m. service. The form of service is the Rite A communion with hymns and with a sermon. In effect, this means holding the form of service usually conducted during mid-morning or late morning at the time of day traditionally reserved for the quiet said communion service. Leslie was intrigued to discover if this kind of service would really work at such an early hour in a small village church.

When Leslie arrived at Thorswell at 8.20 a.m., the village still seemed lost in sleep. There were no cars outside the church. Leslie walked into the church porch and quietly studied the array of notices. All the key information was there, if not attractively set out: the vicar's name, address and telephone number; the churchwardens' names, addresses and telephone numbers; details of the Sunday services and information about weddings and baptisms. Other notices drew attention to the vicar's day off, the results of the PCC election and a forthcoming coffee morning. The readers' rota set out the lesson readers for the year. And in pride of place, if somewhat the worse for age, hung a Certificate of Merit for the best-kept churchyard in 1971.

While Leslie was absorbing the notices in the porch, he was also very conscious of sounds within the church. The organ was playing softly at the front, while three voices were talking very loudly at the back. Just before going in, Leslie looked back at the notice-board; the vicar's name seemed strangely familiar, but he could not place it. Cautiously he opened the door and walked in. The three people talking loudly at the back paused momentarily to stare at him and then picked up their conversation as loudly as before. Leslie looked round for a pile of books, before noticing that books were already in the pews. He sat as close to the back as felt comfortable, without disturbing the conversation.

Sitting down, Leslie first examined the service-books: a new copy of *The Alternative Service Book 1980* and a fairly new copy of *Hymns Ancient and Modern Revised*. Then he gazed the length of the church to the altar at the far end and to the organ which occupied a fair proportion of the chancel. The organist was a man in his seventies, almost completely enveloped in an over-large raincoat. Then, suddenly, the organist looked up from his music and noticed that there was now someone in the congregation listening to him. He stopped in mid-phrase, swung his legs over the organ stool with surprising agility for a man of his age and bore down on Leslie. He shook Leslie by the hand, welcomed him to the church and returned to the organ stool.

By 8.30 a.m. the congregation had grown to a total of sixteen: seven men and nine women. Six of the congregation were clearly in their sixties or seventies, but the other eight were younger: two were a young couple in their twenties. The sixteen members of the congregation were well spread around a church large enough to seat seventy or eighty people; seven of them had been able to find a pew all to themselves, while the other nine sat in four small groups of two or three each.

The service began just one minute late. The vicar, wearing alb and stole, processed alone into his stall and welcomed the congregation in a friendly and sincere manner. He made a special point of welcoming one of the women in the congregation who was attending her first service after coming out of hospital, and of welcoming the young couple who had come to hear their banns. The congregation responded well to this personal touch.

The first hymn, 'Rejoice, O land, in God thy might', got the service off to a good start. In spite of the organ being some distance from the congregation, the organist very skilfully cajoled the congregation into taking up the hymn with speed and volume. After the first hymn, the vicar gave out the page number for the Rite A communion service. From then on, the service charted a recognized path through the Rite A order.

Only two Scripture readings were used. The first was read with care and meaning by the organist; the second was read with equal care by the vicar. The theme of the readings for the fourth Sunday after Easter is 'The way, the truth, and the life'. Between the two readings was placed the hymn 'Thou art the way'.

The vicar took for the text of his nine-minute sermon a phrase from the first reading, 2 Corinthians 4. 13–15: 'No wonder we do not lose heart'. He began by illustrating how the gospel of the afterlife can give hope to those who are oppressed or in a hopeless situation in the present life. But in contrast with this idea of eternal life, he claimed that Paul's message is that 'the taste of eternal life is here and now. And this comes as God's free gift in Christ.' He went on to argue that there are some people who go through life happy: they give us a window on eternal life. We cannot all be like that, but we can be helped by God's free gift of the Holy Spirit. The nine-minute sermon was very clearly structured and crafted. The pace was brisk and the linguistic and conceptual levels quite complex. The actual cutting edge of the sermon was, however, difficult to grasp.

Like the sermon, the intercessions had been well thought through and carefully constructed. The five main sections of the prayer for the church and for the world were each prefaced by some topical reference from international, national or local life. The congregation prayed for Andrew and Julia who were to be married in three weeks' time.

The notices, too, were short and well focused. Information was given about the coffee morning and about the next meeting of the Parochial Church Council. Attention was drawn to the mid-week Thursday morning service in one of the other churches. The main news of the morning was a plug for the new-style family service to be tried for the first time next Sunday, again in one of the other churches in the benefice.

The peace was not celebrated in Thorswell church. The collection was taken by a fifty-year-old man and the bread and wine were taken to the altar by a seventy-year-old woman. During the offertory the congregation really enjoyed singing four verses of the hymn 'O Jesus, I have promised'.

The service closed at 9.21 a.m. with the hymn 'How sweet the name of Jesus sounds'. Leslie was surprised how early it was and how much of Sunday still lay before him. He felt as if he was just leaving a mid-morning service, not an early morning service. In Thorswell early worship seemed to work.

The vicar stood by the church door and spoke to each member of the congregation as he or she left. Leslie was last in the queue, having waited patiently in the church while other members of the congregation walked past him and ignored him. The vicar began to interrogate him: 'What are you doing here? Where do you come from? Where are you staying? What is your name?' The vicar was obviously enjoying himself at the visitor's expense and eventually gave the direct challenge: 'You are Leslie Francis, aren't you?' Leslie confessed; the vicar explained that some years previously, as an ordinand, he had taken part in a church watch weekend. Leslie's bluff was called and he now knew why the vicar's name on the notice-board had seemed so familiar. The vicar apologized for needing to rush off, but he had a 9.30 a.m. service to take a few miles away and he now suspected that one or two students would be there with stop-watches checking on the lateness of his arrival!

After the vicar had gone, the organist came to talk with Leslie and told him quite a lot about the life of the parish. He confirmed that the idea of a weekly 8.30 a.m. communion service with sermon and hymns worked well for Thorswell: 'We'd rather get up early here and know where we are than have something different every week.'

South Hagworth

South Hagworth is a village built on either side of a single, narrow street which winds its way up the steep hillside. Two or three relatively new small residential developments blend not unhappily alongside the ancient stone cottages and the massive eighteenth-century manor-house. The 1950s row of council houses stands out more obtrusively on the high bank, halfway up the street.

This new development has brought the population of South Hagworth up to about four hundred and helped to secure the precarious survival of the village hall and the post office. In the last rounds of educational cuts, the village school was closed.

There is a sense in which the village of South Hagworth is clearly bounded by its religious heritage. At the bottom of the hill the visitor is welcomed by a picturesque complex of three buildings. The centre piece is the ancient parish church. Opposite the church, proud in its own grounds and shielded by trees, stands the majestic late seventeenth-century parsonage, The Old Rectory. The group is completed by the village pub, the Hagworth Arms. At the top of the hill, where the village street becomes a winding country lane, the visitor is bade farewell by the Methodist chapel.

Susan and Stuart arrived in South Hagworth at noon on a bright mid-September Friday. They parked their car at the Hagworth Arms, looked at the lunch-time menu and decided to build up their appetite by exploring both church and chapel before settling down to eat in the pub garden.

They began by visiting the parish church. Walking through the lych-gate, they were impressed by the care which had so obviously been lavished on the churchyard and on the church building itself. This care in presentation was carried over into the way in which the church porch had been used. Inside, both walls were flanked by large notice-boards. One side had been filled with children's artwork; the other side was used to publicize local and area events. The door into the church was open and welcoming.

Inside the church they found a professionally produced guidebook, postcards, an up-to-date parish newsletter, a well-chosen selection of Christian paperbacks, intended to attract both visitors and parishioners, and a set of attractive full-colour free leaflets published by the Bible Society, relating passages of Scripture to aspects of daily life. They bought a copy of the parish newsletter and then set out for their walk through the village.

Thirty years earlier South Hagworth had been a parish in its own right. Then it became part of a benefice of two parishes. Now it is part of a group of five. The parsonage has been sold and the local vicar lives elsewhere. The former pattern of three services every Sunday has been replaced by one service each Sunday; the mid-morning parish communion alternates with evensong.

At the other end of the village the chapel seemed much less welcoming. Here the building showed signs of decay and neglect. Paint was peeling off the door, the windows were grubby and part of the guttering had rusted through. The door was locked.

Outside there was no source of information. Susan and Stuart were not sure whether the chapel was still in use or not. On their way down through the village street, back towards the pub, they asked one of the villagers if there would be a service in the chapel on Sunday. They learnt that there was a service there every Sunday at 6.30 p.m. South Hagworth Methodist chapel is now part of a very large circuit. Occasionally the minister comes to take services himself, but usually worship is led by one of the local preachers.

Settling down in the garden of the village pub for lunch, Stuart and Susan continued to overlook the parish church. At half past one they were conscious of a flow of cars into the village and a steady stream of people walking down the village street towards the church. A death had occurred in the village and the whole community was turning out to take part in the funeral service. Susan and Stuart decided to join the villagers' pilgrimage to the parish church.

By 1.50 p.m., when Stuart and Susan stepped into the parish church for the second time that day, every pew in the church was taken, apart from a few rows at the front reserved for family mourners. The sidesmen had opened up the gallery and were shepherding worshippers up the narrow stairway. By 2.00 p.m. the gallery too was crowded and people were left standing at the back.

The hearse arrived promptly at 2.00 p.m. and the timeless sentences of the prayer-book funeral service brought the congregation to their feet. The prayer-book service was conducted with dignity and simplicity. Downstairs the congregation had books in which they could follow the service; the lack of prayer-books in the gallery did not seem to trouble the people crowding either side of Susan and Stuart. Downstairs the congregation were sharing well-worn copies of *Hymns Ancient and Modern Revised*; upstairs in the gallery they were sharing even older and more battered copies of *The English Hymnal*. The two hymns chosen were 'The King of love my shepherd is' and the evening hymn 'The day thou gavest, Lord, is ended'. They were sung slowly and with great feeling.

The Scripture reading was from St Paul's first letter to the Corinthians, the selection of verses from chapter 15 set out in *The Alternative Service Book 1980*. It was read by the churchwarden from the Revised Standard Version with conviction and power.

The service was being conducted not by the present rector of the five parishes, but by his predecessor who had retired at the age of seventy some four years previously. As rector of just two rural parishes he had built up a depth of relationships with parishioners which had lasted through the four years of retirement and still provided a reference point and spiritual resource in times of death and bereavement. With five parishes in his care, and living in one of the other communities, the new rector accepted help on occasions like this.

From the direct simple sermon, Susan and Stuart learnt a great deal about the deceased and the church and community of which he had been part and to which he had contributed throughout the seventy-five years of his life. He had joined the church choir as a boy; as a teenager he had joined the ringers in the bell tower; as an adult he had joined the parochial church council and had remained an active member. For years he had taken responsibility for cutting the churchyard grass and had taken great pride in making it one of the best-kept churchyards for miles around. Love of God and love of neighbour, said the preacher, had made Reg's life a witness. Today we have come to give thanks for that life.

From the evidence of Friday's funeral, the religious life of South Hagworth seemed well and strong. Susan and Stuart returned to share in the Sunday worship of that same community. It was a Sunday when the parish church had an evening service, but no morning service. That Sunday evening they decided that one of them would go to the Church of England and the other would go to the Methodist chapel.

Stuart went to the parish church. When he arrived at 6.20 p.m. the teenage girl organist was playing one of Bach's short preludes and fugues. A woman in her early forties was standing by the open door with her teenage daughter; they were sharing the job of giving out books and greeting the worshippers. They welcomed Stuart to the service.

The congregation consisted of a man sitting alone on the back pew, a row of three elderly women sitting near the front and two retired couples. Stuart was later introduced to two of the men, Colonel Granger and Major Pluckett. Major Pluckett and Mrs Granger read the two lessons. The robed choir consisted of two men in their seventies.

The service was conducted and the sermon preached by the

woman who had given out books before the service began. She was a licensed reader who lived in the parish and had effectively taken responsibility for the fortnightly evening services since the parish had lost its own rector. On the other Sundays, the fortnightly communion service was left in the hands of the parish priest.

The service was conducted with a great deal of care and sensitivity by the woman reader. It was obvious that there was a considerable rapport between her and the members of the congregation. The sermon was thoughtful and well constructed. The hymns had been chosen to be singable by a small congregation. The psalm was said and the canticles were led confidently, if not musically, by the two-man choir.

After the funeral, the church looked and felt empty. Friday's great show of faith in the countryside had largely evaporated. However, what was left in its place was the firm commitment of a small worshipping community to keep the tradition alive and to do so, as far as evensong was concerned at least, entirely on the strength of local resources.

While Stuart was attending Anglican evensong, Susan had walked up the hill to the Methodist chapel. Here she was greeted by the two Goodmayes brothers. Their father had lived in South Hagworth and had been the mainstay of chapel life. They had both moved away to neighbouring villages, but continued to come back to South Hagworth every Sunday evening. When their father died, they took over running the chapel. They were delighted to welcome Susan and showed her to one of the pews near the back which had a cushion on the seat. She remembered seeing the two brothers the previous day at the funeral in the parish church.

After Susan had been sitting there for a few minutes, one of the Mrs Goodmayes started practising the evening hymns on the ancient harmonium, while her husband put up the numbers on the hymn board. His brother was busy talking with the preacher. This week the preacher was an elderly man in his seventies. While in the Anglican church down the hill the same reader was responsible for all the evening services, in the Methodist tradition of local preachers the circuit plan provided South Hagworth chapel with someone different every week. Susan felt that as a consequence of this there was little apparent personal rapport between preacher and congregation.

The local preacher was responsible for leading the whole of the service himself, apart from reading the notices, a job undertaken by one of the Goodmayes brothers. In the notices Mr Goodmayes mentioned Friday's funeral and asked the congregation to pray for Reg's wife and family. The sermon was long and rambling, going on for about twenty-five minutes. Mrs Goodmayes spent the time turning the pages of her hymn-book; her husband folded his arms and closed his eyes. The rest of the congregation was made up by an elderly couple in the back row, three elderly women sitting together and a fifty-year-old woman sitting with her invalid mother. Susan was amazed by the volume of singing which came from such a small group of people; she felt sure that they would be heard at the other end of the village down by the parish church!

After the services, Susan and Stuart had arranged to meet up again in the Hagworth Arms to talk over their experiences. It seemed to them sad that two small groups of Christians should still need to go to opposite ends of the village on a Sunday evening for their denominational worship, especially when both groups had apparently met two days earlier in the same church for Reg's funeral. But they recognized that the rift between church and chapel can still go deep in English village life.

Much Chipping

Much Chipping is a picturesque village in the heart of National Trust country. The resident population of the community is just over 250 people. A number of the stone houses carry 'bed and breakfast' notices. The village shop and post office combined survives, but markets much more strongly to the passing tourist trade than to the needs of the resident population. Half the post office has been converted into a tearoom. Pensioners wait for their pensions while young walkers are served with afternoon tea. An increasing number of the cottages are now second homes for city dwellers or let out as holiday homes.

In the nineteenth century, Methodism played a prominent part in the life of the community. A new Methodist schoolroom was built in 1851 and the chapel was completely rebuilt in 1879 in a lofty Gothic style. Chapel and schoolroom still stand proudly at one end of the village. The chapel has now been converted into a comfortable house. The notice-board which once proclaimed service times now advertises 'bed, breakfast and evening meal in the old chapel'. The schoolroom has been converted into the base for rural industry, producing 'handmade furniture'.

At the other end of the village there is the medieval parish church and solid early nineteenth-century vicarage adjoining the churchyard. The vicarage has now become The Old Parsonage Guest House, while the stables and outbuildings have been converted into self-catering holiday accommodation. The establishment has been awarded two crown classification by the English Tourist Board.

The parish church contains clear signs of Norman origins, including a splendidly sculptured Norman chancel arch. From the tourists' point of view, the finest feature of the church is its rich Jacobean woodwork. The two-decker pulpit and magnificent box pews are all dated during the late 1630s. Liturgically this fine woodwork makes the church very inflexible.

The parish of Much Chipping is now joined with four other villages, providing a total population of less than a thousand within the care of one full-time clergyman. Basically, three services are held in Much Chipping church each month, although the pattern changes from time to time to accommodate fluctuations in the local situation. The basic pattern provides for one mid-morning communion service, one evening communion service and one service of evensong each month.

The parish church is dedicated to St Peter, and Bob's visit coincided with the patronal festival. By local tradition, Much Chipping Wakes happens at Petertide. Village and church celebrate together. At 6.30 p.m. the silver band from a neighbouring village and some of the parishioners assembled on the green in front of the Royal Oak. Then the band led the way round the village into the church.

Not feeling part of the local community, Bob made his own way into church ahead of the procession. Inside the church he was warmly greeted by a sidesman, a man in his sixties, given a set of books and shown to a pew. The sidesman held open the door to the box pew and closed it once Bob had settled inside. Very quickly Bob discovered that box pews were not designed for comfort. The set of books he had been given included copies of the Book of Common Prayer, *Hymns Ancient and Modern: Standard Edition*, *100 Hymns for Today* and *More Hymns for Today*.

Like Bob, a number of other people had come on ahead of the procession, including several of the senior bandsmen who felt unable to march to church.

Much of the chancel in Much Chipping church is occupied by the organ. At 6.55 p.m. the organist, a lady in her mid-seventies, walked into church. She placed her handbag on the organ stool and began to unpack it slowly until eventually she found the key to unlock the organ. For the next five minutes she played an interesting medley of hymn tunes from memory, sufficiently softly for the sounds of the organ to be drowned by the silver band outside.

All told, the band was made up by nineteen musicians, ranging from several teenage boys and girls to some very senior men. They sat in the choir-stalls, largely concealed from the congregation by the huge organ case. Sitting there, cut off from the rest of the congregation, the band appeared to participate little in the worship. During the prayers they were sitting looking around or gently whispering among themselves.

The band's job was to play for the five hymns while the organist accompanied the two canticles. The hymns were chosen to display the band's love for fine tunes, like 'All people that on earth do dwell' and 'Now thank we all our God'. They played these tunes at a slow pace, giving the congregation plenty of opportunity to savour each note. Their conductor filled the chancel with arm movements. The band expected a different number of verses for some of the hymns than appeared in the congregation's hymn-book.

A good proportion of the community turned out to support the Wakes service. In addition to the organist and the nineteen people in the band, there was a congregation of fifty-four: seventeen men, thirty-five women and two tiny children. Looking at the congregation more carefully, Bob judged eleven of the adults to be under forty, twenty-three to be in their forties or fifties and the remaining eighteen to be over sixty years of age.

When the service began, the vicar took his place in the lower level of the two-decker pulpit, facing the congregation. The service followed the formal pattern of the Book of Common Prayer evening service, except that the psalm was replaced with the metrical version of the twenty-third psalm, sung to Crimond, thus enabling the silver band to provide the accompaniment.

The first lesson, from Ezekiel 3, was read by a layman in his fifties; the second lesson, from 1 Peter 2, was read by the vicar.

When it came to the notices, the vicar was careful to thank everybody who had helped to prepare for the service: the ladies who had arranged the flowers so beautifully, the gentlemen who had given so much time in the churchyard, the band who had so kindly come from the neighbouring village and everyone who had processed from the Royal Oak. The vicar went on to lament the fact that fewer people had taken part in the walk in recent years, since the village school had been closed and the children no longer took part. He suggested that the village would really have to review whether it should continue with this old custom if so few people really wanted it. On this rather sad note, the vicar welcomed the archdeacon to be the guest preacher.

The archdeacon emerged as a very fluent and warm speaker, if none too structured in what he had to say. He preached for twenty-eight minutes, taking care from time to time to lean dangerously round the pulpit and to peer behind him at the band sitting in the chancel.

The archdeacon took his text from the Old Testament reading, 'All my words that I shall speak to you receive in your heart and hear with your ears'. He then deliberately related the text to the musicians by picking up one of the hymns by John Newton. He told the story of John Newton's conversion and the consequence of receiving the love of God into his heart. This was followed by a series of short word pictures which, for the archdeacon, illustrated the power of Christ to change lives. He concluded his sermon with a classic appeal for members of the congregation to dedicate their lives anew to Christ and to repeat in their hearts a short prayer of dedication:

Lord Jesus Christ, you gave yourself for me upon the cross to bear my sins. I now give myself to you, all that I have, all that I am, all that I hope to be. Give me in return your forgiveness, your love, your life, and lead me by your light for Christ's sake. Amen.

Then the archdeacon invited anyone in the congregation who wanted to know more about giving their lives to Christ to ask him, as they went out, for a free leaflet called 'You have come to a point when you want to know God in your own life'.

After the service, however, Bob suspected that the congregation were keener to follow the silver band back to the Royal Oak than to follow up the archdeacon's invitation. The procession walking away from church looked somewhat stronger than the procession into church before the service. The band took up its place on the forecourt to the pub and Bob joined the long queue at the bar. Neither the vicar nor the archdeacon had followed the band for the next part of the village celebration.

Huntersbrook

Huntersbrook is a compact village of ancient stone houses nestling around a pond and green at the foot of a steep hill. The population is about 240 people, in a community where a number of houses are now clearly second homes which do not have all-the-year-round occupation.

The medieval parish church stands at the top of the hill, a mile or so away from the village settlement. It is now part of a benefice of five parishes and is used just on the third Sunday of the month for a mid-morning Eucharist. It has seating for about four hundred people. In the centre of the village a small Methodist chapel was built in 1833. The chapel continues to hold a 2.30 p.m. service every Sunday afternoon and runs a club for children at 6.00 p.m. on a Friday evening. It has modern comfortable chairs for thirty-five people and a gallery which can be used on special occasions.

When Laurie visited Huntersbrook it was not the third Sunday in the month, so the Methodist chapel provided the only service in the community that day. He arrived at the chapel at 2.20 p.m. and checked the handwritten notice pinned to the notice-board which confirmed that the service was to be taken by the Reverend Pamela Short. Inside the chapel, Pamela Short was discussing the hymns with another woman sitting at the harmonium. Both women were in their early sixties. Laurie was the first member of the congregation to arrive. After the hymn board had been put up, the minister came across to welcome Laurie and offer him a copy of the Methodist hymn-book, *Hymns and Psalms*. While Laurie sat waiting, he was very impressed by the display of children's models which had been produced by the Friday Club. The children were studying the exodus, and had made a number of tents as used in the wilderness.

By this time two couples, both in their sixties, had come in and sat on either side of the back row of chairs. Then a man in his seventies came and sat on the second row from the back on the left-hand side; a woman in her sixties took up her position opposite him on the right-hand side. Just on 2.30 p.m., a young couple arrived with a four-year-old girl and two boys aged six and eight. The older of the boys went to sit with his grandparents in the back row. The other two children and their parents filled the front row.

At 2.30 p.m., the minister began the service by inviting the congregation to sing the first hymn. The organist had her music open at the first hymn number on the board and seemed surprised when the minister announced the last number on the board. The congregation waited patiently while the organist found the new page. Just as the organist was about to start, the minister recognized her mistake, apologized and announced the correct number. There was another long pause while the organist found the page again. This whole operation was pro-longed by the fact that the new hymn-book seemed larger than the music stand on the organ, and its very newness made the pages reluctant to stay open anyway. Eventually the harmo-nium wheezed into life with 'Come, let us join our cheerful songs'.

After an opening prayer, the minister said how surprised and delighted she was to see so many children there. The two children in the front row peered round to check just how many others were lurking behind them. The six-year-old boy pulled a face at his eight-year-old brother. The minister then proceeded with a children's address.

'The other day', she said, 'I lost something very small and very precious to me', and she held her finger and thumb about an inch apart to demonstrate the point. 'Can any of you tell me what it was?' Father sitting in the front row whispered the word 'coin' into his six-year-old son's ear and instantly the child's hand flew up. 'No, dear, it was not a coin.' Mother whispered the word 'ring' into her four-year-old daughter's ear and instantly her hand flew up. 'No, dear, it was not a ring. Well, I'll have to tell you. It was a key. Now what do you think the key was for?' The scenario repeated itself. Father whispered 'car'; mother whispered 'front door'. 'No, dear, it was not the car; it was not the front door.

Well, I'll have to tell you. It was the key to my garden shed. Now what do you think I did next? Well, I have a friend I talk to when I lose things like that. So I went and told my friend all about it. Do you know who my friend is?' This time mother whispered the word 'Jesus' and her daughter's hand flew up again. 'Yes, dear, I told Jesus all about it. And do you know what he said? He said go and look in the dustbin. And do you know what? That is where I found my key. Now when you lose things, you must remember to ask Jesus to help you find them.'

The second hymn, perhaps specially chosen with the children in mind, retold the Old Testament story of God revealing to the young child Samuel what the old priest Eli could not see. The notices which followed concentrated mainly on thanking people for their involvement in a ninetieth birthday celebration which had recently taken place in the village; the collection the previous Sunday had amounted to £9.74; and the preacher next Sunday would be Mrs Farrow.

After the third hymn, the minister read the story of the transfiguration from St Mark's Gospel and preached on that theme for twenty-seven minutes. The story of the transfiguration, she said, reveals to us three important truths. The first truth concerns the certainty of the afterlife. Moses and Elijah had been away from this world for hundreds of years and now they are clearly seen by Peter, James and John, talking with Jesus. This is proof of life after death, she said. And we know from the Gospels that after death both heaven and hell wait for us. Only by claiming Jesus as our saviour can we be assured of going to the glory land. The second truth concerns the surety that we will recognize our loved ones when we are taken to the glory land. If Peter, James and John recognized Moses and Elijah whom they had never seen, how much more will we recognize those whom we have known and loved. The third truth is that Jesus was transformed on that mountain because he was praying to God. The glory simply shone from him. We, too, must pray that God's glory will shine through us.

After the final hymn, the members of the congregation and the minister began to chat with each other and they were all very keen not to let Laurie feel excluded. They seemed genuinely pleased to have a visitor among them. At the same time, however, Laurie could not help feeling that they also seemed slightly relieved that he was not hoping to become a regular member of their small, closely knit congregation.

5
MEDIUM
VILLAGES

Great Telfer and Little Telfer

GREAT TELFER AND Little Telfer are two very separate communities, situated on either side of a busy trunk road. Because of the road, they tend to look naturally for their social networks in opposite directions. However, twenty-five years or so ago pastoral reorganization brought these two parishes together under one incumbent. Now, during an interregnum, they are waiting to find themselves joined with the neighbouring group of parishes on Great Telfer's side of the trunk road.

The names of these two parishes are rather misleading. Great Telfer is the smaller of the two, with a population of some 200; Little Telfer now has a population of some 500. During the nineteenth century these two parishes fostered very different styles of churchmanship. Little Telfer was greatly influenced by the Tractarian movement and still possesses some fine continental vestments, artwork and other artifacts. Great Telfer, on the other hand, refuses to use vestments and claims an evangelical heritage.

The main Sunday morning worship alternates between the two churches, depending on the Sunday in the month. Little Telfer has become a Rite A parish. Great Telfer keeps to its prayer-book, with matins on the second Sunday of the month and communion on the fourth Sunday.

Andrew was visiting Great Telfer and Little Telfer at the beginning of October. Autumn leaves were already falling and it looked as if harvest for that year had well and truly finished some time earlier. Great Telfer and Little Telfer churches, however, were now both preparing for one of their major festivals during the year, the harvest festival. According to the parish magazine, harvest festival was to be celebrated in Little Telfer on the first Sunday in October and in Great Telfer on the second Sunday in October. Andrew thought that it would be interesting to compare the two experiences and to come back to these parishes on both Sundays.

Andrew's first visit to look round the churches was made on the Saturday immediately before Little Telfer's harvest festival. There had been a wedding in Little Telfer church at noon on Saturday and, consequently, the parishioners were later than usual in decorating their church for the festival. When Andrew arrived during mid-afternoon, the church seemed to be in utter chaos. Outside there were a Land-Rover, a four-wheel drive pick-up truck and several large estate cars, all with their rear doors open. The porch was completely cluttered with produce and flowers. Inside, a number of women were busy arranging the flowers and sorting the produce. The floor was strewn with the cut-off ends of flower stalks and reject pieces of Oasis. Andrew decided to come back later.

When he returned about 4.30 p.m., the scene was transformed. The vehicles had gone, the produce and flowers had been exquisitely displayed and the floor was spotless. Just one woman remained. She was busy, not displaying flowers and produce, but arranging the artwork produced by the pupils of the village school. She had already flanked both sides of the porch with a beautiful display of children's work and she was now fixing a picture to the bench end on every pew. She was happy to talk with Andrew and explained that the village school would be taking a full part in tomorrow's service.

She then asked Andrew to lend her a hand in moving the grand flower display which had been arranged in front of the rood screen. 'Mrs Smith-James', she said, 'has always done her harvest display there. But tomorrow it will be in the way. You see, when children come we bring a portable table and put it just here to act as a nave altar.' 'Won't Mrs Smith-James mind when she comes tomorrow and finds her flower arrangement moved?' asked Andrew. 'She won't know', said the woman, 'because she doesn't come to church any more; not since we changed the form of service. She'll be going across to Great Telfer next week. Anyway, we can move it back tomorrow, as soon as the service is over.' Andrew was fascinated by Mrs Smith-James' commitment to decorate the church for services she would not attend.

Andrew arrived for the service on Sunday morning at 9.50 a.m. The body of the church was already full and people were now being directed towards the gallery by the forty-year-old sidesman. A teenager was handing out a service leaflet and a copy of the Rite A service booklet to people as they came in. By 9.55 a.m. the gallery was full as well and the sidesman was now packing people into the space under the tower, where they would have to stand. Andrew found it almost impossible to count the congregation, but he guessed that there were more than 220 people crowded into the small church.

While the congregation were arriving, the school recorder players were joining with their headteacher's guitar to provide a background of music. But the general excitement of the children and the conversation of their parents tended to drown the best efforts of this small group.

Because of the difficulty involved in getting everyone into the church, the service began five minutes late. The leadership of the service was clearly in the hands of the reader and the headteacher of the school, a woman and a man both in their forties. The reader began the service by welcoming the congregation and the school and by introducing the visiting priest. Today was the first Sunday of their new interregnum. The opening hymn 'All creatures of our God and King' led into the prayers of penitence and the harvest collect. Then the headteacher took over the ministry of the word, sequencing the work which the school had prepared to share with the congregation.

Some of the older pupils began the ministry of the word by reading short sentences they had composed about harvest and by introducing the theme of 'daily bread'. One of the teachers read a short extract from Deuteronomy 26 (GNB):

> each of you must place in a basket the first part of each crop that you harvest and you must take it with you to the one place of worship. Go to the priest . . .

The congregation sang 'He's got the whole world in his hand' and stood while the reader read the gospel from John 6:

> my father gives you the bread from heaven,
> the true bread which gives life to the world.
> I am the bread of life.

After the gospel the pupils of the school presented a wide collage of their project work on harvest.

Now it was the congregation's turn to join in 'We plough the fields, and scatter the good seed on the land', and a collection was taken. During this hymn the nave altar was moved into place. The priest gave a short commentary on what was happening, emphasizing the continuity between the annual offering of the produce of harvest time and the weekly offering of the bread and wine of the communion service. Part of the harvest loaf was broken off to become the bread for the communion and part was placed alongside all the other harvest offerings.

After the prayer of thanksgiving, simple instructions were given about receiving communion and those who were not communicants were invited to come for a blessing. Almost everyone went up to the altar rail. Out of a congregation of over 220, there were about sixty communicants. During the distribution of communion, three teenage girls skilfully played a variety of woodwind instruments, including recorders, flute and oboe.

The service closed with the hymn 'Praise, O praise our God and King'. After the service people seemed in no particular hurry to leave. Coffee and squash were available at the back of the church and in the churchyard and the rest of the harvest loaf was broken up and shared with the adults and children.

Talking with some of the people afterwards, Andrew learnt that some of the regular worshippers had stayed away because they did not like the changes from their usual form of service. Looking back inside the church, Andrew saw two women busy bringing back Mrs Smith-James' flower display into its place before the screen. Someone else was busy removing the children's paintings from the bench ends. Andrew could not help thinking that before long the 'disturbance' of the morning would be forgotten and all would be restored to normal.

The following week Andrew arrived to share in the much more traditional harvest festival at Great Telfer. Great Telfer church seats about seventy to seventy-five people and by 10.00 a.m. all the seats were taken. The congregation today were generally older than the previous week. There were three families with children present: one with two teenage boys, one with four girls between the ages of seven and twelve, and one with a three-year-old boy and three-month-old twins. The twins helped to enliven the service considerably.

Before the service the organ was played well by a teenage musician. No sidesperson was on duty to welcome worshippers to Great Telfer church. Andrew walked in and looked for a seat towards the back. Copies of *Hymns Ancient and Modern Revised* and the Book of Common Prayer were already set out in the pews.

Today the service began precisely at 10.00 a.m., when the choir of three men and two women emerged from the vestry. They were followed by the visiting minister and the church-warden. The churchwarden welcomed the visiting minister and also invited people to stay for coffee in the churchyard after the service. The service began with the harvest hymn 'Come, ye thankful people, come'.

The form of service was the traditional prayer-book service of matins. The psalm, Psalm 65, was said, but the Venite, Te Deum and Jubilate were all sung. The congregation knew the canticles well and raced through them joyfully. The first lesson was read from the Authorized Version of the Bible by a seventy-year-old woman; the second lesson was read from *The Jerusalem Bible* by a sixty-year-old man. The sermon was preached between the Jubilate and the creed.

After the collects, the collection was taken during the hymn 'To thee, O Lord, our hearts we raise', and the minister moved into the sanctuary to prepare the altar for communion. Matins completed, the communion service was begun with the comfortable words. Throughout the comfortable words, Sursum Corda, prayer of humble access and prayer of consecration, half the congregation stood and the other half knelt, presumably distinguishing between those who had been influenced by liturgical reforms and those who had not been so influenced.

During the distribution of the communion, the young organist played an incongruous set of short voluntaries, mainly from a collection of favourite airs by Handel, including the 'Harmonious blacksmith' and 'I know that my redeemer liveth'. Unlike the previous week, the majority of those attending were communicant members of the Church of England. Out of a congregation of seventy-five, fifty-five received communion. The children who were not confirmed came up to the altar rail for a blessing but, today, the adults not intending to receive communion preferred to stay in their pews.

The service closed with the hymn 'Fair waved the golden corn'. The previous week, coffee had been served inside the church and people chose whether to congregate inside or outside to drink it. Today coffee was served outside and people were discouraged by the churchwarden from bringing their coffee back into church. One of the eighteenth-century table tombs in the churchyard provided the ideal context for the hot-water urn and for counter service.

People were very friendly towards Andrew and quickly he learnt all sorts of things about the life of the church in the parish. The woman who read the first lesson from the Authorized Version told him how much she objected to the new forms of service and how she now only came to church when the old form of service was used. One of the choirmen told him that he had joined the choir at the age of ten and how sad he was that they had not sung that morning 'We plough the fields, and scatter the good seed on the land'.

Andrew had now seen both Great Telfer and Little Telfer at their best. But what he also learnt was that on a 'normal' Sunday the 10.00 a.m. service, alternating between the two churches, would be attended by congregations of between fifteen and twenty-five.

Clifton Berriffe and Clifton Magens

The country lane leading into the Cliftons carries two name boards, one each side of the road. The houses on the east side of the lane are in Clifton Magens; the houses on the west side of the lane are in Clifton Berriffe. Each community has its own medieval church, both showing traces of their Saxon origin. The two churches are no more than three or four minutes walk apart.

St Peter's at Clifton Magens is the larger of the two churches and has been a parish church in its own right since medieval times. St James' at Clifton Berriffe began life as a chapel-of-ease, but not associated with Clifton Magens. St James' became a parish in its own right as late as the 1860s and was eventually linked with St Peter's in the 1920s. Today these two churches share their vicar with two other neighbouring villages. Together Clifton Berriffe and Clifton Magens now have a combined population of about 550.

During a normal month, matins is held in Clifton Magens on the first Sunday at 10.00 a.m. and in Clifton Berriffe on the second Sunday at 10.00 a.m.; on the third Sunday there is family communion in Clifton Magens at 10.00 a.m. and evensong is held in Clifton Berriffe on the fourth Sunday in the month. When there is a fifth Sunday in the month, Holy Communion is celebrated in Clifton Berriffe at 8.00 a.m. This regular pattern, however, seems to be varied frequently to meet specific local needs. For example, whenever one of the four churches celebrates its patronal festival the other three churches are closed down for that Sunday in order to share in a 'family communion for the villages'.

As well as the two Anglican churches, there is also a United Reformed church in Clifton Magens. This church has a very long history, dating back to the 1660s. The present chapel is a charming red-brick building, dated 1782. A service is held here every Sunday morning at 10.30 a.m.

Derek and Christine visited the Cliftons during early November. Finding it difficult to park near either of the parish churches because of the narrowness of the lanes, they stopped first at the United Reformed church, leaving the car in the chapel's own car park. The chapel was locked. Behind the chapel there was a modern hall and set of rooms. Peering through the windows, Derek and Christine saw a room set out for children's activities, a kitchen, a comfortable lounge and a study, complete with telephone and office equipment. The United Reformed chapel seemed well equipped for ministry in the 1980s. The notice-board outside was unpretentious, but gave all the essential information about service times, together with the minister's name, address and telephone number.

Following a footpath round from the chapel, Derek and Christine quickly came to Clifton Magens parish church. Here there was no notice-board outside. The back page of the parish newsletter was pinned to the gatepost giving the times of services for November. Already, so early in the month, the page was looking damp and weather-worn. The church was unlocked. Inside it was cold, damp and musty. At the back there were piles of the Book of Common Prayer, *The Alternative Service Book 1980* and *Hymns Ancient and Modern Revised*. Although these books were all relatively new, they had taken on the damp mustiness of the church itself.

Another short walk and Derek and Christine came to Clifton Berriffe parish church. The notice-board outside gave the name of the church, but no further details. Here service times were not pinned to the gate. Again the church was unlocked. Again the inside was cold, damp and musty. But here the effect was made much sadder by the fact that the paint and plaster were peeling from the walls. At some stage the interior of the church had been decorated with an emulsion and now the ancient fabric was protesting. This church, too, had copies of the Book of Common Prayer and *Hymns Ancient and Modern Revised*, but not of *The Alternative Service Book 1980*. While service times had not been advertised outside, or in the porch, a few copies of the parish newsletter had been left on one of the pews. They provided information about services and gave the vicar's name and address.

As far as could be gleaned from the parish magazine, very little takes place in the life of the four village churches during the week, apart from Wednesday mornings when a mid-week communion service is held. Once a month this mid-week communion service comes to Clifton Magens.

The parish newsletter also made it plain that the normal pattern of services for the second Sunday in the month would be different during November, in order to accommodate Remembrance Sunday. Remembrance Sunday at Clifton Berriffe is kept by holding an outdoor service at the war memorial at 10.55 a.m., before processing to the church.

On Remembrance Sunday morning, Derek and Christine parked in the chapel car park at 10.20 a.m., next to two other cars. Christine walked across the damp grass to the chapel; Derek set off down the road towards the war memorial to join in the Anglican service.

Christine stood for a moment or two outside the chapel door, listening to the organist rehearse 'O God, our help in ages past'. Then she opened the door and walked in. The chapel was empty apart from the organist and two people standing at the back, a man and a woman in their early sixties. The man introduced himself as the minister and welcomed Christine to the chapel. She was given a photocopied order of service, a copy of *The Psalms*, published by Collins in 1977, and the *Church Hymnary*, revised in 1973 under the auspices of the General Assemblies of the Church of Scotland, the Presbyterian Church of England, the Presbyterian Church of Ireland and the Presbyterian Church of Wales.

Inside, the chapel retained much of its early simplicity and character. Although electricity had been installed for concealed lighting in the roof, the old oil-lamps had been retained at the end of each pew. By 10.30 a.m. the congregation had grown to twenty-one adults and five children. The adults comprised seven men and fourteen women, covering a wide age span from mid-twenties to mid-seventies.

The service began promptly at 10.30 a.m. A layman carrying a large Bible led the minister into the chapel, placed the Bible on the reading desk and switched on a tape recorder to record the service. The minister called the congregation to worship with a short prayer and introduced the traditional Remembrance Sunday hymn, 'O God, our help in ages past'. After the opening hymn the minister read a few well-chosen contemporary-language prayers on the themes of war and peace and led the congregation in the Lord's Prayer and the recitation of a short psalm.

Next the minister gave an address for the five children present in the congregation. He began by asking them short questions: 'Children, you must know what today is? – Why do we have Remembrance Sunday? – Which war do we remember today?' The children answered confidently and willingly. The minister then shared in a relaxed way some of his own memories of the war as a child, growing up in London and being evacuated to the countryside.

He told the children: When the Second World War began I was only ten years old. Living in London we saw bombers and Spitfires and the war came very close. What worried me most was that a bomb would fall on my house and destroy my train set. I was evacuated to stay in the country. I was lucky because I stayed with family, but many boys and girls left in school groups to stay with people they did not know. They went away from home with just a bundle of clothes and a gas mask. Many came to this village. Many found that living in the countryside was very different and many were upset because of what they experienced. Many children are still suffering because of wars today. And we remember how Jesus had to leave his home when he was a baby because of Herod. Jesus was evacuated too.

The children's talk was followed by Rudyard Kipling's patriotic hymn:

> Land of our birth, we pledge to thee
> our love and toil in the years to be.

Then came the notices, offering, doxology, dedication and the opportunity for the five children and two of their parents to leave for the Sunday school.

A short Scripture reading from Isaiah 11. 1–9 (NIV) concluded with the famous verses:

> They will neither harm nor destroy
>   on all my holy mountain,
>   for the earth will be full of the knowledge of the LORD
>   as the waters cover the sea.

One verse of the hymn 'Christ is the world's true light' brought the time to 11.00 a.m. The congregation stood to observe the two-minute silence and then sang the hymn 'Father eternal, ruler of creation'. The sermon which followed was a very carefully crafted and clear meditation on the theme of remembrance.

The minister began his sermon by saying that he did so without a biblical text because he could find nothing that truly fitted in with what they were doing on Remembrance Sunday. Today is not a church festival, but a state occasion. It does, however, provide Christians with a clear focus for prayer and thanksgiving. So what is the idea of remembrance? It is a complex idea and involves much more than the psychological act of remembering.

First, Remembrance Sunday means something very special for those who experienced war. For them it is a calling to mind of past experience, especially for those in the armed forces. Names and situations come flooding back. They remember individuals who were killed and whole families who were wiped out. We remember how the Presbyterian Church of England lost most of its leaders in 1945 when a bomb fell where they were all meeting; a sad blow for a small denomination.

Second, Remembrance Sunday means to commemorate; a solemn corporate act of naming, mourning and giving thanks. Our naming invokes God's memory of those who died in war, not just those recorded on our memorial, but those who have no one to remember them, but whose names are inscribed in God's eternal book of remembrance. Our mourning concerns that aspect of the human condition which gives rise to wars in the first place. Our thanksgiving rejoices for the seed of good in every human life so cruelly destroyed in war.

Third, Remembrance Sunday puts us in mind of Jesus' words at the last supper, 'Do this in remembrance of me.' In Greek the word is *anamnesis*. It means not remembering something in the past, but actually making present in the here and now. It is the calling to mind which is making something real, bringing something to reality. What we are helping to make real today by our act of remembrance is the peace of the world. When Jesus' peace takes hold of the human soul, the urge to kill and destroy will die. In the peace which Jesus offers lies a whole new future for humankind. What we are doing today helps to bring that future to come to pass. So may it be.

The service closed at 11.25 a.m. with the hymn 'O day of God, draw nigh' and the benediction. Then Christine joined the minister and many of the congregation in the schoolroom for coffee. The members of the congregation were friendly and articulate and wanted to continue discussing the sermon. No one was in a hurry to go home. The close relationship between minister and people was very obvious. Christine wondered how a small congregation like this could support a minister and benefit from such a high quality of ministry. The answer appears to be that the minister is not paid by the chapel but works in psychotherapy at a neighbouring hospital. Without this part-time ministry, Clifton Berriffe's United Reformed church may well have ceased to exist.

Derek arrived at the war memorial at 10.50 a.m. The war memorial stands on a corner by a road junction. Two elderly men were standing on the opposite side of the road, wearing their military badges. By 10.55 a.m. the crowd had grown to twelve men and fifteen women, all aged between fifty and eighty, and a teenage boy. Noticing Derek as a stranger, a group of local people engaged him in conversation and asked where he had come from. He learnt that the chapel and church used to take it in turns to lead that service at the war memorial, but now the chapel no longer takes part. He was told that the chapel does not have much to do with the village itself. Most of the congregation for the chapel drive in from other places.

A woman handed round an order of service and the vicar processed across from the church. He was a gentle, white-haired man in his sixties. His cassock, surplice and cloak were blowing in the wind as he took up his place by the war memorial. The crowd continued to stand on the opposite side of the road. The vicar beckoned them across; they seemed reluctant to move. The vicar started the service in a low voice, while they were still out of earshot. Short-sighted, the vicar held the service sheet close to his face, his features disappearing behind it. A noisy aeroplane flew overhead. Undisturbed and unheard, the vicar continued to read the names of those local people who had died in the two World Wars. Colonel Flinders stepped forward and declaimed from memory:

They shall grow not old, as we that are left grow old; age shall not weary them, nor the years condemn. At the going down of the sun and in the morning, we will remember them.

Another plane flew overhead during his words. The vicar announced the two-minute silence and nervously kept checking his watch to make sure that the silence did not go on for too long. Then one of the men wearing military medals stepped forward to lay a wreath of poppies on the war memorial. Half a dozen other people placed poppies and crosses in the grass around the war memorial. The atmosphere was charged with memories, sadness and loss.

The vicar turned and led the silent procession from the war memorial to the church. The teenage boy broke away from the procession and made his way home. The two men who had come wearing their military badges took it in turns to photograph each other replacing the wreath by the war memorial. Then they, too, went off home. A depleted congregation completed the procession into church.

The vicar began the service in church by announcing hymn 166. The organist began by playing hymn 165 and the congregation chose to follow the organist rather than the vicar:

O God, our help in ages past,
our hope for years to come,
our shelter from the stormy blast,
and our eternal home.

After the first hymn, the vicar led an act of penitence from the duplicated order of service. The printing was faint in places and gave the vicar's failing eyesight some difficulties. The second hymn was announced somewhat apologetically. The vicar explained that people would recognize the tune, if not the words. He then asked the congregation to read the words through silently before the organist played over the tune, so they could appreciate the relevance of the words of the hymn for Remembrance Sunday. The hymn was 'Son of God, eternal saviour':

As thou, Lord, hast lived for others,
so may we for others live;
freely have thy gifts been granted,
freely may thy servants give.

After the second hymn, Colonel Flinders read a passage from John's Gospel, chapter 15, in the Authorized Version: 'Greater love hath no man than this, that a man lay down his life for his friends.' The lesson was followed directly by the fifteen-minute sermon. The sermon had been nicely prepared but was spoilt by poor delivery. The vicar appeared to be working from a full text of what he wished to say, but once again to be having difficulty in reading what he had prepared. He began by painting a skilful word-picture. It was a pleasant little cul-de-sac of Georgian houses. Through the summer the avenue of trees had given shade. But by November the leaves had fallen. The council sweepers were on strike. The drains blocked. And it was a very wet November. The street flooded. But the people did not pull together and no one would sweep away the leaves. Some of them thought of the war, with longing, with nostalgia, when everyone was willing to lend a hand and to pull together.

The vicar then invited his congregation to think about the good aspects of war, those examples which shone as a light during the dark years of war, and to think of Christ as the true light which darkness would never quench. He gave three examples of what he had in mind. First, there is the light of pulling together. Today our country is torn apart by sectional interests, for example workers and employers. If only we could all pull together as we did in the war, things would improve. Second, there is the light of a common purpose. Today the common enemy of inflation stares our country in the face. If only we could agree on a common purpose against it. Third, there is the light of sacrifice. And we need to be willing to make sacrifices again to get our country back on its feet. More could be demanded of our people now, and more would be given by them all. During wartime, lamps were lit by which we could see our way for a better Britain. If only we could lift those lamps up now. Jesus rose again and his light shines forever. Today our country lacks faith. We must believe in Jesus because his light never goes out.

After the sermon, the vicar led an act of rededication. Then, during the third hymn, the collection was taken for the Earl Haigh Fund by two men, one in his forties and the other in his sixties:

> Thy Kingdom come, O God,
> thy rule, O Christ, begin;
> break with thine iron rod
> the tyrannies of sin.

Next the vicar led the prayers of intercession, praying for our nation, the commonwealth, the Queen, our allies, those whom we fear, those who work for peace, those who suffer as a result of war, the Royal British Legion, the church's gospel of love and peace,

> that men and women everywhere may be able
> to live in the freedom and fellowship of
> your kingdom.

The service closed with the national anthem and the blessing at 11.45 a.m. The vicar went into the church porch and smiled at people as they went out. The worshippers drifted away quite quickly.

The tradition of Remembrance Sunday at the village war memorial had been observed for yet another year. For some people who had gathered there to keep the two-minute silence it had been a very moving experience, as they remembered and as they grieved. But the one person under the age of fifty who had come to the war memorial had not stayed on for the service in church. The two men who had come specifically to lay the wreath had fulfilled their duty at the war memorial and they too had gone home without attending the service. The chapel had, in recent years, disassociated itself from this act of village piety. The Royal British Legion was no longer represented through its colours and standards. In fact only a very small proportion of the inhabitants of the two villages had decided to keep Remembrance Sunday in this way. Today's service had made such good sense largely because the vicar, too, had remembered those years of war and understood the needs of those parishioners who were not regular churchgoers and yet who felt the desire to continue to keep the memory alive of Remembrance Sunday. Derek could not help wondering, however, what a younger country parson would make of it all when the present vicar retired in a few years' time.

East and West Hemsbourne

The two communities of East and West Hemsbourne have so grown together that it is no longer easy to tell where the one ends and the other starts. Today they have a joint population of some 1,450 inhabitants.

George visited East and West Hemsbourne during May on the Saturday before Whit Sunday. The morning had been over-cast but dry; when George set out after lunch, a light drizzle was already settling into a persistent rain. The road wound round past the butcher's, the pub and the small red-brick Methodist chapel. The chapel was set back from the pavement, behind iron railings. The gate in the railings was sealed with a large padlock. George shook the gate lightly to confirm that it would not yield. The only notice outside the chapel made it clear that there was a service there every Sunday at 3.00 p.m., but no other information was given about the life or ministry of the chapel.

Leaving the chapel, George followed the road round past the post office, another pub and a row of delightful thatched cottages, set back from the road up on the side of a rising bank. Then on the left he came to the beautiful medieval parish church. Some of the church stands as it did in the early thirteenth century; much of the church, however, was remodelled in the Perpendicular style with a large five-light east window.

As he approached the church, George saw that there were lights on inside and he was greeted by the sound of music. Stepping inside the church, George saw the nave and chancel taken up by a group of teenagers practising a liturgical dance, to the accompaniment of stately early eighteenth-century music coming from a cassette-player. They were being supervised by a young woman in her twenties.

The space beneath the massive west tower and the immediate area at the back of the church had been professionally converted into a parish room, complete with wooden wall panelling, cupboard space and a small kitchen area. Here George discovered another group of young people working out some form of dramatic presentation. They were being supervised by two young men in their twenties.

While the dance group took a five-minute break, George talked with their leader, Rachel, to discover what was taking place. Rachel explained that the parish had arranged a Pentecost project day for families and young people. The parish had been planning the day for some months as an opportunity to encourage more people, especially young people, to take a part in designing and preparing for a special Sunday service. The planning group had chosen two of the key images underlying the celebration of Pentecost and then looked for ways in which local people and local resources could explore and enrich those images. The images chosen were wind and fire.

Rachel described how the project day began at 10.00 a.m., when young people and families met in the village school and spent around half an hour singing hymns, choruses and songs, and discovering the opportunities of the day. After this introduction, five different visits or activities had been arranged to develop the themes of wind and fire.

One of the choirmen was a steam enthusiast. Not far from the Hemsbournes there is a railway preservation society which happened to be in steam over that weekend. Along with some other adults, he had led a party to visit the steam engines, to discover something about the power of fire to drive these giant locomotives.

A family in the congregation was keen on sailing. They

arranged to take a party to their sailing club, some ten miles away, to look at the boats, to discover something about the power of the wind to drive these little boats across the lake.

Another family in the village operated a small forge. They offered to get the forge going on Saturday morning and to demonstrate how it works. Those who visited the forge saw the bellows fan the flames into great heat and they watched the metal glow in the flames. They saw the craftsman take the hot metal and hammer it into shape. Again, they discovered something about the immense power of fire.

Someone else knew a local fireman and arranged a trip into the neighbouring town to have a guided tour of the fire station. They climbed on the fire-engines and listened to the firemen talk about the power of fire to destroy as well as to create.

The church organist had said that a lot of young people rarely got the opportunity to build and to enjoy a really good bonfire. The rector had offered the rectory garden as an appropriate site for a bonfire. The fifth party had, therefore, spent part of the morning collecting fuel for the bonfire and the rest of the morning smoking out the local neighbourhood.

After lunch in the school, a range of different workshops had been organized to build on the experiences of the morning. By coming into church, George had discovered the dance group and the drama group. Rachel suggested that he should go across to the school to discover what was happening there.

Several different activities were going on in the school hall. An elderly man, in his seventies, was working with a small group of children in one corner, making a weather-vane, to tell the direction of the wind. In another corner a twenty-year-old girl was helping children to blow up balloons, to see how they floated when full of air. Elsewhere a mother was helping to design a kind of tapestry pattern of leaping flames, to decorate a chasuble for Sunday's service. A fourth group was making origami models and other paper crafts, including aeroplanes to fly.

Away from the main hall, each of the classrooms contained a different type of activity. The infants' room had been taken over by the crèche. The classroom which housed the piano had been taken over for a music group. The two classrooms which opened on to each other were being used for art and craft work. In one, the desktops had been covered with newspaper and children were busy painting pictures, supervised by some of the parents. In the other a group was working alongside a young teacher on a large collage, to become an altar frontal for Sunday's service.

On Sunday morning, George arrived for the service in very good time, which was fortunate since parking space around the church and along the village street was quickly taken up. Children and families were chatting happily and noisily along the path up to the church door. The church porch had been used to display some of the children's work, and children were pointing out to their parents what they had made and contributed to the display. A team of sidespersons were welcoming the worshippers as they came in, giving them a eucharist booklet, a booklet of Pentecost hymns and a service booklet specially produced for the day.

The inside of the church had been completely transformed since George was there on the Saturday afternoon. Someone had obviously taken a great deal of care during the Saturday evening to display all the various things which had been produced in the workshops. A nave altar was now in position by the chancel step, proudly displaying the children's collage altar frontal showing the fire-engine, the steam engine, the sailing boat, the forge and the bonfire. The massive stone arcades, separating the aisles from the nave, were each decorated with posters. The window-sills displayed models and paper sculptures. Each bench end was decorated with a picture or painting. The mass of balloons which the children had inflated the previous day were now streaming from the ancient rafters. At the back of the church the offertory gifts of bread and wine were set out on a table, which was also decorated with balloons.

Before the service started, the church felt rather like a busy railway station, as people moved about, chatting and talking. They seemed to bring with them an air of expectancy and excitement. At 10.00 a.m., the organist began a majestic voluntary. The congregation fell silent to listen. After a minute or two of the organ music, the atmosphere was right for the service to begin. The vicar announced the gentle lilting hymn, 'Spirit of God, as strong as the wind, gentle as is the dove', sung to the tune of the Skye Boat Song. The congregation stood to sing and the choir processed in. The choir consisted of a dozen or so teenage girls, four adult men and three adult women.

The service began with the prayers of penitence, the Pentecost collect and the Pentecost reading from Acts 2. Then, while this reading was still fresh in everyone's mind and before the gospel reading about the Holy Spirit from John 20, the dance group presented their meditative dance on the movement of the wind. After the gospel, various groups of children and young people shared with the congregation what they had prepared the previous day. Their offering was interspersed with choruses and songs.

The service then proceeded with the creed, intercessions, notices and peace. The peace was a happy extended affair, with people moving freely around the church to greet each other and with the parish priest trying desperately to greet each member of the congregation individually. After the peace, the offertory procession included not just bread and wine, but examples of all the various activities of the previous day. Even balloons were brought up to place around the nave altar.

During the prayer of thanksgiving some of the younger children played happily in the aisle; some of the older children thumbed through the various booklets trying to follow what was being said by the priest. Like the peace, the distribution of communion was an extended affair, as a couple of hundred people made their way up to the altar and waited to kneel down to receive either communion or a blessing from the priest. George thought that on a normal Sunday Hemsbourne church was probably used to dealing with a smaller congregation. During the distribution of communion, the choir led the singing of a series of hymns and songs.

After the post-communion prayer, the service closed with the hymn 'Blow, thou cleansing wind'. As soon as the choir processed out, balloons were released from the rafters. Children clamoured to find a balloon to take home. George helped one young boy to pluck a long red balloon from the cluster of strings in which it had become entangled and watched him rush up to the vicar waving it triumphantly and shouting 'I blew this balloon up yesterday!' Certainly as far as this child was concerned, the celebration of Pentecost in Hemsbourne church had been an exciting and a memorable weekend.

Having enjoyed the morning service in the parish church, George decided to stay around to attend the Methodist service in the afternoon. He arrived at the chapel at 2.50 p.m. There was one other car parked immediately outside. The door was closed. George pushed the door open and walked in. Inside, the building smelt damp and musty. Sitting in the front row of pews on the left-hand side were a man and a woman in their seventies. The man looked round and seemed surprised to see an unfamiliar face. He came across to greet George. Shaking him warmly by the hand, he offered George a hymn-book, *Hymns and Psalms*, and a copy of the *Sunday Services* and said how nice it was to see a fresh face.

He took George up to the front to meet his wife. They explained that they did not actually live in Hemsbourne, but had been coming to chapel there for a number of years because the wife played the piano. She had suffered a stroke six years ago and since then had partly lost the use of her left hand, but since no one else could be found to play she kept on doing so. Then with the aid of her walking-frame she moved slowly across to the piano ready for the service. George went and sat in the second row of pews from the back, because he did not feel it right to go to the very back.

At 2.55 p.m., two other elderly men came in and sat in the row behind George. Then a woman in her sixties came and sat in the row immediately in front of him. At 2.58 p.m. the minister arrived. The pianist's husband told the minister that they had a visitor that afternoon. The minister eyed George up and down but said nothing.

The Whit Sunday service began with the hymn 'Holy Spirit, hear us'. The pianist gave an uncertain lead and both George and the minister sensed that it was best to leave the singing to the other four members of the congregation. The minister read both lessons himself from a very tatty Bible, choosing passages from Joel 2 and Acts 2. Between the lessons came the hymn 'Breathe on me, breath of God'. After the second reading, the vicar announced the previous week's collection of £6.50 and the following week's preacher. Then he said that he had something very important to say which he had intended to leave to the end, but perhaps was better said straight away.

The congregation apparently already knew that the architect's survey had identified a major structural weakness with their building. Unless £5,000 could be spent immediately on repair work, the insurers had refused to renew public liability insurance on the building when the present period of cover expired in

October. Now the Methodist church in the neighbouring town had considered the congregation's appeal for help and had decided, of course with considerable reluctance, not to come to their aid. As a consequence, the minister said he could see no future for the chapel beyond October. The church in the neighbouring town had, however, offered to organize a car rota to ferry worshippers from the Hemsbournes to both their morning and evening services, if they would accept that invitation.

After hearing this announcement, the small congregation had even less enthusiasm to sing the third hymn, 'Our blest redeemer, ere he breathed his tender last farewell'. The sermon which followed drew heavily on the minister's earlier missionary experience in Zambia of bushfires, and on Wesley's conversion experience. The sermon lasted for nineteen minutes.

The next hymn, 'Spread the table of the Lord', led into the prayer of thanksgiving from the *Sunday Services*. The minister brought the bread and individual communion glasses round the seated congregation. He hovered while the worshippers drained their glasses and returned them empty to the rack. The service closed at 3.57 p.m. with the hymn 'Holy Spirit, truth divine'.

After the service George talked with the minister about the future of the chapel. He learned that the minister had care of four village chapels as well as the large town church. The minister confessed to being tired and very uncertain about the future viability of village Methodism. His preference was to concentrate his ministry and energy on the larger town congregation. In fact his only real contact with Hemsbourne chapel was the monthly Communion service.

George could not help contrasting the experiences of the morning and afternoon services. But he also wondered whether Hemsbourne parish church would be able to sustain its thriving ministry after the present vicar moved on and the diocesan plans were implemented to amalgamate the Hemsbournes with the neighbouring benefice.

6
LARGE
VILLAGES

Sheepton

SHEEPTON IS A community of 1,500 people, built at the intersection of two roads. Traffic lights at the centre of the village control the incessant flow of traffic. Just a short distance from these traffic lights, a narrow street leads to a secluded square. On one side of the square there stands the medieval parish church; on the other side a closed chapel now houses a small public library. A row of five stone houses carry the date 1674 and another stone cottage is dated 1665. A couple of minutes' walk from the square in one direction brings us to the Victorian Methodist chapel; a couple of minutes' walk in another direction brings us to the modern Catholic church.

Arriving in Sheepton on a Saturday afternoon, Henry and Judith visited all three of the active churches. The parish church has a fine thirteenth century west tower; the rest of the church was completely rebuilt during the 1870s and 1880s. The last hundred years has begun to take its toll on the fabric. The outside of the building now has a rather sad, decaying and neglected feel. The churchyard was also in need of care and attention.

There was no notice-board outside the parish church, so Henry and Judith walked into the porch to see what they could discern about the life of St Peter's church. Here the notice-board clearly set out the details of the Sunday and weekday services, and the arrangements made for baptisms and weddings. There was also an up-to-date table of fees in the porch. The vicar's name, address and telephone number were clearly displayed, although there was no information about the lay officers or the lay leaders of the church.

The vicar of Sheepton also has care of Lighton, the neighbouring village of 150 people. The service pattern between these two churches has been devised to achieve variety rather than consistency. On the first, second and fourth Sundays of the month there is an 8.30 a.m. Holy Communion service at Sheepton; on the third Sunday in the month this early morning service takes place in Lighton. On the first, third and fourth Sundays in the month, there is an 11.00 a.m. service at Sheepton; on the second Sunday the late morning service at Sheepton takes place at 11.15 a.m., rather than 11.00 a.m., to make a 10.00 a.m. service possible at Lighton. On the second and fourth Sundays in the month this late morning service is matins; on the third Sunday in the month it is a family communion, and on the first Sunday in the month a non-eucharistic family service is held. An evening service takes place every Sunday in Sheepton at 6.00 p.m. On the first, second and third Sundays in the month it is an evensong; on the fourth Sunday in the month it is a non-liturgical praise service.

Finding the parish church unlocked, Henry and Judith went inside. The church guidebook was professionally produced. The parish magazine was rather less well produced. Reading the parish magazine, they were struck by the vicar's letter about children's work. He was appealing for Sunday school teachers. He would like to start a Sunday school at Sheepton, but was unable to do so until someone volunteered to lead it.

The Methodist church in Sheepton gave its secrets less easily than the Anglican church, but all the key information was clearly posted on the notice-board outside. The neat Victorian red-brick building nestled comfortably behind the locked iron gate and railings. The ironwork had been recently painted and it looked as if the front of the chapel had also been recently repointed. Henry and Judith saw from the notice-board that there were two services held every Sunday at 11.00 a.m. and 6.30 p.m. Junior church met every Sunday at the same time as the morning service. The Methodist minister actually lived in the manse next to the chapel. So this meant that there were two resident ministers, an Anglican and a Methodist, living in this village of 1,500 people.

The Catholic church was set back from the road in its own grounds, with a lot of parking space around it. The large notice-board by the gate simply gave the name of the church and the priest's telephone number. The Catholic priest was not resident in this village. The Catholic church was built to a modern design and looked no more than ten years old. The main door was standing open, leading into a light and airy foyer. In the foyer the notice-boards gave full details about the life of the Catholic community in the neighbourhood and information about the Sunday and weekday services in this and in the neighbouring churches. A bookstall contained a range of Catholic literature. Between the foyer and the church itself there was a glass partition and door. The door into the church was locked, but it was possible to see the altar through the glass screen and there were chairs and a prayer desk in the foyer itself. Sunday Masses were celebrated in Sheepton Catholic church every week at 6.00 p.m. on Saturday evening and at 10.00 a.m. on Sunday morning.

The Sunday when Henry and Judith were visiting Sheepton there were, therefore, three services held in the Anglican church, two in the Methodist chapel and one in the Catholic church. The early morning service in the parish church was attended by a congregation of twenty-five. The mid-morning services were attended by seventy-four people in the Catholic church, forty-one in the Anglican church and thirty-four in the Methodist chapel, including fifteen children and an adult who withdrew from the main service into the junior church. The evening services in the Anglican and Methodist churches both drew congregations of ten adults.

Henry and Judith attended the evening service in the Methodist church. When they arrived at 6.20 p.m. the chapel steward was standing outside by the iron gate, looking up and down the street for his congregation. He welcomed Henry and Judith very warmly, enquiring whether they were 'Sheeptonians or visitors'. He was excited to be able to tell them that they had come on an evening when their minister would be taking the service himself. 'But tonight there is not going to be a sermon', he said. 'When you go in you will see that there is a television set on the communion table. We are going to have a video tonight.' So saying, he led Henry and Judith up the steps into the entrance area of the chapel. He gave them a pew leaflet and a copy of the Methodist hymn-book. He then held the door open for them to go into the chapel.

The chapel was the usual design of two aisles and three blocks of pews, one in the centre and one at either side. Each block had thirteen rows of pews. Henry and Judith were fascinated how the congregation of ten adults spread themselves round this large area. In the centre block it was just the front and the back rows which were occupied. A sixty-year-old man sat alone in the front row; a fifty-year-old woman sat alone in the back row. Two rows were taken in the left-hand aisle, one occupied by a forty-year-old woman and the other by a fifty-year-old woman. In the right-hand aisle four rows were occupied; one was occupied by a couple in their seventies and the other three by three men, all in their sixties, sitting alone. The other person present was the organist, who was the minister's wife. She was playing a two-manual pipe-organ and greatly enjoying opening and closing the swell-box during some sentimental Victorian church music.

The minister began the service by announcing the theme as 'Rededication'. The first twenty minutes of the service were a tightly packed hymn sandwich. Four hymns were sung: 'Let earth and heaven combine', 'Thou art the way', 'O word of God incarnate' and 'God of all power, truth and grace'. After the first hymn the minister offered a short prayer of rededication and the congregation joined in saying the traditional Lord's Prayer. After the second hymn, the minister read from the beginning of Mark's Gospel: the call of the first four disciples, followed by the call of Levi. After the third hymn, the minister led the prayers of intercession:

We pray to thee, O God, for all who seek to bring health and healing. We pray for all doctors, health visitors, district nurses, dentists. We pray for all those who are sick, especially for our brother Ken. Hear our prayer, O God, for all who work among the poor in every society; for all who serve the handicapped, distressed, elderly and isolated; for all who work to improve farming and the crops; for all who work in education, teachers and lecturers; for all who lead our worship, ministers and lay preachers; for the couple who were married here yesterday; for ourselves.

After the prayers of intercession, the minister read the notices, about a jumble sale and about the services next Sunday. He then explained how Isabel, one of the women in the congregation, had recently seen a Christian video and recommended that it should be used in church. Isabel had managed to borrow the video and Mr Jenkins had kindly brought his television and video recorder along to church. The minister then apologized for the fact that those sitting at the back or along the sides of the chapel probably would not be able to see; he suggested that once the video had started to play, they might care to move a little closer. Having said this, the minister tried to switch the video on, but could not puzzle out how to work the machine. Isabel came forward to help him.

The video lasted about thirty minutes and was a prime example of the unimaginative use of video as a medium by Christian communicators. For the whole of the thirty minutes the video camera was trained on the preacher. The preacher was shown sitting in a swivel chair, behind a large desk. He was smartly dressed in a blue suit and wearing a blue tie. On the desk there was a reading stand which held the preacher's notes. He read closely from these notes, spending much more time looking at the reading desk than at the camera. When he looked up to the camera, there always seemed to be the fear in his eyes that he would not find the right place in his notes again. Also on the desk there were three large books. The presentation began with him picking up one of these books, the Bible, and reading a lengthy section from Romans 3. Behind the desk there was a large pot plant.

The theme of the video was said to be 'What is a Christian?' The answer to the question was expressed as someone who recognizes failure, repents of failure, receives Jesus as saviour and responds by living the new life. The primary image through which this theme was developed was from exegesis of Paul's Greek word for sin: 'Sin', said the preacher, 'means missing the mark.'

The preacher, using video to paint a word-picture, asked his listeners to imagine an archery contest. Imagine an archery contest, he said, and not a single man has hit the target. We are like that. Then one man comes along and shoots at the target and every shot goes into the bull's-eye. Jesus is like that. Jesus offers the divine exchange of his righteousness for our failure. Jesus will shoot his arrows through you.

When the video ended, the people went back to their own favourite seats, all round the chapel. The minister announced the final hymn 'Just as I am, without one plea' and the chapel steward took the collection.

After the service, several people spoke with Henry and Judith. One man asked them how they liked the video. The minister's wife said there were not as many people in chapel that night as usual; some did not like the idea of showing a video in church and so stayed away. The minister invited Henry and Judith back to the manse for coffee. 'Do you always treat visitors as well as this?' joked Henry. 'I don't get much chance', said the minister, 'we don't see many visitors here.'

Grandbythorpe

Grandbythorpe is primarily a commuter village. The old village centre of High Street and Church Street is surrounded by ribbon development along the main road towards the neighbouring town and by a series of compact housing estates, occupying areas of land which until recently were open fields. Today Grandbythorpe has a population of some 3,200.

Marianne and Roy came to visit Grandbythorpe on a bright late October afternoon. At the corner of High Street and Church Street they stopped to look at the red-brick Methodist chapel. The notice-board told them the regular pattern of Sunday worship: Junior Church at 10.30 a.m. and evening worship at 6.00 p.m. This week the evening service was being conducted by their minister. The minister's name and address were clearly given on the notice-board. He lives in the neighbouring town, some six miles away. The notice-board also said that the chapel key could be obtained from the 'Post Office or 17 High Street'. Marianne went to both of these addresses in search of the key, but found no one at home at either address.

The Anglican church was five minutes' walk away at the other end of Church Street. The Anglican church had been built in yellow stone at the end of the 1850s. An imposing Gothic church school had been built next to the parish church in the same colour stone. The church school had been recently enlarged to cope with the growing population.

The church notice-board gave the vicar's name and address and set out the Sunday pattern of services: Holy Communion is celebrated on the first and third Sundays in the month at 8.00 a.m. A family service is held every Sunday at '10.15 a.m. for 10.30 a.m.', including Communion on the second and fourth Sundays in the month. The 6.15 p.m. service is evensong on the first, third and fourth Sundays in the month, but Holy Communion on the second Sunday in the month. The vicar of Grandbythorpe lives in the parish, and also has care of a neighbouring village of 310 inhabitants.

The door to the church porch was unbolted. Inside the porch there was a splendid flower arrangement and nothing else. There were no notices on the notice-board and the door into the church was firmly locked. Walking back up Church Street, Marianne and Roy stopped to talk with an elderly couple who were busy gardening: 'Can you tell us how we can get into the church?' they asked. 'Oh, I think the vicar has the key', they said. 'You had better go and ask him.' They gave Marianne and Roy directions on how to find their way to the vicarage.

The vicar was at home and pleased to welcome visitors. Emphasizing that the church had to be kept locked because of vandalism, he gave Marianne and Roy the key, a large heavy object about nine inches long. 'Take care with it', he said, 'it's the only one; so if that went missing we couldn't get into church and we have a meeting there tonight.' The vicar was a man in his early fifties, wearing a bright red pullover with a Lee Abbey badge on it and a friendly smile on his face. He started to chat with Marianne and Roy about where they had come from and what they were doing in Grandbythorpe. The conversation was cut short by another visitor arriving.

Letting themselves into Grandbythorpe church, Marianne and Roy were impressed by all the signs of life they found. At the back of the church by the door there was a very well-stocked cassette-tape lending library of Christian lectures and Christian music. There was a table of up-to-date Christian literature and a well-organized display screen. The display screen included a large map of the parish, the names of key church leaders and the names of 'area church representatives'. Arrows led from the names to the map, pinpointing where each individual lived. Marianne and Roy thought that this was a wonderful resource for people wanting to make contact with the ministry of the church; but the usefulness of this resource was reduced by the fact that the church was kept locked and no clues were given as to how to gain access.

An area at the back of the church had been screened off to make a small, but useful, kitchen and coffee bar. Around the walls of the church there were bright and colourful collage banners, each conveying a simple text:

- New wine of the Kingdom
- I will build up my church
- Enthrone Jesus on our praise
- From his fullness have we all received
- I will be with you
- Go in my name.

The front of the church had been nicely reordered. A nave table had been brought well forward into the chancel and a simple reading desk served as both pulpit and lectern (the large Victorian wooden pulpit was stored away in a general junk area under the tower). The traditional pipe-organ occupied the end of the north aisle. The end of the south aisle was occupied by a piano, a set of drums and sophisticated amplification equipment. Marianne and Roy could now understand why the vicar found it necessary to keep the church locked.

Marianne came back to Grandbythorpe for the 8.00 a.m. communion service on Sunday morning. A congregation of thirteen met in the choir-stalls behind the nave altar table for a straightforward communion service from the Book of Common Prayer. This service was conducted entirely by the vicar, wearing a surplice and preaching scarf and celebrating from the north end of the eastward-facing altar. Marianne found the congregation mainly elderly, but very friendly.

Roy came back for the mid-morning family service which had been advertised as 10.15 a.m. for 10.30 a.m. He arrived at 10.10 a.m. to find that the school playground was already full of cars. As soon as he stopped the car engine, he could hear sounds of singing coming from the church. A couple of the regular worshippers, a man and a woman in their mid-forties, met Roy on the church path and started to chat with him, welcoming him to the church. They walked into church just ahead of him. A West Indian woman in her mid-thirties was waiting inside to welcome worshippers. She gave both the man and the woman a big hug before offering them a set of books. She gave Roy a set of books, but sensed that he was not expecting to be hugged. The vicar was standing at the back of the church, also hugging people as they came in. He recognized Roy from the previous day.

Although it was only 10.10 a.m., a number of people were already in church singing modern hymns and songs. The singing was being led by the vicar's wife, who was holding her hands high in the air. People of all ages in the congregation were following her example, from young children to the very elderly. The accompaniment was provided by two guitars, a pianist and a drummer. All this was being fed through the church's professional amplification equipment and carefully monitored by a young technician who was wearing headphones and continually making adjustments to the amplifier. Roy had come to a charismatic Anglican service.

Roy took a seat near the back, next to a man in his mid-forties, who immediately held out his hand and introduced himself. They sat there chatting for five minutes or so while people all around them were singing, clapping or holding up their hands. Watching other people come in, Roy recognized that the welcome and conversation was all part of the style of this church. From the conversation he learnt a lot about the house groups and junior work of the church. He also learnt that the PCC was hoping to enlarge and refashion the church building.

Looking through the books he had been given, Roy found two hymn-books, *Songs of Fellowship, Books 1 & 2* combined, *Songs of Fellowship, Book 3 and Hymns of Fellowship* combined, and also the little booklet, *Family Worship*, published by the Church Pastoral Aid Society. Reading the weekly notice sheet, Roy realized just how much was going on in this church. The Young People's Fellowship meets on a Sunday evening after the evening service; Pathfinders meet on Monday; youth leaders meet on Tuesday; Explorers meet on Wednesday; house groups meet on Thursday; on Friday the adult musicians meet to practise and a coffee evening is being held this week to raise funds for mission work; a young persons' music group meets on Saturday morning.

The service proper began promptly at 10.30 a.m. The vicar and a visiting preacher from the South American Missionary

Society walked to the chancel step, both dressed simply in lounge suits. The vicar welcomed the congregation and visiting preacher and read the introduction from the family worship service. A traditional hymn, 'Stand up and bless the Lord', was accompanied by the organ. Then after the prayers of penitence and the versicles and responses of praise from the family worship service, piano, guitar and drum accompanied the chorus 'From the rising of the sun'. This was sung through three times, with the vicar and visiting preacher standing at the front encouraging the congregation to reflect the words of the song in actions. Each time the sun rose, so their hands rose to reflect the sun's journey across the sky.

After the song, the vicar called on a forty-five-year-old man to read a lesson, Acts 16, about one of Paul's missionary journeys. This was followed by another song, 'As we are gathered, Jesus is here'. After the creed, the congregation said the Lord's Prayer, and the vicar offered three prayers, for those in South America, for missionaries and for our own families and friends. Next they sang 'There is a sound on the wind like a victory song'. The vicar gave out some notices and the visiting preacher said that he was going to make a 'sales pitch' for the South American Missionary Society's literature he had brought with him.

Now it was time for the young person's music group to share something with the rest of the congregation. Thirteen children, between the ages of seven and twelve, came out to the front to sing, 'If you can sing a song, then praise the Lord'. Mime had been carefully choreographed to accompany the words. The *pièce de résistance* was the verse which included 'if you can turn a somersault' when a ten-year-old girl somersaulted across the chancel step. The congregation applauded so loudly that the young persons' music group was brought back for an encore; 'Okay kids', said their thirty-five-year-old woman leader, 'raise the roof', and they did.

After the excitement of the somersaults, the organist took over accompaniment of the more traditional hymn 'Master, speak! Thy servant heareth'. During this hymn, seven infants were taken out to a crèche in the neighbouring school in order to make way for the sermon.

The sermon lasted thirty-three minutes; the emphasis was primarily on entertaining the children. The visiting preacher began by setting up an overhead projector and screen. His first slide was designed to teach the congregation a new song, 'Listen, listen, can you hear his heartbeat'. His first point was that mission begins with listening for God's call. Then, switching off the overhead projector, the visiting preacher began to test the congregation's knowledge of geography, mentioning places like New Zealand, China and Japan. 'Why', he asked, 'is geography important?' Several children gave predictable answers about helping us to find places. 'But why else is geography important?' pressed the preacher, before providing his own answer: 'I'll tell you. It shows you God's world. God loved the world so much, what did he do? He gave his only son.' This excursus on the value of studying geography paved the way for the second slide, a map of the Pauline missionary journey described in the portion of Acts read earlier. His second point was that Paul's missionary journey was undertaken in response to God's call.

The third slide was another map, this time turning attention to South America. The preacher outlined the various countries of South America. His third point was that missionary Ian was working with the South American Missionary Society in Brazil, in response to God's call.

During the exposition of Paul's missionary journey, Roy found the opportunity to count the congregation. He was sharing worship with a young and lively group of worshippers. He reckoned that there were in church that morning thirty children and young people under the age of twenty-one, twenty-five people in their twenties and thirties, another twenty people in their forties and fifties, and fifteen or so in their sixties or seventies. Towards the end of the lesson on South American geography, Roy found himself listening to the inviting sound of the coffee urn bubbling away at the back of the church.

After the sermon, the congregation stood to sing the traditional hymn 'Stand up, stand up for Jesus'. This hymn was accompanied by organ, piano, guitars and drums. The majority of the worshippers lifted their hands high as they sang. The congregation remained standing for a closing prayer and blessing.

When the clergy had walked to the back of the church, the junior choir assembled at the front again to sing a short song. As they finished singing, the organ burst in with a triumphal voluntary. The congregation showed no signs of haste to leave.

As a visitor, Roy quickly found himself caught up in a sequence of conversations over coffee. Regular worshippers were keen to make him feel welcome, but not to press him into saying too much about himself or to express his Christian commitment.

That Sunday evening Marianne went to Granbythorpe parish church to attend the 6.15 p.m. service. Although the outside church notice-board had led her to expect evensong on the third Sunday of the month, inside Marianne found that she was participating in a Rite A communion service. This time she was sharing in worship with about thirty other people, again a comparatively young congregation. In the evening there was another visiting preacher from the South American Missionary Society; he preached for twenty-eight minutes.

While Marianne attended the evening service in the parish church, Roy went round the corner to the Methodist chapel. The congregation here was much more elderly. There were thirty-five people, sixteen men and thirteen women in their sixties or seventies, a couple in their fifties and another couple in their forties, with their two children. The service was conducted by the minister who had travelled from the neighbouring town. Although this service had a very different feel from the one which Roy had attended in the parish church that morning, once again he found himself among a warm and welcoming congregation. He had chosen to sit in a pew by himself during the service, but as soon as the service ended one of the sixty-year-old men came across to sit beside him and began to engage him in conversation. Other members of the congregation joined them as well.

Talking with the regular worshippers about their chapel, Roy learnt that until very recently they had maintained a morning service as well as an evening service. The morning service had been disbanded because the circuit was short of lay preachers and could no longer staff two services every Sunday in Grandbythorpe. A number of people who used to attend the morning service had not transferred their allegiance to the evening service and so, by cancelling the morning service, Grandbythorpe Methodist chapel had also reduced its active membership.

Roy then mentioned that he had attended the Anglican church for the morning service. From the following conversation, Roy learnt that the Anglican church developed its charismatic tendencies over the past two or three years and that some of the established villagers were very suspicious of it. 'It has been very good for our Sunday school', said one of the Methodists. 'Our Sunday school has risen from the teens to thirty or forty now. Parents don't want their children to get mixed up in all that charismatic stuff so they send them here instead.'

Willow Fen

Willow Fen is a long straggling village, surrounded by miles of flat open countryside. A few small new housing developments nestle alongside older established cottages and a handful of large Victorian houses. Today the population stands at nearly 2,000 people. To serve this rural community there are two pubs and three churches. Colin, Terry and Helen visited Willow Fen on a mid-November Sunday morning so that they could attend the mid-morning service in all three places of worship.

The first of the mid-morning services to begin was in the Fen Street Baptist church at 10.30 a.m. By 10.15 a.m. Fen Street was beginning to fill up with parked cars and a small queue was forming outside the chapel door. Then a minibus arrived, proudly displaying the name 'Fen Street Baptist Church' along both sides. Colin joined the queue to enter the chapel.

Inside, the chapel was still comparatively empty, because a number of the regular congregation were making their way directly to the schoolroom to join the pre-service prayer meeting. One of the stewards on the door, a man in his thirties, recognized Colin as a visitor and asked him if this was his first visit to Fen Street: 'You can sit anywhere you like, upstairs in the gallery or downstairs. Only the pulpit and organist's seat are reserved.' He gave Colin a hymn-book, a Bible and a duplicated notice sheet. The hymn-book was a looseleaf binder of hymns and songs specially compiled and printed for Fen Street church.

While the congregation was settling, a group of young people played guitars, woodwind and percussion instruments. The leaders of the chapel were walking about trying to catch the attention of individuals and talking with them. Groups of teenagers mingled talking and laughing. Senior citizens greeted each other and exchanged the week's news. The atmosphere was busy, noisy and happy.

Fen Street church is well organized to look after babies and children. Four separate crèche groups operate throughout the service for babies, wobblers, toddlers and under-fives. The junior church offers a series of classes for five- to fourteen-year-olds.

The chapel itself has seating for about 350 people. Colin counted a congregation of around 220. The chapel was particularly strong on young people under the age of forty. Colin learnt that this was an eclectic congregation with some people travelling twenty or thirty miles to attend services. Listening to their accents, Colin recognized that quite a number travelled in from the American air force base.

The front of the chapel is dominated by a tall pulpit, reached by eight steep steps. At 10.30 a.m. the pastor, a man in his early fifties, and two deacons, men in their early thirties, climbed into the pulpit. One of the deacons welcomed the regular congregation and visitors: 'We give you a warm welcome and pray God will really bless you this morning.'

The first half hour or so of the service consisted of open praise. The minister set the mood by suggesting the song 'Give thanks with a grateful heart, give thanks to the holy one'. Then individuals in the congregation gave testimonies, spoke in tongues, sang solos and led congregational singing. Some of the congregation had brought their own tambourines, some held hands high, others sat and listened. Two teenage girls sitting near Colin began to play noughts and crosses on the back of the notice sheet. Throughout this part of the service new worshippers arrived and others got up to leave.

At around 11.00 a.m., a member of the congregation said that the Lord was telling her that there were people in the church that morning who had special needs. The minister said that the Lord only spoke to a purpose and invited those in need of ministry to come forward to the elders. While the rest of the congregation continued to sing, six or seven people went forward and were met by the elders.

One couple in their fifties, who apparently had never been to Fen Street church before, spoke of their daughter's terminal illness. The pastor related their tale to the congregation and prayed 'Father, we look to you this morning for this miracle in the name of Jesus'. Someone else led the congregation in singing 'God is good'.

At around 11.30 a.m. a change was introduced into the mood of the service and some of the younger teenagers left for their own teaching session. The congregation was asked to pray for five members of Fen Street church who were away 'on the King's business' preaching in other places, as far apart as London, Norfolk and Yorkshire. Then a fifty-year-old woman and her husband were invited to talk about their experience the previous week of visiting and ministering to the fellowship which Fen Street church was establishing among English-speaking families in a European capital. They asked for the tape recorder to be switched off and spoke with considerable passion of the English-speaking church in that community as 'a barren wilderness in the midst of luxury'. The congregation prayed for God to bless the couple whom the chapel was sponsoring to found the Christian fellowship there.

At 11.43 a.m. the pastor read 1 Samuel 4 (RSV):

So the Philistines fought, and Israel was defeated, and they fled every man to his home; and there was a very great slaughter, for there fell of Israel thirty thousand foot soldiers. And the ark of God was captured; and the two sons of Eli, Hophni and Phinehas, were slain.

What we need to ask, said the preacher, is why God gave the victory to the Philistines. The answer is that there was sin in the nation and God chose the Philistines to teach his people a lesson. And 30,000 foot soldiers were killed in one day. There was sin in the spiritual leadership of the people. No wonder God gave the victory to the Philistines.

They had brought the ark of the covenant with them and they thought that was a lucky charm, sufficient to keep God on their side. But God saw right through to the wickedness in their hearts. Do we treat God as a lucky charm in our daily lives? I have asked you, and I'll ask you again.

But, friends, I want to ask you another question this morning. What about spiritual fraud and spiritual deception? Jesus is there all the time. The Lord is there when you are driving the car, watching the TV, lusting after that person walking down the street. If there is spiritual fraud, the Lord will allow you to be defeated, trodden down, unless you turn from your wicked ways.

Friends, the fellowship at the moment is going through hard times. Somehow we are not getting it right. We have known better days. Perhaps some folk have even lost the vision of God. What we need is God on our side and that will mean a clean-up job in many ways. As I look in my own heart and in the heart of the congregation I see that we are guilty of many things. We are guilty of complacency, taking God for granted. We are guilty of compromise, doing things today and condoning things we would not have done five years ago. This is sin.

Pray for the leadership that God will reveal himself to us and that we may know God in the very midst of his people. Pray for yourselves that you may obey God because God is looking for a people of obedience.

The sermon ended at 12.10 p.m. and the service closed with a great chorus of praise: 'I declare your majesty'. The pastor asked the congregation to leave quietly so that they could reflect on the message of the sermon.

The weekly notice leaflet revealed Fen Street Baptist church as a church busy seven days a week, not simply on Sundays. On Monday evening a group meets to pray 'for the outworking of God's purposes in the fellowship and for a greater outreach to those around us'. On Tuesday afternoon there is a social meeting and on Tuesday evening a time of prayer 'to seek God's blessing and guidance upon us as individuals and as a fellowship'. On Wednesday morning there is a time of praise and prayer 'for all ladies who would like to come', and on Wednesday evening an open house for girls aged twelve and over. Thursday begins at 7.00 a.m. with a men's prayer breakfast. Mid-morning there is an evangelistic Bible study group and in the evening three meetings take place: the junior section of the Girls' Brigade, an evangelistic Bible study and a Bible workshop. Three meetings also take place on Friday evening: a youth group with a special speaker for thirteen- to fifteen-year-olds, an 'at home' for fifteen- to twenty-year-olds and a workshop for men. On Saturday there is a group for five- to eleven-year-olds. On Sunday there is an evening fellowship at 6.30 p.m. as well as the morning service.

The second of the mid-morning services to take place in Willow Fen begins in the Anglican church at 10.45 a.m. The Anglican church, too, is in Fen Street, but by the time Anglican worshippers begin to arrive all the parking space has been taken up by Baptists. Helen waited until a few people had already gone into the Anglican church and then entered herself at 10.35 a.m.

Inside, the church appeared large, airy and empty. The tall arches were brightly adorned by home-made collage banners, and the lofty roof echoed with rich classical organ music. A churchwarden, a woman in her mid-forties, welcomed Helen and gave her a copy of the Rite A communion service, *Hymns Ancient and Modern Revised* and the church's home-produced 'Hymn Supplement'. After Helen had settled down in a seat the churchwarden came over to talk with her. She emphasized that on this particular Sunday the deanery clergy all exchange churches and that the service was, therefore, not being conducted by their usual vicar. Helen appreciated this explanation, because it soon became apparent that the visiting priest, a man in his late sixties, had very little sense of relating to the congregation or to the form of service.

Fen Willow parish church is a large building. Although the pews had been removed from one whole aisle, there was still seating in the nave for about 330 people. Today the congregation comprised twenty-three women, twelve men and two babies, scattered throughout the building. There was also a choir of three women, an elderly man and a boy. The choir robed but did not process into place.

At 10.42 a.m. the priest walked to the chancel step, and gradually the congregation stood. He looked at his watch, said that it was too early to start and the congregation gradually sat again. The churchwarden came to the front to try to persuade the priest to use the microphone. Three minutes later, the priest moved away from the microphone and announced the page number where the collect and readings could be found in *The Alternative Service Book 1980*. Since the worshippers were not equipped with copies of *The Alternative Service Book 1980*, and since the readings used were not those appointed anyway, it hardly mattered that most of them could not hear. Omitting the customary opening hymn and not waiting for the congregation to stand, the priest spoke the salutation and read the collect for purity and the Gloria. Very few members of the congregation joined in.

Both readings, from the Old Testament and the gospel, were read by the elderly choirman. The readings chosen were from Numbers 21, where Moses sets up an image of a bronze serpent to heal snake bites, and John 3, where Jesus draws on this image to illustrate the healing nature of his crucifixion. Between the readings came the hymn 'We sing the praise of him who died'.

Just before the sermon, the churchwarden made sure that the visiting priest was wearing the necklace microphone positioned near the pulpit. The priest began his sermon by slowly retelling the two Scripture readings. The Israelite people gazed on the brazen snake to be healed of their snake bites. We gaze on Jesus to be healed of the bites of sin. What is common in these two acts of gazing is faith. Our celebration of Christmas is determined by our preparation for it. Today we are given the opportunity to prepare for Christmas by gazing on these two models of salvation, gazing in faith at the brazen snake and gazing in faith at the crucified victim. Christ takes our human nature and reshapes it, straightens it out by unqualified obedience to the Father's will wherever it may lead. What our religion is all about, concluded the preacher, is the knowledge that this life which is offered for us and on our behalf on the cross is offered in order that, in the power of his risen life, imparted to us by the Spirit in the meal which we share in the eucharist, we may be healed of the snake bites of sin. The sermon, with all its many subordinate clauses, finished at 11.10 a.m. and the congregation awoke to join in the creed.

The rest of the service was conducted at an erratic pace with long pauses. The first pause occurred between the intercessions and the confession. The congregation rose from their knees, sat, waited for something to happen and then kneeled again. Another long pause occurred after the prayer of thanksgiving while the priest broke the roll of bread into many fragments.

After the distribution of communion, the Sunday school children and their teachers came into church for the children to receive a blessing at the altar rail. An impressive procession of twenty-four young people up to the age of about ten came waving paper snakes on wooden sticks. The third long pause occurred while the priest consumed the remainder of the bread roll used for communion. The Sunday school children chatted in the front pews and the adult members of the congregation became restless as well. Then the priest came down to the Sunday school children and asked them, 'Can you tell me what you have been doing in Sunday school?' He then proceeded to repeat his summary of the two Scripture readings for their benefit.

After the second homily the priest led the closing prayer and the congregation spontaneously sang the chorus 'The grace of our Lord Jesus Christ'. While they were singing, the priest walked to the vestry and the service petered out. The last hymn on the hymn board, like the first, was left unsung.

Unlike the Baptist pastor, the Anglican vicar no longer lives in Willow Fen. Willow Fen is now part of a three-parish benefice. The mid-morning service within the benefice takes place in Willow Fen parish church each week: on the first Sunday in the month it is a family service at 11.00 a.m.; on the other Sundays it is the family communion at 10.45 a.m. The 9.00 a.m. family communion and the 6.30 p.m. evensong alternate between the other two parishes.

During the week a ladies' group meets in the church hall on a Tuesday morning. The bell ringers practise on Wednesday evening and the youth group for the over-elevens meets in the church hall at the same time. On Thursday evening a Bible study group meets in a private house and on Friday evening the choir practice takes place in church.

The third of the morning services in Willow Fen begins in Sheep Lane Free church at 11.00 a.m. When Terry walked down Sheep Lane at 10.50 a.m., he could hear coming from the chapel the sound of young voices singing choruses. The foolish man was building his house upon the sand and the chapel walls reverberated as the children's hands thundered together to imitate the collapse of the house. At the door Terry was given a copy of *Mission Praise* by a shy man in his early fifties and left to push his way through the two stiff doors which separated the small foyer from the chapel.

Inside, the chapel looked quite dark and shabby. Paint and plaster were peeling from the grubby yellow walls. The three front rows of pews were filled with the Sunday school pupils, twenty-two children between the ages of three and eight, together with a teenage girl and four mothers. A short bouncy man in his mid-fifties, dressed in an untidy grey suit, stood at the front waving his arms to lead the choruses. Some of the children were by now feeling quite restless. Terry was surprised how loud they seemed to be singing until he realized that the chapel sound system was turned on and the microphone stood facing the children. The whole effect must have sounded more impressive to those walking past the chapel on their way to the parish church than to those venturing inside.

At 11.00 a.m. the pastor walked in. A man in his early sixties, his complexion, hair, sports jacket, hand-knitted pullover and tie all blended as slightly different shades of grey, strangely off-set by a deep red shirt. 'Good morning, boys and girls', he said, ignoring the twenty-eight elderly adults in the back of the chapel. 'Good morning, Pastor Williams', the children replied.

After the opening hymn from *Mission Praise*, 'This is the day the Lord has made', the pastor led the children in prayer, giving thanks for their homes and families, and praying for their diligent attendance and attention at Sunday school. The pastor followed the prayer with a five-minute children's address. Producing a green plastic bag, he invited the children to guess what was inside. Then he asked, on a cold morning, what will mum give you to put on your hands . . . on your head . . . on your feet? And he pulled out from the bag a pair of muddy boots. We all need clothes to protect us. I need these heavy boots when I am pushing a barrow of cement on the building site. If you go to a Church of England service up the road you find the vicar wearing fine clothes to worship God, to cover up the old clothes he is wearing underneath. In the Bible it says that Jesus offers a wedding garment to cover us up. The Lord Jesus wants to clothe us all over with his lovely righteousness. Now, boys and girls, I want you to remember that you have to be suitably attired with Jesus' lovely mantle of righteousness.

The Sunday school children left the chapel to go home during the next hymn, 'The Lord is King! Lift up thy voice', and the pastor turned his attention to the adult worshippers. He read the whole of Zechariah 10 and announced the hymn 'My soul doth magnify the Lord'.

Next, the notices were read by a fifty-year-old woman. After welcoming visitors to the chapel she welcomed their pastor to the pulpit. Then she listed the activities of the coming week. On Tuesday evening the fellowship meets; on Thursday evening there is a meeting of the prayer and Bible study group; on Friday afternoons the ladies meet for fellowship. All these meetings take place in the manse. She thanked the lady who had been responsible for the chapel flowers that morning and announced who was responsible for the flowers the following week. Then the offering was taken. Last week it had amounted to just over seventy pounds.

After another hymn, 'Master, speak! Thy servant heareth', the pastor settled down to his half-hour sermon at 11.37 a.m. He began by rereading a few key verses from Zechariah 10 (AV): 'I will sow them among the people: and they shall remember me in far countries.'

My first encounter with Jews, he said, was at school. They were always different. They always stood out. They did not attend the religious education classes. Then in the army the man in the next bed to me was a Jew. He was different. He ate special food. When we were all queuing up at the mess room, he went in through a special door. We all booed him because he did not have to join the queue like the rest of us. He could not eat our food because it had not been blessed by a rabbi. He could not eat meat. Every so often his mum would send him a food parcel of all sorts of things that had been blessed by the rabbi. He would eat them under the bedclothes at night. When the next food parcel came in we got it first to punish him for his meanness.

Most of us encounter Jews, one here, one there, always a minority, always apart, always a bit different. They have been scattered in our own time by Hitler's pogrom. They are God's people and God wants them scattered. Nothing, even Hitler's gas chambers, has been successful in exterminating them. God wanted them to survive.

We, too, are God's people. The Bible speaks of us as a new Israel. It is true that we too live as a minority in the world. If you go to school and you are a Christian, you find you are in a minority. You do not want to be different, but you are. At school, at college, at your place of work, you are one of God's scattered people, thinly spread. Yet it is hard to find any place totally without Christian witness. There may not be a place of worship in a nonconformist sense in many villages today, but there are still Christians living there. You are leaven. You do not have to be a *cordon bleu* cook to know that only a small amount of leaven goes a long way.

But let me say something about the future of God's people. In Zechariah, God says 'but I will bring them back'. To find out what this will be like we have to turn to Revelation 19, the final book of the Bible, which deals with future events. This is the great eschatological event in the future, the reuniting of those who wait for the day.

But let me say something of the reuniting of God's people now. There are small gatherings of God's people today. The

Jews have their synagogues and we have our congregations. Synagogue is a Hebrew word and congregation a Greek word, but they both mean the same thing. This is the place where God's people are gathered now in the hope that they will be gathered together later. Let us treasure it in practice and look at the day when it will be eternally real.

The sermon finished at 12.10 p.m. when the theme of the service carried through into the closing hymn 'We are gathering together unto him'.

After the service, several members of the congregation made a real effort to welcome Terry and to discover if he was likely to be coming again. In conversation the pastor's wife explained that her husband had oversight of only the one congregation, but that he had to have a full-time job as well. She said that it was hard work and that he would like to be able to devote more time to his pastoral ministry; he is grateful when other members of the church help with the preaching.

At the door the pastor, too, welcomed Terry and was curious to know why he had decided to come to Sheep Lane church. Had he, perhaps, heard about the growth at the Fen Street church and then mistakenly come to the wrong one?

7
SUBURBAN
VILLAGES

Didford and Shotsfield

DIDFORD IS A prosperous market town which expanded rapidly at the beginning of the present century. Expansion to the east pushed housing development across the river and into the neighbouring civil and ecclesiastical parish of Shotsfield. Shotsfield now has a population of 4,500 people. Just over a thousand of these inhabitants live in the picturesque village of Shotsfield itself, which is dominated by the 1840s parish church. The ruins of the medieval parish church lie a little to the north. To the west there is an expanse of open countryside before coming to that part of Shotsfield which looks more naturally to Didford. Almost all the development in this area is owner-occupied and some of it looks very prosperous.

To care for the spiritual needs of this new part of Shotsfield, the Anglican church established a corrugated iron mission church, St Stephen's, some two and a half miles away from the parish church. Sometime later, after the First World War, the Catholic church also responded to the needs of the developing part of Shotsfield and established St Mary's chapel. Today St Stephen's mission church is still looked after from the parish church of Shotsfield; St Mary's chapel is served from the Catholic parish of Didford. Every Sunday there is one service in each of these churches. The vicar of Shotsfield takes a 9.00 a.m. communion service at St Stephen's mission church between the 8.00 a.m. and 10.00 a.m. services in the parish church; the parish priest of Didford celebrates Mass in St Mary's chapel at 10.00 a.m., between the 8.30 a.m. and the 11.00 a.m. Masses in his main church. Since the two churches are only a mile or so apart, Gordon decided to attend morning service in both.

Driving across the river at 8.30 a.m. on Sunday, Gordon's first problem was to find St Stephen's mission church among the labyrinth of suburban roads. He asked the paper-boy on his early morning rounds; the paper-boy did not know. He asked the milkman; the milkman could not help. Then he saw an elderly woman carrying a handbag and a prayer-book. She was making her way towards St Stephen's church; she refused the offer of a lift, but gave clear directions. Gordon drove off in pursuit. So well was the shabby tin tabernacle shielded by a high hedge from disturbing the amenities of a desirable residential area that Gordon drove right by without noticing it. Then he saw an elderly gentleman, smartly dressed in Sunday suit. He asked again, turned the car round and discovered St Stephen's mission church.

Behind the tall hedge, the notice-board clearly confirmed the time of the morning service. It also gave the vicar's name and telephone number and the names and telephone numbers of two readers. The church itself looked sadly neglected and decaying. A sidesman in his late sixties was standing outside the main entrance to the mission church. He greeted Gordon as he walked up the path, ushered him in, gave him a copy of *Hymns Ancient and Modern Revised* and a copy of the Rite B communion service. Gordon sat towards the back on the right-hand side. It was now 8.50 a.m. The church was quite small. Instead of pews there were chairs; eight rows of four chairs each side of the central aisle. As well as the sidesman, there were three women in the church standing at the front talking quite loudly to each other about the happenings of the past week. One of them was carrying a jug of water, ready to recharge the flower vases on the altar. They were not disturbed by Gordon's arrival.

By 9.00 a.m. the total congregation of eight had assembled. The three women had sat down, but were continuing their conversation. Three other women were each sitting on their own in different parts of the church. Two men sat together at the front. No one in the congregation was under the age of sixty.

Exactly at the stroke of nine the vicar walked to the sanctuary step. People stood up and the three women stopped their conversation. The vicar made a gentle and relaxed comment about the weather and announced the first hymn, 'Lord of beauty, thine the splendour'. He then moved across to the organ, swung his legs over the organ stool, found the page in the hymn-book and switched on the blower. The organ was a two-manual harmonium harnessed to an electric fan. The organ wheezed into life, complete with a permanent cipher or two. The vicar was a skilful musician and seemed to massage the hymn tune from the creaking mechanism. His green chasuble danced as he exerted considerable pressure on some of the keys. One of the older women in the congregation led the singing in a quavering soprano. After the hymn the vicar made a jovial comment about the organ being more asthmatic than usual, perhaps due to the weather. Then he walked back into the sanctuary to begin the service.

The Rite B order of communion was followed faithfully. The collect and readings were taken from the Book of Common Prayer. After reading the epistle from the right-hand side of the altar, the vicar returned to the organ stool to accompany the hymn 'O Holy Spirit, Lord of grace'. Then he returned to the left-hand side of the altar to read the gospel.

The nine-minute sermon was preached from the centre of the sanctuary, without notes. It quickly became apparent that the preacher was relaxed and at home with his band of faithful worshippers. The sermon was clearly structured and well thought through. It was delivered in a direct and personal style which kept the attention of the congregation. Gordon found himself watching the preacher very closely. He was a rotund man with a jovial podgy face. From time to time he would pause to structure his next sentence and while pausing his tongue gently caressed his upper lip, a distinctive mannerism.

The sermon began by retelling the tale of the sinking of the *Titanic*. The preacher emphasized the unnecessary nature of the tragedy as a consequence of a series of 'lost opportunities'. He then reflected on his own recent holiday and the conversations that he had enjoyed with fellow holiday-makers. So many of them, he said, had failed to respond to the gospel, again a story of missed opportunities. He concluded by exhorting his congregation not to allow their mission church to miss the opportunity of ministering to the local neighbourhood. This was an important message, well put, but Gordon could not help feeling that the present condition of the church and congregation made real action rather unlikely.

After the creed and intercessions, the words of the peace were said while the congregation remained kneeling. No sign of peace was exchanged. Then the vicar returned to the organ stool to accompany the offertory hymn, 'My God, how wonderful thou art', while the sidesman took the collection. The hymn ended, the vicar returned to the sanctuary to receive the collection and to prepare the bread and wine for the communion. The altar in St Stephen's mission church remained fixed to the east wall. The vicar, apparently preferring a westward position, faced the congregation for much of the prayer of thanksgiving, with his back to the altar.

Following the blessing, the vicar once again became organist to accompany the final hymn 'Stand up, and bless the Lord'. After the hymn he returned to the altar to pick up the collection and the eucharistic vessels before processing out. As soon as the service was over the three women resumed their conversation. The sidesman shook Gordon by the hand and said how good it was to have a visitor. The vicar, too, welcomed Gordon to the church and wished him a good holiday in the area. It was now 9.46 a.m., leaving Gordon plenty of time to move on to St Mary's chapel.

St Mary's chapel is built on the main road out of Didford, so Gordon had no problem in finding it. He did have a problem, however, in finding somewhere to park the car. By 9.55 a.m. the road outside St Mary's chapel was already well congested. After parking in a side street, Gordon joined the small queue of people pushing their way through the narrow entrance into the ante-chapel. Inside, Gordon met with a surprise. A building project was under way to create extra meeting rooms at the back of the chapel. No attempt had been made to clear away the signs of 'work in progress' for the Sunday service. Copies of the newsletter *Sunday Plus* were strewn on a dust-covered table. Gordon picked up a copy and filed into the chapel itself. St Mary's chapel, like St Stephen's mission church, had originally been set out with seating for sixty or so people. Now an extra thirty seats were crowded at the back. Gordon looked round for somewhere to sit. A family moved up and he squeezed in beside them. To his left was a teenage girl who offered to share with him her copy of *Celebration Hymnal*; to his right was a grandmother in her wheelchair who passed him a copy of the service leaflet, *The New English Missalette*.

Not being familiar with a Catholic service, Gordon spent the rest of the time before the service began looking through the leaflets he had been given. *The New English Missalette* provides the complete service for each Sunday. The opening sentence for the day, the collect for the day, the three Scripture readings, the responsorial psalm and the appropriate eucharistic prayer are all printed in full at the appropriate point in the service. This makes following the service very easy. The *Sunday Plus* is an A4 weekly news sheet produced by Redemptorist Publications. On the back the parish prints its own weekly information. The parish of Didford produces this one leaflet for its three churches, noting all the week's activities and a list of subjects for prayer. This leaflet revealed a busy and active parish. In addition to the Saturday evening Mass, three Sunday Masses in the parish church and the Sunday Mass in each of the two chapels, there was a morning Mass every day of the week except Tuesday, and an evening Mass on Tuesday, Wednesday and Friday. A range of clubs and activities met during the week, including the Catholic Women's League on Wednesday and the Senior Youth Group on Friday.

At 10.00 a.m., people were still coming into St Mary's chapel and having difficulty in finding somewhere to sit. The priest was already hovering at the back by the vestry door, but waited there patiently until 10.05 a.m., by which time the congregation had settled down for a very squashed service. The congregation included people of all ages, from babes in arms to the very elderly. There were a number of children of primary school age range, and teenagers were notable by their presence. There were young couples in their twenties, some alone, some with their own parents and some with two or three infants.

The service began quite abruptly when the priest pushed his way through the people crowding the back of the chapel and walked casually to the small altar at the front. He announced the first hymn from *Celebration Hymnal*, the gentle and lilting refrain 'We are gathering together unto him'. The accompaniment was provided by two young musicians standing in the sanctuary, the only area of the chapel affording unrestricted space for their music stands. An eighteen-year-old youth played the guitar; a fifteen-year-old girl played the flute. The combined effect of these two instruments and the relaxed singing of the congregation got the service off to a very good start while some of the younger children continued to play in the centre aisle.

After the opening hymn, the priest introduced the greeting, the prayers of penitence and the Gloria in an unenthusiastic and matter-of-fact way. A fifty-year-old layman took the priest's place at the lectern to read a short passage from the Old Testament, to lead the responsorial psalm and to read a short passage from the New Testament. Young children continued to chatter throughout, without anyone seeming to mind. Those who could not hear the readings too clearly were able to follow the printed text in *The New English Missalette*. The congregation joined in the responsorial psalm with an air of practised familiarity.

Following the New Testament reading, the reader and the priest changed places at the lectern and the congregation stood to sing the gradual hymn 'Make me a channel of your peace'. This was enjoyed particularly by the children of primary school age, who had obviously learnt and practised this song in their Catholic primary school. The congregation remained standing for the reading of the gospel from Luke 14. The priest moved on directly from the gospel reading to a short three-minute homily. The homily was read from three pages of text. The pace was fast; the tone of voice was dull. The priest did not look up from his text. The children carried on talking and playing. The theme was the need for faithful and regular attendance at Mass. Building on the day's New Testament reading from Hebrews 12, the priest argued that, although we do not expect to see anything spectacular at the eucharist, we should trust to the power of God's grace in the sacrament. The homily ended abruptly; almost without pause, the priest led the profession of faith in the creed.

The prayer of the faithful was also led by the priest who read out a series of short formal biddings, to which the congregation dutifully replied 'Lord, graciously hear us'. The prayer of the faithful reached its climax in a spirited recitation of the 'Hail Mary'. Before announcing the offertory hymn, the parish priest drew attention to the fact that there had been a ciborium by the door into which intending communicants could have transferred a wafer. He asked those who were intending to communicate but who had failed to do this to put up their hands. Nine hands shot up and were duly counted.

The rather formal and rigid atmosphere of the way in which the liturgy was being led once again gave way to a softer, more relaxed mood during the offertory hymn. The guitar and flute played a gentle swinging introduction to Patrick Appleford's hymn 'Living Lord'. The congregation showed all the signs of knowing and enjoying the familiar words. As the congregation sang, two men, a thirty-year-old and a fifty-year-old, passed the collecting dishes around from pew to pew.

The offertory procession, bringing wafers and wine from the back of the church, was a task entrusted to a whole family. Mother, father, twelve-year-old daughter and two sons aged eight and six, filed from their pew, walked casually to the back of the church and carried the elements to the altar in a matter-of-fact manner.

In the Catholic rite, the peace comes at the climax of the 'liturgy of the eucharist', following the eucharistic prayer and the Lord's Prayer. There was quite a lot of activity in the confined space at the back of the chapel, as people moved around to greet each other. Young children were rushing up to the woman in the wheelchair to grab her by the hand. Strangers greeted Gordon as if he were a regular member of the Sunday fellowship of St Mary's chapel.

After the spontaneous joy of the peace, the congregation settled back on their knees for the 'Lamb of God' and for the invitation to communion. The hosts were distributed by the priest standing at the centre of the sanctuary step. The congregation formed a perfunctory queue. Nearly one hundred people had received communion in a surprisingly short space of time and then the priest brought communion to the woman in the wheelchair at the back of the chapel. Gordon felt very sad that church discipline did not permit the Catholic priest to welcome him, as a communicant Anglican, to share the sacrament along-side those with whom he had already shared the peace so warmly.

The Mass concluded with another lilting hymn to guitar and flute accompaniment, 'Lord, for tomorrow and its needs I do not pray; keep me, my God, from stain of sin, just for today'. As soon as the hymn was over, the congregation rose to its feet and made for the door. Mass was ended and the Catholic community was dispersing to the four corners of Didford and Shotsfield. The teenage girl who had shared her hymn-book with Gordon, and the family who had welcomed him so warmly in the peace, were gone without exchanging another word with him. As Gordon pushed his way through the crowd, he glanced into the open vestry. Already the priest was out of his vestments escaping towards his car. The service had started five minutes late and lasted for thirty-eight minutes. The priest was needed to say Mass in the other chapel at 11.00 a.m.

Many of the congregation seemed to be racing the priest to their cars. Three mothers and their children had gathered outside to talk. Gordon hung back to read the church notice-board. But no one was inclined to speak to him; so he joined the rush to get his car back on the road.

Thinking through the experiences of the day, Gordon was fascinated by the stark contrast between the Anglican and Catholic churches in this growing part of Shotsfield. It was the Anglican priest who had taken considerable care to prepare his sermon, who had led the liturgy with thought and insight and who had made an effort to welcome a visitor. It was the Anglican church where a sidesman had been on duty ready to welcome the congregation and to greet them as they left. But all this was shared with an elderly congregation of only eight people. It was the Catholic priest who read a dull homily, who led the liturgy without particular care or feeling and who made no personal contact with the worshippers. It was the Catholic church where no one was responsible for welcoming visitors. But this was shared with a full church, with one hundred worshippers from babes in arms to the granny in her wheelchair. Of the two, it was the Catholic church which represented life and it was the Catholic church to which Gordon felt that he would wish to belong were he a resident in Shotsfield.

Hathaden

The centre of Hathaden is the narrow picturesque High Street. On either side of the street, two timber-framed inns rival each other for attractiveness and for the tourists' custom. Pedestrians squeeze their way along the narrow pavement; cars and lorries race through the one-way system from west to north. In the 1830s, a small chapel was built on a parcel of land squashed between the pavement, a house and one of the inns. The chapel and the Kings Head literally join on to each other, their ageing and sloping walls offering a mutual support against the ravages of the passing traffic which shake their inadequate foundations.

Today the chapel is part of a group of Elim Pentecostal churches; the Kings Head is part of the Berni chain of inns and restaurants. Each in its own way has adorned the adjoining walls with posters to proclaim its message and to peddle its distinctive wares. The Elim chapel's colourful wayside pulpit proclaims that 'the wages of sin is death'; a somewhat more colourful and more varied bill of fare outside the Berni proclaims the price of steaks, grilled fish and their special dish, styled 'surf and turf', which combines the delicacies of tender juicy steak and succulent prawns.

Away from this picturesque village centre, Hathaden has grown into sprawling suburbia. To the south, ribbon development has now joined the village to the neighbouring town, and a series of patchy and rather uncoordinated private developments have filled in the fields either side of the main road. To the north, a large between-the-wars council estate has continued to decay and to grow. Row after row of terraced houses line a labyrinth of roads and culs-de-sac, relieved only by the occasional cluster of shops or the school.

Historically, the small hamlet of Hathaden has never been an ecclesiastical parish in its own right. As the large council estate developed between the wars, the neighbouring town parish established a new chapel of ease a couple of miles north of the village centre, on the main road and just to the west of the new estate. Green fields still separate the Anglican chapel of ease from the council houses. As the crow flies, the church and estate are quite close together; the parishioners who do not fly and who prefer to travel by road would find the village centre as accessible as their new chapel. In 1973 the Catholics opened a new church to service this growing area as well.

On her visit to Hathaden, Philippa made for the heart of the old village to join the morning congregation at the Elim Pentecostal church. The handwritten poster on the notice-board read 'Communion, 11.00 a.m.; gospel service, 6.30 p.m. A warm welcome to all visitors.' Philippa was looking forward to discovering the way in which the Elim Pentecostal church celebrated communion.

At 10.45 a.m. Philippa drove through the one-way system of the village street. Double yellow lines prevented parking outside the chapel. There was no chapel car park. The car park attached to the Berni inn next door was firmly marked 'for patrons only'. So she drove on through the old village street and parked her car in the first residential cul-de-sac she could find.

Walking back towards the chapel, Philippa followed a smartly dressed couple and their two daughters, aged about seven and nine. Both the girls were carrying a black Bible; their mother was carrying a tambourine. Philippa guessed that they, too, were making their way towards the Elim chapel. As the family of four turned to go into the chapel the father noticed Philippa following them. He grabbed her by the hand, welcomed her to the chapel and said 'God bless you'. Philippa smiled nervously.

Inside the chapel door, there was a squashed reception area. A short, deaf man in his seventies was shaking everyone by the hand as they came in and giving them a set of books. The father of the family in front shouted a short exchange of greeting with the chapel steward, whom he addressed affectionately as 'John'. John looked up at Philippa and handed her some books; he too said 'God bless you'.

The chapel was a small building; fifty-four chairs were set out in rows either side of a centre gangway. At the front there was a raised platform. The centre of the platform supported a pulpit; to the right there was an electronic organ. A woman in her early thirties was sitting at the organ gently playing through some hymn tunes from memory and looking over the top of the organ to the row of chairs in front. The row immediately in front of the organ was occupied by her husband and their eleven-year-old son. In the row behind them were three elderly women, all wearing hats. In the next row there was one fifty-year-old woman by herself and behind her two other women in their sixties. The family of four who had gone in before Philippa took the next row back. The row behind them had just one solitary chair, reserved for John when he had finished giving out the books. This completed the pattern on the right-hand side of the church. On the left-hand side, the back row was already occupied by two elderly women. The row in front of them was taken by a grandmother, a mother and her three-year-old girl. Philippa took the next row forward and sat directly in front of the three-year-old. There were two women sitting in front of Philippa, one in her forties and the other in her sixties. The congregation was now complete.

No sooner had Philippa sat down than the woman sitting by herself on the other side of the chapel came across and greeted her. She welcomed Philippa to the chapel and asked if she was new to the area or just visiting. Philippa explained that she was just visiting. 'Where are you from, dear?' the woman enquired. 'London', said Philippa evasively. 'Which part?' the woman persisted. 'Wimbledon', Philippa replied. 'Well, I never, my husband and I used to be there too!' Philippa now realized that she was talking with the pastor's wife and the rest of the congregation were following the conversation with interest. At the sound of 'Wimbledon', the pastor interrupted his pre-service meditation and came across to join in the conversation. He was a large, thickset man in his early sixties. He towered over Philippa as he welcomed her to share their fellowship. 'God bless you', he said.

Feeling herself to have been well and truly welcomed, Philippa began to look through the literature she had been given by John. There were two hymn-books: a battered copy of the Elim songbook *Redemption Hymnal* and a smart new copy of *Mission Praise*. There was also a home-made booklet of fifty or so other hymns and songs. Finally there was the monthly newsletter.

Reading through the monthly newsletter, Philippa was slightly disappointed to realize that the regular pattern of Sunday communion at 11.00 a.m., advertised outside, was not what was going to take place inside. On the first Sunday in the month, she discovered, things are different, and today happened to be the first Sunday in the month. On the first Sunday in the month communion took place at 6.30 p.m. instead of the gospel service. In the morning communion was replaced by a family service. Looking round the congregation, Philippa wondered how different the attendance had been from the usual communion service. Today's family service seemed to mean two young families, a grandmother with her daughter and grandchild, John the chapel steward and a group of elderly women.

At 11.00 a.m., the pastor climbed the steps on to the stage and took his place behind the pulpit. The organist stopped playing and reached for her music copy of *Mission Praise*. The first fifteen minutes or so of the service were filled by a sequence of hymns and songs: three hymns from *Mission Praise*, followed by two from the duplicated song sheet and one from *Redemption Hymnal*. The singing was led by the pastor's fulsome baritone, and each hymn was repeated until he was satisfied with the congregation's participation. He suggested ways in which each repeat could improve on what had gone before. The congregation were told in turn to stand, to sit, to clap, to raise their hands. Throughout these fifteen minutes the young woman whom Philippa had followed into the chapel made full use of her tambourine. Watching from the corner of her eye, Philippa was most impressed by the virtuoso performance, as the moods changed from gentle drum-like tapping with the right hand, to more rigorous shaking by the side of the body, to flamboyant waving over the head.

The six hymns which opened the service were chosen to create a mood rather than to develop a specific theme. The pastor made no attempt to introduce the hymns nor to draw out their individual messages. From *Mission Praise* the service began with the gentle repetition of the simple chorus, 'All hail King Jesus, all hail Emmanuel'. The pace and volume crescendoed in the second hymn 'Alleluia, alleluia, give thanks to the risen Lord' and climaxed in the third, 'You are the king of glory'. The two following hymns from the song sheet were 'I delight greatly in the Lord' and 'Surely goodness and mercy shall follow me'. Then the mood changed with the more traditional 'To God be the glory' from *Redemption Hymnal*.

The pastor drew this period of introductory singing to a close by reminding the congregation that they had sung the word 'Alleluia' frequently in the preceding songs and he expressed the hope that the congregation would feel moved to use that great word of praise throughout the service. His wife responded with a fervent 'Alleluia' and the tambourine clattered gently as its player placed it on the floor. The pastor then welcomed the worshippers and introduced Philippa as someone visiting their fellowship on holiday from Wimbledon. Eyes turned and faces smiled to reinforce the pastor's words of welcome. Philippa appreciated this personal touch.

After the welcome, there was a period for extempore prayers. The pastor started off and invited others to follow. The first person to respond to the invitation was the organist who stood up behind her instrument and offered a prayer of praise for God's goodness. A second woman stood up in the body of the church to continue the same theme; a third offered prayer for a young man who had been hurt in a motorcycle accident and for his parents. The silence which followed these three contributions to the opening prayer session was terminated by the pastor's singing 'I will bless the Lord and give him glory'; the congregation slowly picked up the refrain and joined in.

Then followed a more formal hymn from *Redemption Hymnal*, 'The Lord is my shepherd, I'll follow him alway'. This paraphrase of the twenty-third psalm provided a natural link to the reading of Scripture, Psalm 23 itself. It was read by the nine-year-old daughter of the tambourine player. She read from the Authorized Version of the Bible. The pastor welcomed her on to the stage by name, 'Rebecca'.

While the reading was taking place, Philippa studied the delightful child-made poster hanging near to her seat and signed 'Rebecca'. The central motif of the poster was the multicoloured rainbow which signalled the end of the great flood. In the top right-hand corner was a picture of Noah's ark, stranded on the top of Mount Ararat. Below this a large red heart proclaimed the message 'I love Jesus'. On the left-hand side a teddy bear proclaimed 'Everything is bearable with Jesus'.

The pastor took the theme of the twenty-third psalm for his ten-minute message 'for the children'. He began by explaining that, while English shepherds drive their sheep in front of them, Palestinian shepherds led the way and the sheep followed. Then he produced a car sticker carrying the message 'Don't follow me, I'm lost'. This message was illustrated by a range of personal and second-hand anecdotes of car drivers following other drivers who were lost. The moral was plain: the children in the congregation should take great care in choosing the models whom they follow. Some young people follow pop stars; many pop stars, said the pastor, are lost, hooked on drugs, leading evil lives. Some young people follow their teachers; many teachers are lost: they are atheists, agnostics, humanists and if you follow their ideas you will be lost as well. The pastor then went on to warn the children present (the eleven-year-old boy, the nine- and seven-year-old sisters and the three-year-old) of the dangers of university and college life where clever people with clever ideas lead you astray. The theme of choosing the right leader was further amplified by telling stories about Good King Wenceslas, an Indian chief and the chorus 'Following

Jesus'. The pastor concluded his ten-minute message for the children with the advice: 'But you can be absolutely sure of your way if you take the Lord Jesus to be your shepherd. One thing is sure about the Lord Jesus. He is not lost. He says 'I am the way.' This theme of following Jesus was taken up in the next hymn from *Redemption Hymnal*, 'Where he may lead me I will go'.

The reading of a passage from Luke 19 began a new phase of the service, by introducing the theme of the parable of the pounds. This reading, too, was taken from the Authorized Version of the Bible; this time read by the pastor himself. Immediately after reading the lesson, the pastor gave out the notices. He spoke about Richard's accident, regarding which the congregation had already been informed through the extempore prayer session, and exhorted the church to pray for him and his family. The major emphasis in the notices was reserved for the day of prayer and fasting called for by the Elim movement to take place on the following Sunday, to pray for the movement of the Holy Spirit. He spoke about the virtues of fasting and exhorted the congregation to come thirty minutes early to both of the services the following week, in order to have more time in church for prayer. Another hymn followed the notices, again from *Redemption Hymnal*: 'It was down at the feet of Jesus'. The collection was taken during this hymn.

The pastor then began his main preaching at 11.50 a.m. on the parable of the pounds. First he retold the parable in a humorous and engaging manner. The man who traded his one pound to make ten pounds was the sort of fellow he had been seeking for his church treasurer, but he would be content to take the man who had made five pounds. Then he developed three lessons from the parable. The first lesson is that we have but a limited time to accomplish our work for the Lord; we are waiting for the return of our king and time is running out. The second lesson is that our service is to be fulfilled in a hostile environment; we should expect the world to hate us and, for our part, we should not be too accommodating. As an example of this point the pastor quoted the instance of the previous Sunday when the landlord of the Kings Head complained that the worshippers' cars were obstructing his trade. The third lesson is that we need to look for opportunities for service; the old Elim saying 'We are saved to serve' is as true today as it has ever been. Some day we shall be called to give an account of our service. Although our eternal salvation does not depend on service, what we are entrusted with in God's kingdom will depend on how we responded to that trust here. Down here we are training for up there, to be fitted for further responsibilities; the time for rest is up there, not down here. The pastor closed his sermon notes at 12.24 p.m., having preached for thirty-four minutes. The congregation were listening intently throughout and occasionally signalled their involvement with an 'Amen' or an 'Alleluia'.

The mood which pervaded the sermon was one of urgency. The points were frequently illustrated by anecdotes from the preacher's reflections on his own personal ministry and his awareness of approaching retirement from full-time ministry and of death. This personal evaluation of a lifelong ministry, flowing through the sermon as a kind of hidden agenda, added a poignancy which left a clear impression on Philippa's mind.

After another hymn from *Redemption Hymnal*, 'There is joy in serving Jesus', the pastor closed the service with prayer at 12.29 p.m. The pastor moved directly to the door to greet people as they went out, but no one seemed in a hurry to leave after their ninety-minute service. The organist came down from the rostrum at the front and made a point of coming across to Philippa's chair to talk with her. Other members of the congregation went out of their way to make sure that she felt welcome. At the door John took her books and said 'God bless you.' The pastor pumped her hand warmly, towering over her slightly, and wished her a good holiday.

Philippa had been somewhat apprehensive of attending a Pentecostal service in case she stood out as not properly belonging to that kind of church tradition. She came away realizing just how much effort the congregation was taking to make visitors like her feel wanted and welcome. At the same time, she was slightly disappointed that the church had not afforded her an opportunity to witness prophecy, glossolalia or other signs of charismatic worship.

8
MARKET
TOWNS

Woldbridge

WOLDBRIDGE IS A small market town of 2,785 inhabitants, the
largest community in a very rural area. Woldbridge is served by
three churches: Anglican, Catholic and Methodist. In the nineteenth century there had been both a Wesleyan and a Primitive
Methodist chapel. The Primitive Methodist chapel now serves as
a garage. The Pentecostal church has also closed and now serves
as a fish and chip shop.

Mid-morning Sunday worshippers today have a choice in
Woldbridge of an Anglican service at 9.30 a.m., a Catholic Mass
at 11.00 a.m. and a Methodist service at 10.45 a.m. The Anglican
church provides other services at 8.00 a.m. and 6.30 p.m., while
the Methodist church also holds an evening service. Robin's
choice was to attend the Methodist morning service.

The previous day Robin had gone to look at the Methodist
chapel, a most imposing building just off the main road through
the centre of Woldbridge. It was built in the 1860s in a sturdy
Grecian style. Behind the iron railings, which separate the
chapel from the road, the red-brick front is adorned with a
massive Ionic portico and pediment.

Close up, it became obvious that the yellow plaster was
crumbling on the Ionic arcade and the blue paint on the main
door was faded and blistered. Robin was not surprised to
discover that the door was locked; he was surprised not to find
any kind of notice-board outside the chapel. He wandered
around the town centre, to check whether he had found the

right place. He passed the old Primitive chapel, but finding no
other likely candidate to be the Methodist chapel he began to
make local enquiries. It was the reader from the Anglican
church who confirmed that the Methodist church met at 10.45
a.m. every Sunday morning for divine worship and junior
church.

On Sunday morning Robin arrived at the chapel fifteen
minutes early. The iron gates from the pavement were open to
welcome worshippers. He climbed the six or seven steep steps
which were all part of the Grecian design and wondered how
Woldbridge Methodist chapel provided for the disabled. The
faded blue-painted doors stood open, leading into the ante-
chapel. Immediately in front of the door the visitor was welcomed by a long table covered with a deep blue serge cloth and
a pile of books. Three notices were pinned to a board behind the
table, one as an eye-catching poster, the other two in small
typescript. The message proclaimed by the eye-catching poster
read simply 'Your church needs money'. Leaning over the table
to read the small print of the typescript, Robin identified the
flower rota and the circuit link newsletter. There were no other
notice-boards or notices in the chapel and the only copy of the
current newsletter was the one pinned to the notice-board, so
Robin was not able to discover much more about the life of the
chapel or anything about the circuit's minister.

At either end of the long table stood one of the stewards,
both men in their fifties, ready to welcome worshippers and to
hand them a copy of the 1933 edition of the Methodist hymn-
book. Robin moved towards the shorter steward on the right.
He was given his hymn-book and the door was held open for
him to enter the chapel.

The interior of the chapel was as lofty and as imposing as the
exterior. The front was dominated by the large organ and the
huge pulpit. The pulpit stands about nine feet above floor level,
like the bridge on a ship, allowing the preacher unrestricted
view across the pews and into the galleries. It is said that in its
heyday this galleried chapel accommodated a congregation of
eight hundred.

When Robin arrived, the organist was already well into his
voluntaries and twenty or so people were in church listening to
'Jesu, joy of man's desiring'. Robin looked round for somewhere
to sit. The chapel was furnished with boxed pews, each pew

having its own door. In order to protect the congregation at the back of the chapel from the draughts off the street, these doors had been built up to a height of six feet and included glass windows. Robin had not experienced anything quite like that before and felt very cut off from the other worshippers as he closed the door to his pew and settled down in the comfortable shadow of the gallery.

By 10.45 a.m., a congregation of fifty-nine had assembled. This is a large number for a rural church, but when dispersed throughout a chapel designed to accommodate eight hundred, the congregation still appeared remarkably thin. The junior church had been lined up in a pew towards the front. These eight boys and four girls were accompanied by three male leaders: a teenager and two men in their thirties and forties. The rest of the congregation tended to sit as far towards the back of the chapel as possible, where the pews were protected by the higher doors, leaving much empty space between themselves and the preacher. Apart from the junior church and their leaders, there were twenty men in the congregation and twenty-four women. Of these forty-four people, thirty-five were clearly over the age of sixty. On the whole, the congregation appeared to be friendly. While people often came into the chapel individually, many of them sat with friends and began a conversation above the organ music. Only five people were sitting in a pew by themselves.

The service began just one minute late, when the minister arrived in the pulpit. He was a tiny man, now in his eighties, who had retired to live and help within the circuit. His clerical suit and collar had been purchased for a younger, straighter and plumper man. Standing alone in the huge pulpit, which could have supported a team of ministers, he looked rather lost; but peering over the pulpit edge into the huge church, he quickly asserted his leadership of the worship. He was obviously a well-loved and respected pastor within the chapel. His sensitivity to the needs of the worshipping community and his alertness to the issues of the contemporary world were much in evidence as he called the people to worship and offered their needs and the needs of today's world to God in prayer. Robin quickly realized that the frail frame and infirm voice of an octogenarian minister were not about to proclaim a geriatric gospel.

The pattern of service followed the Free Church tradition of prayer, Scripture, preaching and notices, interspersed with hymns. Five hymns were sung, all from the Methodist hymn-book: 'Meet and right it is to sing', 'O Jesus, king most wonderful', 'Spirit of wisdom, turn our eyes', 'My heart and voice I raise', 'Father, let thy kingdom come'. The junior church was present for the first hymn and left during the second. Generally the singing was rather weak, perhaps unusually so for a Methodist church, but the size of the building militated against participation. The organ provided a good lead for the hymns, but the church suffered from having neither choir nor individuals within the congregation who gave a positive lead to the singing.

The whole leadership of the service was in the hands of the minister. He read both passages from Scripture himself, led the prayers, read the notices and preached the sermon. Apart from the two stewards who gave out books and also took the offertory, the lay involvement was in the hands of the three men leading the junior church and the sixty-year-old male organist.

The prayers began after the second hymn by giving thanks to God for the great hymns of the church, especially making reference to the hymn just sung, and by giving thanks for the young people of the junior church who had just left during that hymn. Then thanks were given for the worldwide church, the Methodist heritage and the outpouring of the Spirit in 1738. Prayer was offered for Methodist local preachers, the local circuit and for the chapel in neighbouring Little Wold where the members were 'few in number but strong in faith'. All this seemed to Robin rather parochial and remote from his own experience as a visitor who did not belong to the Methodist tradition. But after this the prayers turned to the contemporary world situation. The catalogue of topics was well informed and up-to-date; the treatment of them was perceptive and sensitive.

The notices revealed a church which was in business not only on Sunday morning, but also on Sunday evening and throughout the week. The preacher for the evening service was announced and the members of the congregation were exhorted to attend. On Monday evening the leaders of the junior church were meeting. On Tuesday it was the turn of the Ladies' Group, while on Wednesday the Women's Fellowship was supporting a meeting in a nearby chapel. The prayer circle meets on Thursday. No notices were given out about Friday or Saturday. The notices finished with the announcement of the collections for the previous Sunday, a total of £84.76.

The sermon was an exposition of Acts 4. 1–30 (NEB) on the theme of God's power. The minister began the theme by reading the whole of that portion of Scripture himself:

> They were still addressing the people when the chief priests came upon them, together with the Controller of the Temple and the Sadducees, exasperated at their teaching the people and proclaiming the resurrection from the dead – the resurrection of Jesus. They were arrested and put in prison for the night, as it was already evening. . . .

After the singing of a hymn, the minister developed the theme by retelling the scriptural tradition in his own words. He then linked this Scripture to his theme of power by drawing attention to the way in which the prayer at the end of this section addressed God as 'Sovereign Lord'. Sovereign Lord, he said, is a title about God's power. The next section of the sermon invited the congregation to think about sovereign power in human hands. He illustrated his point by producing a long list of rulers, from Pharaoh to Hitler, via Herod, and by referencing the abuse of power in South Africa. The congregation seemed neither particularly stirred by their minister's political views, nor enraged by them. There was no response. The third part of the sermon proceeded to contrast the power of earthly rulers with the weakness of the crucified Christ. The congregation were exhorted to follow the model of Christ, presumably in preference to the models offered by Pharaoh, Herod and Hitler. The sermon lasted fourteen minutes and kept Robin's attention throughout.

After the service the minister and the stewards were standing by the door to greet people as they left. The minister was doing his best to shake everyone by the hand. Recognizing Robin as a visitor, he made a special point of welcoming him to the chapel and asked him where he was from and wished him a good stay in Woldbridge. Several members of the congregation also engaged him in conversation as he lingered on the chapel steps. They were keen to make him feel at home and insisted that he take back greetings from the Wold circuit to his own chapel. Listening to their conversations, Robin learnt a great deal about the immense problems faced by their church. Their building was in need of restoration; their junior church was struggling to keep up its membership; the circuit needed more preachers. Yet under the inspiring leadership of their octogenarian retired minister, Robin got the impression of a friendly church, trying hard to consolidate and extend its ministry during difficult times.

Spears Cross

Spears Cross is a large and prosperous market town, with strong historic associations which support a bustling tourist industry. When Jane arrived in Spears Cross at the end of April the town was already full with visitors and traffic.

On a Sunday morning Spears Cross' 10,000 inhabitants and the numerous visitors can, if they so wish, choose between a range of places of worship. All within a few minutes' walk of each other there are a large medieval Anglican church, the Catholic church, the Methodist church, the United Reformed church, the Baptist church, the Salvation Army citadel, the Christadelphian hall and the Quaker meeting house. Contemplating the rich smorgasbord of mid-morning services, Jane decided that she would become a Baptist for the morning and a Christadelphian for the evening. Jane had never experienced Baptist or Christadelphian worship, so this would be a good opportunity to do so.

The Baptist church in Spears Cross is in a narrow side street behind the town centre bus station. Jane almost missed the narrow turn off the main road. The street name was high up in small letters and hard to see from a distance; the church was not signposted from the main road. The narrow side street was a no-parking area, but a number of cars were drawing up near the chapel to let their passengers out. There seemed to be a steady flow of young couples in their twenties or thirties, shepherding young children and senior citizens along the church path. Jane drew up outside the church to check the service time on the notice-board. A lady in her mid-thirties immediately spoke to her, asked her if she was coming to the service and whether she knew where to park. Jane appreciated the help, listened carefully to the parking instructions and drove off to find the private office car park 'which the church is allowed to use on Sundays'.

Two stewards, a man and a woman both in their fifties, were waiting by the door to welcome Jane and to give her an 'order of worship leaflet'. Since it was still only 10.55 a.m. when Jane arrived, she was surprised to hear singing already coming from inside the church. She checked with the stewards whether she was late for the service. They explained that, while the service proper did not begin until 11.00 a.m., ten minutes were always spent before the service singing songs of fellowship. One of the stewards opened the door into the church for Jane and apologized for the fact that it might be difficult to find a seat at this time in the morning. They walked up the aisle until the steward saw space and asked an elderly couple if they could squeeze up a little to make room for a visitor. They did so willingly and Jane sat down rather self-consciously.

Jane found herself sitting next to a plump woman in her late seventies, wearing a bright pink hat perched over a neat, grey bun. She moved her walking-stick out of Jane's way. On her knees she was nursing the *Baptist Hymn-book*, the *New English Bible* and *Songs of Fellowship*. She nudged Jane to tell her they were singing song 64 and then she offered her all three of her books, saying 'They're no use to me. I've left my glasses at home. But I know most of the words.' And she went on singing song 64.

The whole church seemed alive and happy. The singing was being conducted by a man in his early thirties and supported by a motley crew of musicians. To begin with there was both an organ and a piano, being played *fortissimo* at the same time and each tuned to a slightly different pitch. Both were being played by men: a thirty-year-old and a forty-year-old, two very competent musicians. There were also two guitars, a double bass and a violin being played by young adults in their twenties.

Before finding her place in the song book, Jane looked through the service sheet. The front page gave the names of the minister, the church secretary, the church treasurer, the leader of the junior church and the stewards on duty that morning. Then there was a word of welcome:

We extend a warm and friendly welcome to visitors worshipping with us today. We hope you will enjoy your stay in Spears Cross and that in our services you will find fellowship and peace.

Please sign our Visitors' Book as you leave the church and convey our greetings to your own church upon your return home.

   If you are newly resident in the town or area or are worshipping with us for the first time, the minister would like to arrange to call upon you. Please make yourself known to him or to any of the stewards today.

The first page concluded with the invitation, 'This service sheet may be taken away.'

   Looking round the church Jane began to realize just how full it really was, with a few people standing at the back. Jane reckoned there were 180 people crammed into space for 160. The second thing to press itself home on Jane was that the congregation was fairly evenly balanced between men and women. There were a number of young families and a number of children. At the same time, the elderly were not absent from this church. The service sheet described the morning service as 'family worship' and that was most certainly the feel of the inter-generational congregation.

   The service proper began promptly at 11.00 a.m. when the singing stopped and the minister, a man in his mid-fifties wearing a lounge suit, announced 'Let us stand to worship God'. The minister then led the people in a series of simple versicles and responses, conveniently printed in the service sheet:

> M: O God, you are enthroned in holiness.
> P: It is you whose praise Israel sings.
> M: Our fathers put their trust in you.
> P: Unto you they cried and were delivered.
> M: The people of all nations worship before you.
> P: We worship you and bow before you.

   The first hymn was a rousing rendition of 'God is in his temple' with both *organo pleno* and *piano fortissimo*. Jane was fascinated by the sheer physical energy which both keyboard instrumentalists were exerting on this hymn. Then the congregation remained standing through the extemporary opening prayers and to join in the Lord's Prayer. The mood of the opening hymn was developed in the scripture reading from Isaiah 62, a prophecy of Zion's vindication, read by a forty-year-old man, whose name was printed in the service sheet.

The notices helped Jane to appreciate just how much was going on at Spears Cross Baptist church, especially among young people. Monday night is practice night for the music group who are preparing for a youth service. Tuesday is Girls' Brigade at 6.00 p.m. Wednesday is prayer and Bible study night at 7.30 p.m. Thursday is choir practice night at 7.00 p.m. and Boys' Brigade (Company Section) at 7.30 p.m. On Friday the Boys' Brigade (Junior Section) meets at 6.15 p.m. On Saturday there is an early morning prayer meeting at 6.30 a.m. and an evening celebration of praise at 7.30 p.m. The young people's group meets on Sunday at 8.00 p.m. after the evening worship. The notices led into the offertory which was taken up by the two stewards who had been on duty at the door, assisted by two young girls, aged seven or eight.

After the offertory there was 'the presentation of infants' when a young couple brought their first child for a form of dedication. The couple were obviously well established and well liked members of the congregation. Both the minister and the congregation welcomed them warmly. Before the presentation took place, the minister said that he was going to speak for a few minutes; in fact he spoke for about ten minutes. His first points were to welcome the young infant by name, Claire Louise, and to stress the wonder and privilege of sharing in God's gracious gift of parenthood. Then the minister developed a trenchant attack on denominations which practise infant baptism. He emphasized the lack of scriptural precedent for infant baptism and praised Claire Louise's parents for bringing her up in a Christian household and leading her to believers' baptism later in life.

During the next hymn, 'Father, in thy presence kneeling', the forty or so children of the junior church left their pews and gathered around the minister. After the hymn the minister prayed with them. Then they filed out for their own classes while the congregation enjoyed two more songs.

Now the children had left the service, the adults could spread themselves out a little more comfortably in the pews and the serious stuff could begin. In practice this meant the prayers, the preaching of the word and two more hymns. The prayers, led by the minister, were relatively short and direct. The main themes of the prayers were also printed on the service sheet. Jane found this very helpful.

The sermon began at 11.43 a.m. and lasted until 12.14 p.m., a solid thirty-one minutes. The minister announced his theme as 'a noble example' and quoted Daniel 3.16–18 as his text. Jane thumbed quickly through *The New English Bible* which she had been given in the pew in time to discover that the minister was using a more traditional translation, the Revised Standard Version:

> Shadrach, Meshach, and Abednego answered the king, 'O Nebuchadnezzar, we have no need to answer you in this matter. If it be so, our God whom we serve is able to deliver us from the burning fiery furnace; and he will deliver us out of your hand, O king. But if not, be it known to you, O king, that we will not serve your gods or worship the golden image which you have set up.'

The first five minutes or so of the sermon were a basic retelling of the Nebuchadnezzar tradition from the book of Daniel. Then the main heart of the sermon speculated about the many various excuses which Shadrach, Meshach and Abednego might have made to justify the worship of Nebuchadnezzar's statue. Since there is no scriptural indication that such excuses were ever made or even contemplated, the preacher felt at complete liberty to range over all the issues which he might imagine his own congregation would be tempted to evoke as excuses to deviate from their commitment to the faith. The sermon concluded with a useful summary of what the minister understood to be his main point: We must follow our consciences to do what is right. We must follow the commands of the Lord, whatever the consequences may seem to be. Then it is God's responsibility to see us through it.

In some ways, Jane thought the sermon was a stark contrast to the rest of the service. To her the presentation and content seemed dull and boring. Looking round at other members of the congregation, the life and vitality which characterized them at the beginning of the service was slowly draining away. The pews seemed increasingly uncomfortable and people began to shift and change their positions. Sitting at the front, the pianist and the organist began to drift off into their own worlds, turning the pages of their music books. By the time twenty-five minutes had passed by, interest had reached a very low ebb indeed.

After the sermon had finished, the musicians, choir and congregation sprang back into life for the final hymn 'Christian, seek not yet repose'. At the end of the hymn the minister pronounced the blessing and the service closed with a sung Amen at 12.18 p.m. Then the musicians began to play over some modern hymn tunes.

The congregation seemed in no hurry to leave. Some listened to the musicians; others began talking one to another. The woman sitting next to Jane turned to her and asked if she was a visitor. They sat chatting for several minutes about Spears Cross Baptist church and about Jane's home congregation, until the people trapped on the inside of their pew wanted to make a move. When Jane's neighbour got up, she removed a large cushion from her seat, tucked it under her arm and prepared to carry it home. Progress out of Spears Cross Baptist church was very slow, as the congregation talked with each other and welcomed guests. The minister stood at the door speaking to everyone as they went out.

On the way home, Jane decided that she had enjoyed and appreciated the friendliness and the liveliness of the worship that morning. She would not be reluctant to go back to Spears Cross Baptist church, but next time she would arrive earlier to get a better seat and she would take a cushion for the long sermon.

In the evening Jane made her way to the Christadelphian hall. This was a smart new building. Going through a bright foyer she entered a newly decorated meeting room. She picked up the Christadelphian hymn-book and found a seat. At the front of the room two men in their forties sat behind a table on a raised dais. About fifty chairs were set out in the room in neat rows. By 6.30 p.m. there was a total congregation of twenty-nine: twelve men and seventeen women. These included four couples in their twenties and thirties and a teenage girl. All were smartly dressed and all the women wore hats, except for Jane herself.

At 6.30 p.m. precisely one of the men sitting at the table at the front of the hall stood up. He introduced and welcomed the visiting lecturer who was going to speak to the title 'Who are the angels?' The lecture forms the main substance of the Christadelphian evening meeting. After the opening hymn, the reading of Acts 12, a short prayer and a second hymn, the lecture began at 6.45 p.m. and lasted just over half an hour. Many of the congregation took copious notes during the lecture, between frantically turning the pages of their Bibles to keep up with the lecturer's rapid quotation of texts.

During the course of the lecture, the lecturer posed three major questions: 'Who are the angels? Do angels have wings? and Do we have guardian angels?' Each question was answered by 'considering what God has to say in the Bible'. His conclusions were that the angels are the Elohim of the Old Testament, as distinct from YHWH himself; that angels do not have wings, otherwise Abraham would not have mistaken them for men (Genesis 18); that we should not stand staring at the sky looking for flying people, but we should look for ordinary people doing the will of the Father. These are the real guardian angels.

After the lecture, the lecturer was profusely thanked for his careful, thorough and enlightening talk. Then the notices were given out. Two different visiting speakers were coming to lead the Bible class on Tuesday at 8.00 p.m. and the evening meeting next Sunday at 6.30 p.m. On Sunday the lecturer was going to take for his subject 'The person of God'. Tuesday evening's subject was, however, not yet available.

The service closed with the hymn 'Sun of my soul, thou saviour dear' and a prayer offered by a member of the congregation. The organist then played a sombre voluntary for three minutes while the congregation sat in silence with heads bowed. When the music stopped, no one was in a hurry to go home. Several people came up to Jane and asked her if she liked the lecture and which Christadelphian meeting she belonged to at home. When she confessed that she was not a member of the Christadelphians, they were keen to take her across to the bookstall and to give her some literature about their beliefs. In particular, they wanted her to read a booklet entitled *A New World Coming: God's Plan for the Future*, which offered the following promise:

> The call of the gospel is still open to all who will hear. However, events in the Middle East are moving towards a dreadful climax and we know that this heralds the return of Jesus. If you wish to be among those who will welcome his return with joy and not with fear, the time to look into these things is now.

Clutching her newly acquired literature, Jane stepped back into the busy main street running through the middle of Spears Cross, now secure in the knowledge that angels do not have wings.

Market Lipton

Market Lipton is an ancient market town which received its first royal charter in the mid-twelfth century. Today the medieval pattern of streets is still visible, as are some remains of the old castle. It is said that Market Lipton had ten or eleven parish churches in the twelfth century, but only four in the fifteenth century. Just one of these four churches, St John's, escaped the ravages of the civil war. One was razed to the ground and not rebuilt; the other two, St James' and St Paul's, were reduced to roofless ruins and remained in that state until the end of the eighteenth century. Before the Reformation there was also a small Benedictine priory in Market Lipton.

During the late eighteenth century and the first half of the nineteenth century, the three remaining medieval parish churches were all thoroughly restored and refashioned. St Paul's was the first to receive a completely new nave and tower in the 1760s. In the 1840s the fine Norman nave and apsidal chancel of St James' were given an ugly brick tower and a south aisle. In the 1850s St John's was entirely rebuilt, except for the west tower.

In 1950 there were still three rectors in Market Lipton, one for each parish church. While the rector of St John's had nearly 1,400 people living in his parish, there were fewer than 400 living in the parish of St Paul's. In the early 1950s one rector was appointed to St John's and to St James'. Then in the early 1970s all three parishes were united to form one new parish. In the mid-1970s St Paul's was made redundant. Both the other churches remain in regular use, although they are only a few minutes' walk apart. On Sundays the mid-morning parish communion always takes place in St John's and the 6.00 p.m. evensong always takes place in St James'; the early morning Holy Communion service alternates between the two buildings.

Jennifer arrived in Market Lipton to look round the churches shortly after lunch on a busy Wednesday afternoon just after Easter. She began by visiting St John's, which stands right in the centre of the market place. The large notice-board outside gave the church's name and carried the invitation 'Visitors always welcome'. The notice-board also gave the vicar's name, but not his address or telephone number, and explained that the details of services would be found on the notice-board in the porch. The notice-board in the porch was empty, apart from a forest of drawing-pins. The porch was littered with cigarette ends. Jennifer guessed that the church porch was one of the few public places open in Market Lipton where young people could congregate on a draughty evening. The church was locked and there was no indication of where the key could be obtained.

St James' church, only a few minutes' walk away, was in a more sheltered position. An identical notice-board was placed outside and here the more detailed notices in the porch remained intact. Jennifer was able to learn fully not only when services were held, but also who was responsible for doing the readings and the names of the sidespeople on duty. Again, however, the church was locked and there was no indication of where the key could be obtained.

Another few minutes' walk and Jennifer came to St Paul's. The notice-board outside this church carried a different text:

> This church is maintained by the Redundant Churches Fund, St Andrew by the Wardrobe, Queen Victoria Street, London EC4, with money provided by Parliament and the Church of England and by the gifts of the public. Though no longer needed for regular worship it remains a consecrated building.

Like the other two parish churches, St Paul's was locked; unlike those still in current use, St Paul's made it clear where the key could be obtained. Jennifer fetched the key and let herself in. St Paul's church smelt slightly musty, but looked clean and well cared for. The first leaflet she picked up when she entered the church was designed 'To help you use five minutes in prayer'. Although the church was redundant, it seemed to be taking its spiritual ministry to visitors more seriously than many churches still in regular use.

The short eighteenth-century chancel had been turned into a stage. A leaflet left in the church gave an indication of the kind of performances the stage hosted during the summer festival. Behind the stage the original altar remained in the sanctuary. The church organ was still *in situ*. Pinned to the console was the notice, 'The keys to the church organ are with the vicar. Please do not force open.' The organ had, however, been forced open. The lectern carried a huge Bible, printed in 1770 and presented to St Paul's church after the eighteenth-century rebuilding programme. It was open at the first chapter of the book of Daniel:

> In the third year of the reign of Jehoiakim king of Judah came Nebuchadnezzar king of Babylon unto Jerusalem, and besieged it. And the Lord gave Jehoiakim king of Judah into his hand, with part of the vessels of the house of God: which he carried into the land of Shinar to the house of his god.

A table at the back of the church carried up-to-date leaflets produced by the Redundant Churches Fund. Jennifer learnt that:

> A redundant church is a consecrated church belonging to the Church of England which has been formally declared redundant under the procedure of the Pastoral Measures (1968 or 1983) because it is no longer required for regular worship. Some redundant churches are found other uses – as places of worship for other denominations, as concert halls, cultural centres, offices or even as houses; some are demolished, but there is a residue of churches which are so important to the cultural heritage of the nation that their preservation must be secured. It was to look after churches of this kind that the Redundant Churches Fund was established.

As well as the three parish churches, there are four other denominations active in the centre of Market Lipton, two in the market square close to St John's, one right opposite St Paul's and one tucked away in a side street.

The Catholic church had a good notice-board outside. It gave the times of Sunday services, 8.30 a.m. and 11.00 a.m., the times of holy day Masses, 9.00 a.m. and 7.30 p.m., the times of Saturday confessions, 11.30 a.m. to 12.00 noon and 6.30 p.m. to 7.00 p.m., the parish priest's name and address; and the information that details of weekday activities were available in the church porch. The church porch was locked and nothing was said about the availability of the key. The parish priest lives in Market Lipton.

The Methodist church looked considerably less well cared for than the Catholic church. The notice-board was shabby but informative. It gave the minister's name and address, the times of Sunday services, 11.00 a.m. and 6.30 p.m., the time of the Junior Church, Sunday at 11.00 a.m., and a list of weekday activities. The Wesley Guild meets on Tuesday evening, the Youth Club on Wednesday evening and a children's group on Friday evening. Again the church was locked and nothing was said about the availability of the key. The Methodist minister lives in Market Lipton.

The Baptist church had a huge poster outside carrying the message 'Come and praise Jesus Christ the living God, Sundays, 11.00 a.m. and 6.30 p.m. For details concerning youth meetings, prayer and Bible study groups see the other notice-board inside or telephone the minister on Market Lipton 2552 or 2553.' Again the church was locked and nothing was said about the availability of the key.

The Society of Friends' meeting house was most inconspicuous. Built in the 1720s, it looked like a simple brick cottage and Jennifer walked right past the first time without noticing it. Next time she saw the small notice and learnt that meetings take place on Sunday at 11.00 a.m.

During the present century Market Lipton has expanded considerably from its ancient town centre. Today there is a population of around 7,500 people. While the Church of England, the Methodist, Catholic and Baptist churches and the Society of Friends have all remained concentrated in the town centre, the Assemblies of God have opened a church in the heart of one of the local authority housing estates. This unattractive prefabricated hall is well signposted from all directions through the warren of suburban roads. The notice pinned to the main door gave details of the Sunday services at 11.00 a.m. and 6.00 p.m. and of the Tuesday Bible study and prayer meeting at 7.30 p.m. 'All are welcome', said the notice. No details were given about how to get into the church or how to contact the minister or local leaders.

Later in the day, talking with some local people, Jennifer learnt that there was also a house church meeting on one of the estates. It was thought to have a membership of between thirty and forty people, but Jennifer was unable to find out further details about this.

On Sunday morning Jennifer had a choice, therefore, of

attending a mid-morning service in the Anglican, Baptist, Catholic, Methodist or Pentecostal churches or in the Friends meeting house. She decided to go to the 10.00 a.m. parish communion service in the Anglican church, and for good measure to go to the 8.00 a.m. service as well.

On Sunday she discovered that the vicar was on holiday. The early morning communion service was taken by a retired priest, a man in his late seventies. The service was straightforward, from the Book of Common Prayer. There was a congregation of twenty-one, eight men and thirteen women, all well on in years.

The mid-morning service was taken by a non-stipendiary priest, borrowed from a neighbouring parish, a man in his late thirties. The Rite A communion service was used from *The Alternative Service Book 1980* and lasted just an hour. All told, there were seventy-eight people in church, including three servers, a reader and a choir of eleven. The average age of the congregation was well over fifty; the choir, although including no children, on balance seemed a little younger. There were just four people in the congregation under the age of twenty-one, as were the three servers. The choir sang most professionally and the congregation remained largely silent.

After the service, coffee was available in one of the aisles. About fifteen people stayed for coffee and Jennifer went along to join them. They made her most welcome; before long she was part of a small group earnestly discussing the sermon with the visiting preacher. Talking with the churchwarden, she asked about the other denominations in town. He explained that it was the Baptist church which drew the largest congregation and that the Baptist church was doing particularly well among young people. 'What we need here', he said, 'is a young curate who could build up our youth work too.'

Intrigued by the churchwarden's comments about the Baptist church, Jennifer decided to go there for the evening service. She arrived fifteen minutes before the service was due to start to find the building vibrant with singing from *Songs of Fellowship*. A large choir of children, teenagers and adults was standing in three stepped rows at the front of the building. To one side of the choir there was a small orchestra of guitars, wind instruments and piano. On the other side, the minister stood by a large microphone. He was wearing a bright yellow teeshirt, emblazoned with the name of the church. During the next ten minutes they sang a range of songs, including 'Alleluia, give thanks to the risen Lord', 'Victory is on our lips and in our lives', 'Worship his Majesty' and 'I stand before the presence'. By 6.30 p.m. the congregation had grown to about one hundred people, including young families, babies and teenagers.

The minister began the service proper by spending about six minutes on giving out the notices. The notices indicated how much was going on in the church during the week. As well as announcing their own services for the following Sunday, the minister said that two teams were going from the church to lead services in neighbouring villages. He asked the congregation to pray for the ministry of these teams and for volunteers to go with them to lend encouragement and support to the smaller congregations in the villages.

After the notices, the congregation stood to sing the hymn 'Good Christian men, rejoice and sing'. Then after a brief opening prayer the congregation sat to sing the chorus 'Worthy, O worthy are you' a number of times. Next the minister gave out special prayer requests: 'John prays that Judith may come to know Christ'; 'David prays for the parents of a four-year-old girl who died this week'. While the offering was taken by two men in their early forties the congregation sang 'I am the bread of life'.

Then the minister settled into the first of his extemporary addresses, this one lasting about six or seven minutes. 'I don't know if some of you know this, but before he died Jesus talked about his death to his disciples. He said to them "So with you, now is your time of grief." But this grief will be taken away and then they will have joy. Now, as I thought about our time together this evening this verse came to mind: "No one will take away their joy".'

This text about joy provided the right introduction to the central component of the evening service. The choir had been practising Roger Jones' musical *Jerusalem Joy*. They presented this musical with considerable professional skill. It reached its climax with a brief liturgical dance.

When the musical finished at 7.40 p.m., the minister settled into the second of his extemporary addresses, this one lasting about five minutes. 'I hope you get the message from Roger Jones' musical *Jerusalem Joy*. He is not here. He is risen. I would like us to capture that joy by singing "Jesus Christ has risen today".' For this hymn the small orchestra took a rest and allowed the organ to take over.

After the hymn the minister settled into his third extemporary address, this one lasting about ten minutes. 'Jesus said no one will take away your joy. So many things give us joy. Last Sunday Easter eggs gave us joy, but by this week most of those Easter eggs will be forgotten. Ultimately so many joys pass from us. Life is very real and death is very real too. When we see the crucifix with Jesus hanging on it, that is not the true story. When I see a crucifix I always want to turn it round so we can see the empty cross on the back. He has risen. Last week my wife made a cake for tea. Instead of overflowing the cake tin it remained flat at the bottom. I called it a Bishop of Durham cake; it had all the ingredients but it hadn't risen. For those of us who know the Lord Jesus Christ there is no Bishop of Durham cake this Easter. I trust that as you have listened, seen and heard this evening you have known that joy of the resurrection. If not, come and see me afterwards and I will gladly arrange to talk with you.' Stirred by this address, the congregation stood to sing their final hymn 'I know my redeemer lives'. Then the choir repeated one of the choruses from *Jerusalem Joy* as an encore.

The service ended at 8.10 p.m. The minister stood right in the doorway to make sure that he spoke to everyone as they went out. The number of people in church meant that it was quite some time before it was Jennifer's turn to pass through the door. The minister identified her as a stranger and asked her where she lived. Jennifer would have liked to chat with him for a few moments but she was too conscious of the long queue of people behind her to feel comfortable about adding any further to their delay.

The following week Jennifer returned to Market Lipton to attend the Quaker meeting. She arrived at 10.50 a.m. and found the front door to the cottage open. She was welcomed by a woman in her late seventies and shown through the cottage to the back door. The meeting house was built at the bottom of the garden, totally hidden from view.

Inside, the simple meeting hall had benches arranged parallel with both sides and along the back, focusing on a small table at the front. On the table there were three Bibles, a pot plant and a small battery clock. The elder with oversight for the meeting, a woman in her late fifties, sat facing the clock. At the very back of the room there was a small library of books; at the very front there was a kettle and a tray of cups and saucers.

By 11.00 a.m. the meeting had grown to fifteen people, ten women between the ages of fifty and eighty, a man in his fifties, a youth in his late teens, and a young couple with a toddler. As members came in they sat in silence. The young parents tried very hard to persuade their son, Thomas, to share in the silence, but Thomas had other ideas. By 11.10 a.m. father had decided to take Thomas out. 'Leave mummy behind', said Thomas, 'No, no!' But the reluctant Thomas was firmly taken out.

Shortly after 11.15 a.m. the elder stood up and broke the silence for a few minutes by reading a short section from the *Advices and Questions*. The section contained advice on how to conduct a meeting: pray silently as you gather together; yield yourself and all outward concerns to God's guidance; if the call to speak comes, do not let the sense of your own unworthiness inhibit you; pray that your ministry may arise from deep experience; try to speak audibly and distinctly with sensitivity to the needs of the members.

Just before 11.30 a.m. a member of the meeting, again a woman in her fifties, stood up and said that she had been moved to speak: When Thomas went out he said 'Leave mummy behind'; to find new life we, too, have to leave mummy behind; Thomas also said 'No'; we, too, are reluctant to set out on our own spiritual pilgrimage leaving mummy behind.

Silence was broken for the third time shortly after 11.50 a.m. by the oldest member of the meeting, a woman in her late seventies. Throughout the silence she had been holding, reading and rereading a poem. Now she read that poem aloud.

At 12 noon the elder gave out some notices and made a special point of welcoming visitors and inviting them to stay for coffee. Then the members turned to each other and shook hands. The members made a particular point of welcoming Jennifer and talking with her over coffee. Over coffee the elder explained to her that the meeting room had been built in the 1720s, fell into disuse during the late nineteenth century and reopened in the 1930s. She also described her own spiritual pilgrimage and how she had converted from Anglicanism about ten years earlier. The welcome after the service was so real that Jennifer came away feeling that she had indeed been among a 'Society of Friends'.

9
RESORTS

St Giles Bay

THROUGHOUT THE FIRST half of the nineteenth century, St Giles was a small, inaccessible rural parish. There was a sturdy manor-house; the ancient parish church, dedicated to St Giles; a hamlet of poor dwellings, mainly thatched; and the straggling farmsteads. By the 1850s two neighbouring communities were already experiencing a new form of development and a new source of prosperity. The neighbouring area was being transformed into a coastal resort. Large and substantial houses were being built; new recreations were being discovered.

Then in the 1860s the railway reached the coast by St Giles. The centre of the community rapidly moved down to the water's edge, away from the manor-house and the medieval parish church on the hillside leading up from the coast. A new Victorian centre was created, a new identity was formed and a new name adopted at St Giles Bay. The Victorian era witnessed the development of the Esplanade, the pier, the pavilion, the coastal paths, the grand theatre and the pleasure garden.

The Anglican church responded quickly to the pastoral challenge of the new resort area of St Giles Bay, and did so through the competitive spirits of Tractarian and evangelical initiatives. The Tractarian presence was the first to arrive on the scene when the foundation stone of the church of the Most Holy Redeemer was laid in 1869. In 1875 the foundation stone was laid for the evangelical counterpart, St John the Evangelist, at the other end of an expanding St Giles Bay. Well over a hundred years later, the independent trusts which hold the patronage of these two churches continue to appoint clergy who are sure to maintain the distinctive churchmanships and liturgical traditions.

Three other denominations also remain active in St Giles Bay. The Methodist church and the United Reformed church both occupy grand Victorian buildings. The Catholics opened a new church in the second half of the 1950s. A second Congregational chapel closed after the union of the United Reformed church. The building was sold into secular use and now serves as a youth and community centre. The Saturday night teenage disco now takes place where Sunday morning divine worship had been celebrated in a former age; notices advertising a range of recreational activities now occupy the former wayside pulpit.

Much of the rich Victorian splendour of St Giles Bay has fallen into a shabbier decay. Paint is peeling from the ornate front of the theatre. The shopping arcade is a mixture of vacant units, bric-à-brac shops and a dingy café. The pretentious railway station, once built for two-line traffic and the gracious reception of visiting gentry, is now a mere shadow of its heyday. One of the platforms has been closed and the track removed, as no longer needed in the days of single-line running. The remaining operative platform has been shortened, grass growing through the tarmac, waiting-room locked and toilets broken. The entrance to the pier lacks paint, and the ravages of the summer gales have shortened the welcoming name label to an appetizing 'St Giles Pie'. The grand family homes have been converted into flats, rest-homes for the elderly and innumerable guest-houses and hotels. Bed, breakfast and evening meal is the industry which keeps St Giles Bay in business.

Today there are two different faces to St Giles Bay and two different lives for the permanent residents. The holiday season limps on from Easter to late October, but only during July and August is the tourist industry running anywhere near capacity. By the beginning of September, some of the hotels are beginning to pull down their blinds, some of the cafés are closing earlier in the afternoon and opening later in the morning, the gift shops are running their end-of-season sales before putting up the shutters for the winter months, the St Giles Bay theatre company is playing to rows of empty seats. By the end of October many of the guest-houses have closed for the season. Then the winter months are left to the elderly and to the retired who are trying to make their final home in the shadow of the community where they spent their summer holiday in their younger, more active and more affluent days. The disillusionment of the unrealized dreams of post-retirement bliss hang heavy over the winter months of St Giles Bay.

Godfrey made his visit to St Giles Bay during mid-September, when the bulk of the holiday-makers had already left and signs of autumn were beginning to arrive. Nostalgic for Anglo-Catholic ceremony, he made his way to the church of the Most Holy Redeemer in time for the 11.00 a.m. family Mass. Low Mass had already been celebrated at 8.00 a.m. and evensong and benediction were due to follow at 6.30 p.m.

Like so much of St Giles Bay, the first impression of the church of the Most Holy Redeemer was one of a prosperous past, now fallen on hard times. The Victorian architect had created a sturdy neo-Gothic west tower, crowned by the soaring spire which dominated the neighbouring skyscape. A hundred years of wind and rain borne in across the sea had now taken its toll of the stonework. The first notice to welcome the approaching visitor proclaims starkly 'Danger. Keep away. Beware falling masonry'; and the base of the tower was securely cordoned off to protect the unwary. By the porch, however, a much friendlier notice gave times of Sunday services, the arrangements for confessions, and the parish priest's name, address and telephone number.

When Godfrey arrived, the church porch was quite crowded. Only one side of the large double door leading into the church itself was open. A group of elderly worshippers were carefully negotiating their way through the door and down the step to the church. Immediately inside the door, there was a reception committee of three people. A seventy-year-old woman was handing out two hymn-books, the *English Hymnal* and *English Praise*. A seventy-year-old man was handing out the church's own Mass book and the weekly newsletter. Both were experiencing some difficulty in assembling two items to give out at the same time. It was this which was causing the bottleneck at the door.

The third member of the reception committee was slightly younger than the other two: a stout, formidable woman in her early sixties with short straight grey hair. She was acknowledging briefly the regular worshippers and stopping the visitors. Spotting Godfrey as an unfamiliar face, she asked him the direct and abrupt question, 'Are you a visitor here?' Godfrey nodded. The next question came even more abruptly: 'Where are you from?' 'London', he said and was allowed to pass. On his way to a seat at the back, Godfrey passed a large marrow and a basket full of apples. Today the church of the Most Holy Redeemer was keeping harvest festival.

During the remaining minutes before the start of the service, the organist was playing chorale preludes by Bach; the members of the congregation were kneeling or sitting silently. The church had an aura of reverence, quiet and worship. Godfrey began to look through the weekly news leaflet and the service booklet.

The weekly news leaflet was based on the Catholic Sunday bulletin published by Redemptorist Publications, *Movements of Life*. This is an A5 folded leaflet, printed on the front and back pages, with the inside left blank for the parish's own news. This week the front page contained a well-written article on death; the back page contained short quotations and the readings set for the Catholic Mass. The first paragraph on the inside pages was a warm welcome to visitors:

> Welcome to any visitors worshipping here today. We hope you will be able to join us after the 11.00 a.m. service at the back of the church for tea or coffee and a few moments' chat.

Then followed information about the hymns, readings and page numbers for the service. This included naming the lesson readers, those responsible for presenting the bread and the wine at the altar, and the 'hosts' who had been welcoming worshippers by the door.

The Sunday bulletin also gave the pattern of daily Masses throughout the week and indicated that 'the third of the Vicar's talks on "Questions" will take place on Tuesday at 7.30 p.m.'. The two main pieces of news in the Sunday bulletin showed that the church of the Most Holy Redeemer was busy both at home and overseas. At home the faculty had been received to enable work to begin on the new heating system. Overseas the parish was sponsoring two children from the Lebanon:

> There are new photographs of them together with a short

letter from each and their school reports. They will have returned to their home now after the summer break spent with their families and would welcome hearing from us. The sponsor money allows for a small gift at Christmas but they would be very grateful for something extra.

This church had been built for a growing and thriving resort. Today the congregation was by no means small, but somehow the worshippers still seemed lost in the huge nave. Godfrey counted thirty-eight men and ninety-one women. There were a few young families and a small group of teenagers sitting together at the front, but the general age structure of the congregation was elderly. It is obviously the post-retirement population of St Giles Bay who keeps their parish church in business.

At 11.00 a.m. the parish priest, robed in cassock-alb, came to the front of the nave and said good morning. The worshippers responded to his greeting. Then he made a special point of welcoming the visitors, including those on holiday 'from Cromer, Glasgow, Birmingham, Little Tey, Stratford and London'. Godfrey suddenly realized why the 'host' who had welcomed him into the church was so keen to discover where he had come from. This, he thought, was an impressive strategy for a church with a central ministry among holiday-makers. Then followed the banns of marriage and the notices, both of which were communicated in a direct and friendly manner. The presentation had been well thought through, so as to be clear and brief but not abrupt. After the notices the parish priest returned to the vestry to complete vesting. He was a young bearded man in his mid-thirties, presumably now in charge of his first parish.

The first hymn, 'Come, ye thankful people, come', began without announcement as the congregation stood and the choir processed from the vestry at the top of the north nave, down the north aisle and back up the central aisle into the chancel. The procession was led by a twenty-five-year-old female crucifer and two teenage female acolytes. The choir was much younger than the congregation; ten young teenagers were followed by six women and eight men between the ages of twenty and forty. Then came the teenage male thurifer, two male servers in their mid-twenties, who later acted as deacon and subdeacon, and the parish priest. The disciplined and well-practised singing of the choir and the abundant clouds of incense filled the lofty nave of the church of the Most Holy Redeemer with an aura of mystery, worship and joy.

The order of service employed a version of the Rite A communion, rearranged and adapted as much as possible to approximate the Catholic missal. The epistle was read by one of the women choristers; the gospel was read by the parish priest, with full ceremonial of procession, acolytes and incense. Between the epistle and the gospel there was a responsorial psalm. The choir sang Psalm 8 to the Catholic Gellineau method, with the congregation joining in the response 'God saw all that he had made and found it very good'.

The sermon was delivered from the lectern by the parish priest. The sermon reflected a great deal of preparation and skill in communication. The young bearded preacher's own theology came clearly from a social and political gospel concerned with the poor; his congregation seemed to reflect many signs of social and political conservatism. The sermon grew out of this context of conflict.

The sermon began by drawing a distinction between the preacher and the message proclaimed; the message, he said, was eternal and written in the Gospels. He then reminded the congregation that the previous week two visitors had stormed out during his sermon in protest. They had written to him later in the week, he explained, to object against what they thought was his socialist gospel. At the same time, he said, another visitor had stayed behind after the same service because his life had been changed by the same message. The difference, he said, was that the visitors who had stormed out were wealthy, while the man whose life had been changed was poor and down on his luck. Drawing on the different characters of these two visitors, the parish priest was able skilfully to draw out the contrast between two groups in his own congregation, but by distancing the lesson on to visitors, he was able to avoid some of the danger of pointing a finger towards any of his regular worshippers. The conclusion was that harvest festival is not an occasion to gloat over achievement and possession, but a time to show gratitude by sharing our resources with those in need.

The sermon was followed in the usual way by the creed and the prayers. The second hymn of the morning was sung during the offertory: 'To thee, O Lord, our hearts we raise'. The collection was taken by the two people who had been giving out the books before the service; the bread and the wine were presented at the altar by an elderly couple. The peace had not taken place before the offertory; it was reserved to be celebrated in the position it occupies in the Catholic Mass, after the prayer of thanksgiving.

On the notice-board outside, a Sunday school had been advertised concurrent with the family Mass. Apparently this took place in one of the vestries. At the end of the prayer of thanksgiving, while the congregation was exchanging the peace, the three teenage girls sitting at the front of the nave went off to let the Sunday school know that it was time for them to join in the service. They then helped the Sunday school teachers to shepherd the children to the altar rail for a blessing, following on after the choir and before the congregation. Today there were nine children in the Sunday school and two teachers. After their blessing, the children returned to the vestry.

During the communion of the people, the choir sang Maurice Greene's motet, 'Thou visitest the earth' and then led the congregation in singing 'On this the first of days' from *English Praise*. After the distribution of communion, the congregation stood and enjoyed singing 'We plough the fields, and scatter'. After the closing prayer, blessing and dismissal, the choir and sanctuary party processed out to glorious triumphant organ music.

What seemed so sad after the service was that the carefully planned welcome, extended to visitors before the service began, was not followed through. The two people who had been giving out books were now so busily employed collecting these books and sorting them into neat piles that they had no time left even to raise their faces to smile at those whose books they were intent on taking. The parish priest remained in his vestry out of sight. The regular worshippers congregated around the coffee cups and formed small cliques of friends. By this stage Godfrey felt clearly superfluous to the fellowship of the church of the Most Holy Redeemer and slipped away unnoticed, back into the labyrinth of guest-houses, hotels and rest-homes for the elderly.

Cranton-on-Sea

When the railway came to Cranton in 1865 it helped to bring a new lease of life to this little port. The railway opened up easy access for visitors to come to enjoy the seaside; the railway also opened up an efficient way to transport fish to the markets in the large towns. As a consequence, the small port expanded rapidly.

Today the branch line has gone and a large caravan park has taken over the site of the old station and goods-yard. The fishing industry has largely disappeared and a children's boating lake and playground have replaced the fishermen's sheds. The small shipyard has closed and given place to a marina. Recent development has created a satellite community, mainly of retirement homes. There is a resident population of about 6,000 people.

Ronald was spending Christmas not far from Cranton-on-Sea and arrived to explore this seaside community around 11.00 a.m. on Christmas Eve. The main shopping street was bustling with life; Father Christmas had taken up his stand outside the main supermarket and toy store, tempting children to bring their parents inside.

As Ronald began to look round the shops, his attention was repeatedly caught by a colourful poster displayed on notice-boards, in shop windows and on telegraph poles. The notice read simply:

> Celebrate the King's birthday
> with us at 10.30 a.m.
> on Christmas Day
> in Cranton Baptist church.
> All are welcome.

Amid all the bustle of the Christmas shopping Ronald could hear the sounds of carol singing. An ad hoc band and choir had assembled in the shopping precinct. They too carried on their placards the message 'Celebrate the King's birthday'. Some of their number were pressing leaflets into the hands of the passers-by, while others were trying to engage busy shoppers in conversation. Cranton Baptist church was trying hard to promote its Christmas morning service.

Ronald found the Baptist church just off the busy high street. It had been built in 1848. The large notice-boards outside emphasized the Christmas morning service and the message of Christmas. They also continued to advertise the services for the previous Sunday. Ronald knew now that he had missed the 11.00 a.m. family service, in which the Sunday school children were taking part, and the 6.30 p.m. carol service. But the tall iron gates in front of the church doors were firmly closed and locked.

Next Ronald went off to find the Catholic church, built in the 1960s, more on the edge of the town. Church and presbytery stood next to each other, well set back behind an ample car park. What Ronald found here was a complete contrast to what he had discovered at the Baptist church. Outside there were no notices about the Christmas services at all, but the church door stood open. Inside the entrance area to the church Ronald hunted through the crowded notice-board to see what he could learn about the Christmas services. There in small typescript he read that Mass would be celebrated on 25 December at midnight, 8.00 a.m. and 10.00 a.m. As yet there were no signs of Christmas decorations or festivities in the Catholic church.

Ronald's third visit was to the medieval Anglican church. The service times were pinned up on the notice-board outside, but in small, discreet print. Only those who knew that the information was there would be obliged to read it. According to the notice-board, on 'Christmas Eve' low Mass was said in the morning at 8.30 a.m. and the midnight Mass of Christmas was celebrated at 11.30 p.m. During the afternoon there was a service of 'blessing of the crib' at 3.30 p.m. The parish priest was available in church to hear confessions at 10.30 a.m., 7.00 p.m. and at other times by arrangement. On Christmas Day, Mass was celebrated at 8.00 a.m. and the parish Mass at 9.30 a.m. Matins followed at 11.30 a.m.

Like the Catholic church, the Anglican church was open and Ronald went in. Just inside the door there was a pile of leaflets advertising the Christmas services; Ronald took one. The church itself was a hive of activity. A group of women in their fifties and sixties were busy arranging flowers in the sanctuary, while their husbands seemed to be carrying and fetching for them. A huge Christmas tree had been erected at the front of the north aisle and a couple of men were busy fixing the lights to the tree. A large Christmas crib was being unpacked and assembled at the front of the south aisle, using carefully made figures which had obviously already seen many years of service. Each window-ledge around the nave was being decorated with evergreens.

Down the centre aisle evergreen decorations were being fixed to every bench end. While Ronald was looking round, the vicar came in to encourage those who were busily occupied with the work of decorating the church. Then the organist arrived to practise some Christmas music. The church was alive with activity, but all were too busy to notice the casual visitor.

It was to the parish church that Ronald returned for the midnight Mass of Christmas. By the time he arrived in Cranton at 11.15 p.m., the church bells were ringing the Christmas message across the night sky. He parked some way from the church and walked through the high street towards the sound of the bells. The White Hart, Red Lion and King's Head were still open and doing brisk Christmas Eve trade.

Outside, the church was beautifully floodlit. Ronald was met at the door by two sidesmen, one a man in his fifties and the other a man in his sixties. One gave him a copy of the Rite A communion service; the other gave him a *Bethlehem Carol Sheet*. A group of a dozen or so other sidesmen stood at the back of the church, watching the congregation as they came in. Inside, the church was in almost total darkness. Candles had been lighted on the altar and along the choir-stalls in the chancel. The Christmas tree lights were on and a star shone brightly above the manger. A single spotlight illuminated the entrance and gave some dim lighting to the rest of the nave. The organist was extemporizing softly on a medley of carol themes.

When Ronald arrived the church was already half full, with 150 or so people. Some were kneeling in prayer; some were sitting in silence; others sat chatting. Ronald took a seat towards the back of the north aisle. Almost immediately a group of six people came to sit behind him, a couple in their twenties and three women and a man in their fifties. The younger woman was wearing tinsel around her coat. In the semi-darkness of the church, one of the older women tripped over the carpet and the others fell into hysterical laughter as they tried to steady her. The tranquillity of the evening had been interrupted and the church became charged with an atmosphere of nervous agitation. One of the dozen sidesmen who was standing at the back quietly came over and took a seat beside the revellers.

By 11.30 p.m. the congregation had grown to nearly 250 people. The service started promptly with the vicar announcing the first carol, 'Oh come, all ye faithful'. The organ announced the well-known tune *fortissimo* and all the church lights were suddenly switched on. The congregation rose to its feet. The singing was slow to start, but by the second verse the volume began to build up. The choir, mainly of teenage girls, processed into the candlelit choir-stalls, followed by two servers and the parish priest. The servers were a man and a woman, both in their late twenties.

The language of the church notice-board had led Ronald to expect a very high church form of service. He learnt later that the ritual and ceremony were reserved for the parish Mass on Christmas morning. The midnight service was a more informal occasion, which recognized that a number of irregular church-goers would be present, as well as the regulars. At the parish Mass on Christmas morning the service would be conducted from the high altar; at the midnight Mass the service was conducted from a nave altar.

The midnight service had been constructed to contain as many well-known carols as possible. During the course of the service the congregation sang 'Oh come, all ye faithful', 'While shepherds watched their flocks by night', 'Christians, awake! Salute the happy morn', 'See, amid the winter's snow', 'O little town of Bethlehem', 'Once in royal David's city', 'It came upon the midnight clear' and 'Hark! The herald-angels sing'.

Looking round the congregation, Ronald realized that some people had come specifically to enjoy the carols; they took no active part in the rest of the service. Although there were enough service books to go round and although the vicar frequently gave out page and paragraph numbers, some of the congregation were clearly not interested in following the service. Others did not appear particularly interested in joining in even the carols. The six people behind Ronald continued to talk and giggle among themselves.

The Old Testament reading from Isaiah (RSV) was read by one of the choirmen with care and feeling:

> The people who walked in darkness
> have seen a great light;
> Those who dwelt in a land of deep darkness,
> on them has light shined.

Isaiah's sonorous and familiar words caught the attention of the whole congregation; even those who were not really participating in the service stilled themselves to listen. One of the choir-women had less success with the rather ponderous translation of parts of Titus 2–3 from the *New English Bible*. The acolytes accompanied the vicar halfway down the nave to read the Christmas gospel from the first chapter of John. Because the congregation was asked to remain standing for the gospel reading, many of them could not see the reader, and the gospel failed to attract their attention as powerfully as the Old Testament reading had done.

The vicar preached for just four minutes. His message was simple and direct. He held up the Christmas present he was going to give to his wife and made the point that it is not so much the gift as the love with which it is given that really counts. The significance of Christmas, he said, is that God loves each one of us. During the sermon the congregation was very aware of a great deal of shouting and swearing taking place in the street outside. Something was thrown at one of the church windows; laughter was followed by raucous carol singing in the street. Past experience had obviously taught the vicar that Christmas midnight was not the time to grace his preaching with eloquence and rhetoric.

No sooner had the short sermon ended than the church door burst open and four youths stumbled in. They seemed quickly to sober and walked to the front seats in the south aisle. One of the sidesmen came from the back and sat behind them. There they remained for the rest of the service.

The peace was celebrated by the vicar and the two servers walking round the church and giving a hand clasp to the people at the end of each pew. In some rows the peace was passed along from one person to the next with enthusiasm. In other rows people just stood waiting for the next carol to begin.

When the time came for the distribution of communion, the sidesmen carefully formed up to direct the flow of people, and someone else from the congregation walked up to take the chalice. Less than half the congregation received communion. The choir, meanwhile, led more carol singing.

The service ended at 12.40 a.m. with the singing of 'Hark! The herald-angels sing'. There was now quite a carnival feeling in the church as the vicar stood at the door wishing a happy Christmas to regular and casual worshippers alike. Ronald felt that Cranton church had obviously been fully aware of the difficulties, problems and challenges of a Christmas Eve midnight service when the regular committed worshippers are being joined by many with rather different expectations and needs. All had been made welcome and trouble had been avoided, but there had been people on duty to deal with more serious disturbances had they occurred.

Batsford-on-the-Water

On a winter Sunday, Batsford-on-the-Water appears to be just another quaint deserted market town. The broad market-place, with its ancient stone cross and stately town hall, has been deserted by the cars; the narrow alleys of stone and timber buildings, with their overhanging upper storeys, have been deserted by the pedestrians. The shops are closed and the river and park are silent.

On a summer Sunday, Batsford-on-the-Water takes on a completely different character. The coach park is full and the streets bustle with British and foreign tourists. The shops are busy trading postcards, souvenirs and ice creams. While street traders purvey hot dogs and ice-cool cans of drinks, pubs, restaurants, hotels and cafés vie for a passing trade. Rowing-boats and canoes collide on the river and the occasional horse-drawn carriage ferries sightseers and slows the passing traffic.

Angela, Shirley and Brian visited Batsford-on-the-Water during early September, just before the schools began their new term. The town was crowded.

Batsford-on-the-Water is well served by a wide range of Christian churches. Earlier in the century there were two Methodist chapels, a Primitive and a Wesleyan. Now both Victorian buildings have been closed and a new chapel built. On Sunday there are two Methodist services at 11.00 a.m. and 6.30 p.m. Until quite recently there were also two Anglican churches. Now the parishes have been united. The smaller medieval church in the town centre has been declared redundant and services have been concentrated on the larger medieval church down by the river. On Sundays there are three Anglican services: Holy Communion at 8.00 a.m., parish communion at 10.30 a.m. and evensong at 6.30 p.m. The huge neo-Norman Catholic church was built on the outskirts of the town in the 1880s. At weekends there are four Catholic Masses, at 5.30 p.m. on Saturday and at 8.30 a.m., 11.00 a.m. and 6.30 p.m. on Sundays. The stately neo-classical Baptist chapel was built in the early 1800s. On Sundays there are two Baptist services, at 11.00 a.m. and 6.30 p.m. The large neo-Gothic United Reformed church has recently been declared unsafe and services transferred to the adjoining school-room. On Sunday there is one URC service at 11.00 a.m.

In addition to the Catholic, Anglican, Methodist, Baptist and URC churches, there are also the Salvation Army, the First Church of Christian Science and the Christian Fellowship. Both the Salvation Army and the Christian Science church hold morning and evening services at 11.00 a.m. and 6.30 p.m. The Christian Fellowship meets at 10.30 a.m. in a local youth and community centre.

On Saturday evening, Angela, Shirley and Brian all decided to attend the 6.30 p.m. Mass at the Catholic church. When they arrived at 6.15 p.m. the last wedding party of the Saturday afternoon was still waiting around for final photographs. Wedding cars were parked across the entrance of the lych-gate and wedding guests were thronging the church porch.

Inside, the church was already filling up for the Mass. At the back of the church Angela, Shirley and Brian found a pile of *Sunday Plus* news leaflets, but neither missalettes nor hymn-books. The *Celebration Hymnal* was already in the pews, two copies for a row of six people; missalettes did not seem to be generally available for this service.

The service started quite promptly at 6.30 p.m. The fifty-year-old priest introduced the opening hymn, 'Praise, my soul, the King of Heaven' and began to sing it unaccompanied. He had a pleasantly musical Irish accent. There was no organ or other musical accompaniment. Many of the congregation were without hymn-books and the singing was without enthusiasm. After the hymn the priest announced the theme for the Sunday readings and led the service through to the collect of the day. During the collect, a layman brought a notice sheet to the priest's attention. The priest apologized for using last Sunday's theme and collect by mistake and proceeded to read the proper collect for the day.

During this first part of the service and the readings from Scripture, the congregation continued to grow in size as people squeezed up on the pews to make room for latecomers. The church was filling to capacity with about 220 worshippers. The age groups which predominated were the forty- and fifty-year-olds. There was also a good number of younger families in their twenties and thirties, teenagers, children, babies and older people over the age of sixty.

In place of a sermon, the priest read a homily prepared by the Catholic Missionary Society. The intercessions were read by a layman in his fifties. They were formal and brief. During the offertory there was a modern hymn by Kevin Nichols, 'In bread we bring you, Lord, our bodies' labour'. Again the singing of this hymn was not improved by the lack of hymn-books and an absence of instrumental accompaniment, and being a modern hymn fewer people seemed to know it by heart.

The eucharistic prayer, the peace and the administration all took place with some speed. Many of the worshippers left the church immediately after receiving Communion so it was a considerably reduced congregation which stood to sing the final hymn, 'Holy Virgin, by God's decree, you were called eternally'. The service ended at 7.13 p.m. The rest of the congregation quickly melted away, leaving an empty church. Angela, Shirley and Brian felt themselves to have been anonymous members of an anonymous worshipping group.

On Sunday morning, Angela attended the Christian Fellowship which meets in the local youth and community centre. A simple handwritten notice pinned to the door read 'Batsford Christian Fellowship meets here every Sunday at 10.30 a.m. All are welcome.' When Angela arrived at 10.20 a.m. the leaders of the fellowship were busy unpacking their cars and carrying in overhead projector, screen, portable organ, loudspeakers, guitars, kettles, coffee and so on. Everyone was busily involved in setting out the equipment and arranging the chairs. As soon as Angela arrived, the two leaders of the fellowship welcomed her and introduced themselves by their Christian names.

On her way in, Angela picked up a smart printed leaflet introducing Batsford Christian Fellowship:

We are not part of a denomination, but we welcome fellowship with all God's people, believing that he wants Christians to love one another, rather than overemphasize our differences.

Sunday is an important day for us, because it is when the family comes together. The worship is fresh and alive and open for all to enter in, under the guidance of the Holy Spirit.

We believe in the supernatural; God heals people today, both physically and mentally, sets them free from the power of the devil and changes lives. Jesus Christ, risen from the dead, invades people's lives, getting rid of the rubbish of sin, and replacing the emptiness with new life.

While one of the leaders resumed his task of setting up the overhead projector, the other sat down beside Angela and told her a little about himself and the fellowship. He had been a Baptist minister, but the Lord had told him to leave his church and to set up this fellowship. Now he works in insurance three days a week and for the fellowship on the other four days. His co-leader is a personnel manager. As yet the fellowship is small but the Lord has promised them that it will grow over the next year. As other members of the fellowship arrived, they too introduced themselves to Angela and some hugged her and each other warmly.

By 10.40 a.m. the service was ready to start. The congregation was predominantly young families, casually dressed and from professional backgrounds. All told there were fourteen children under the age of twelve, a couple of teenagers, and twenty-eight adults. Men and women were equally represented in the congregation. The oldest person present was about forty-five.

The first hour or so of the service was unstructured praise. Members of the group called out hymns and songs which the leader then displayed on the overhead projector. Some sang solo; some read from Scripture; some offered shouts of praise; some spoke in tongues. The music was provided by two men playing guitars, three teenage girls playing recorders and a flute, a young woman on the electronic keyboard and the minister's trumpet. Many of the group had brought their own tambourines and percussion instruments. During the singing some clapped in rhythm, some held hands on high, some jumped around with enthusiasm. As the group warmed up spiritually and physically, jackets, cardigans, pullovers and ties were discarded.

Shortly after 11.40 a.m., one of the leaders invited the worshippers to sit down and talked about the fellowship's plans for home groups during the coming week. Then the children were taken out for their own Sunday school lesson, led by the Baptist minister and some of the parents. The overhead projector and screen were cleared away and the other leader sat on the edge of the table to begin his teaching. He announced his theme as 'faithfulness'. This address lasted for sixty-two minutes.

'What I propose to do', said the preacher, 'is to examine what the Bible says about faithfulness.' And this is precisely what he did. He had prepared a long list of texts in which the words 'faithful' or 'faithfulness' appeared and he led the congregation through this list. Some of the congregation copied down the chapter and verse in their notebooks, others simply underlined the key verses in their well-worn Bibles. Angela had not thought to bring a Bible with her, so the young man sitting next to her thoughtfully leaned over and pointed out the verses to her as he looked them up. His Bible had already been well marked from years of note taking during service.

By 12.45 p.m. the Sunday school children were beginning to drift back into the main worship area, so the preacher decided to conclude his exposition quickly. He finished by reeling off a further nine sets of chapters and verses and suggesting that the congregation looked them up when they got back home. 'Basically', he said, 'to be faithful is basically just that: to be full of faith.'

As soon as the sermon was ended, people stood up and started chatting with each other. Both of the fellowship leaders began earnest conversations with members of the group and Angela slipped away unnoticed by them.

Shirley attended the 11.00 a.m. service at the Christian Science church. This church was a light modern room built onto the side of, and entered through, a splendid Georgian town house. The room contained fifty-six chairs facing a raised stage at one end. On the stage there were two solid reading desks in front of two sedate chairs. On either side of the stage were two texts:

> Ye shall know the truth
> and the truth shall make you free.
> *Jesus Christ*

> Christianity is again demonstrating
> the life that is truth
> and the truth that is life.
> *Mary Baker Eddy*

When Shirley arrived she was welcomed by a woman in her early sixties who was wearing a small lapel badge carrying the word 'usher'. She gave her a copy of the *Christian Science Quarterly Bible Lessons*. The *Christian Science Hymn-book* was already in the pews. Shirley took a seat at the back.

The congregation appeared elderly and solitary. The usher sat towards the front with her daughter and granddaughter. The other six members of the congregation sat alone, scattered throughout the building. They comprised two men and four women. Both of the men were in their seventies; the women were aged between forty and eighty.

At 11.00 a.m. the two readers walked on to the stage, a man in his sixties and a woman in her seventies. The male reader began the service by announcing the hymn, written by Mary Baker Eddy, the discoverer and founder of Christian Science:

> Shepherd, show me how to go
> O'er the hillside steep;
> How to gather, how to sow,
> How to feed thy sheep.

After the male reader had read a passage from Scripture, the female reader introduced a period of silent prayer, followed by the Lord's Prayer, 'with its spiritual interpretation from *Science and Health with Key to the Scriptures* by Mary Baker Eddy':

Our Father which art in heaven,
  Our Father-Mother God, all-harmonious,

Hallowed be Thy name.
  Adorable One.

Thy kingdom come.
  Thy Kingdom is come; Thou art ever-present.

Thy will be done on earth, as it is in heaven.
  Enable us to know — as in heaven, so on earth —
  God is omnipotent, supreme.

Give us this day our daily bread;
  Give us grace for today; feed the famished affections;

And forgive us our debts, as we forgive our debtors.
  And Love is reflected in love;

And lead us not into temptation, but deliver us from evil;

*And God leadeth us not into temptation, but delivereth us from sin,
disease and death.*

For Thine is the kingdom, and the power, and the glory, forever.
For God is infinite, all-power, all Life, Truth, Love, overall, and All.

The second hymn, 'I look to thee in every need', was followed
by the notices and a solo sung most beautifully by the fifty-year-
old woman in the congregation, 'Cast thy burden upon the Lord
and he shall sustain thee'. Then came the main teaching ministry
of the service, preceded by the formal explanatory note written
by Mary Baker Eddy:

Friends:
The Bible and the Christian Science textbook are our only
preachers. We shall now read scriptural texts and their correlative
passages from our denominational textbook; these comprise our
sermon.

The canonical writings, together with the word of our textbook, corroborating and explaining the Bible texts in their
spiritual import and application to all ages, past, present and
future, constitute a sermon undivorced from truth, uncontami-
nated and unfettered by human hypotheses, and divinely
authorized.

The evening service is a repetition of the morning service.

This 'sermon' constitutes six blocks of readings. Each block is
made up by a series of scriptural texts read by the male reader
followed by a series of passages from Mary Baker Eddy's *Science
and Health* read by the female reader. All told, that morning
there were twenty-one passages from Scripture and thirty passages from *Science and Health*.

After the sermon, the service closed with the collection, the
third hymn, 'Our God is all in all', 'the scientific statement of
being' from *Science and Health* and the benediction. The elderly
readers proceeded slowly down the steps from the stage and
disappeared into a back room. One of the men in the congregation came over to talk with Shirley and explained to her how she
could use the Christian Science reading room which was open
every lunch-time and on Saturday mornings.

While Angela was attending the Christian Fellowship and

Shirley was attending the Christian Science church, Brian went to the 11.00 a.m. holiness meeting of the Salvation Army. The Salvation Army citadel, situated in one of the narrow back streets, had just celebrated its centenary. Brian waited patiently outside the narrow doorway while a couple of uniformed officers, a woman in her sixties and another in her thirties, helped two elderly women negotiate their walking frames from the car parked outside on double yellow lines to the seats nearest the door.

As Brian came in he was warmly welcomed by the officers and given two hymn-books, *Song Book of the Salvation Army* (1953) and *Keep Singing* (1976). When Brian had settled down at the back row opposite the door, the younger of the two officers came over to talk with him. Discovering that Brian was a visiting Anglican, the officer explained that he might find this form of service rather strange and more lively.

Inside, the citadel was plain and somewhat shabby. What really caught Brian's attention, however, were two large and well-arranged display boards. The first had been designed to celebrate the citadel's centenary. Its theme was the range of work in which the local Salvation Army was involved today and some of the highlights in its history. The second had been designed to introduce a team of young people who were visiting Batsford for a week to run an outreach mission based on the citadel. Brian's visit had coincided with the first day of the mission.

While the congregation was assembling, another elderly uniformed woman officer was playing a medley of hymn tunes on the electronic organ. Brian was very disappointed that there was neither sight nor sound of the Salvation Army band which he had hoped would lead the morning worship.

By 11.00 a.m. the regular congregation had assembled. This consisted of three men and eleven women over the age of sixty, a woman in her fifties, a couple in their thirties and a couple of teenagers. Today, the regular congregation had been augmented by ten visitors who· had come to run the outreach mission, ranging in age from late teens to mid-thirties. At 11.00 a.m. the young officer who had already welcomed Brian to the citadel took her place on the raised platform at the front. She welcomed 'the young friends on the mission' and other visitors.

The leadership of the service was divided between the officer and the mission team. The officer had planned a connected series of readings, songs and an address on the theme of journeys. The mission team introduced a series of testimonies, extemporary prayers, drama and songs intended to challenge the elderly congregation to repent, to rededicate their lives to Christ and to participate in outreach into the community. The interplay between the two themes and styles of leadership created the feeling of two separate parallel services, rivalling each other for attention. The contrast was accentuated further by two separate musical traditions. The officer chose songs from the *Song Book of the Salvation Army* and these were accompanied at a sedate tempo by her fellow officer on the electronic organ. The mission team chose short choruses from *Mission Praise*, displayed on large sheets of paper at the front, and these were accompanied at a more lively tempo by one of the team on the piano.

The officer's theme of journeys reached its climax with her address, which lasted for twenty minutes. She referred to some of the great journeys of the Bible and to the people who travelled with God. She began her theme in Genesis 5, with Enoch who 'walked with God for three hundred years' and who 'was seen no more, because God had taken him away'. 'Enoch', she said, 'was a great walker, and God said to him "Enoch, you have walked so far, you cannot go back now. Come right in."' Then she passed on to Noah who 'walked with God', to Shadrach, Meshach and Abednego, who walked with God through the fire, and many other Old Testament characters. She finished her theme with the two disciples walking the road to Emmaus, and Jesus walked with them. 'When Jesus walked this earth', she concluded, 'he was limited by his humanity. Now Jesus can walk all the time anywhere with us all.'

After this address the congregation sang the song 'We are travelling home to heaven above'. They seemed particularly to enjoy the sentiment, 'My old companions fare you well, I will not go with you to hell'. The mission team's challenge of repentance reached its climax with their dramatic presentation, which they called 'action replay'. Two drivers killed in a road accident met in the waiting-room before being called to the throne of judgement. Each is shown a detailed video of his past life, 'everything he had done and thought'. Each is seen carrying a heavy burden of sin. One, however, had experienced conversion and given his life to Christ. God told him to take his burden of sin to the edge of the cliff and to throw it away. He entered into life. The other man was told to carry his burden down to where it is hot. 'There is coming a great day', concluded the commentator, 'when all shall be judged. When we trust in the Lord Jesus what we have done wrong is removed from us.'

After the drama the congregation sang the chorus 'Ascribe greatness to our God the rock':

> his work is perfect and all his ways are just.
> A God of faithfulness and without injustice,
> good and upright is he.

The service finished at 12.10 p.m. The young officer was busily involved in driving some of the elderly members of the congregation home. The mission team stayed behind in the citadel to talk with any members of the congregation who were not rushing off and to plan their afternoon campaign on the streets. They seemed disappointed that Brian was only a visitor and not a potential convert.

Part Two
TYPES OF COMMUNITIES

The four chapters in part two each look in depth at church life throughout a defined geographical area. In each case the unit chosen is one Anglican deanery and *every* place of worship within that area is described. The four deaneries were chosen to illustrate the four different types of countryside defined by Anthony Russell and discussed in chapter one. These different types of countryside are described as *urban shadow countryside, accessible countryside, less accessible countryside*, and *remote or marginal countryside*. The names given to the communities and to the individuals are fictitious.

10
REMOTE OR MARGINAL COUNTRYSIDE

Church of England

IN MARGINAL DEANERY there are fourteen Anglican parishes and eighteen Anglican churches; sixteen of the churches are in use and two have been declared redundant. Today these sixteen churches serve a total population of 4,023 people, an average of 251 each. The largest parish, where there are three churches, has a population of 953, while the smallest has just ninety-seven inhabitants. Collectively, the sixteen churches provide seating for about 2,580 people, nearly two-thirds (64.1%) of the total population. The electoral rolls of the fourteen parishes contain 379 names, representing one in ten (9.4%) of the population.

The fourteen parishes and sixteen churches are now in the care of three full-time clergymen and one part-time clergyman who also holds a diocesan post. Two of the full-time clergy, including the rural dean, have benefices of five churches each, one with a total population of 1,556 and the other with a total population of 946. The third full-time clergyman has responsibility for four churches and a population of 1,262. The clergyman who shares his parochial responsibility with a diocesan post has care of two churches and a combined population of 259. Currently each of the four groups of parishes is organized in a different way.

The benefice of four churches has until recently been operated on the pattern of providing one service in each church every week. The form of service and time of day alternate throughout the benefice. In this way, each church had one mid-morning, one late morning, one afternoon and one evening service per month. Nine months before the survey of marginal deanery was conducted, however, the vicar of this benefice was taken ill. In marginal deanery the other clergy were already too heavily committed to their own pattern of services to be able to pick up the schedule in this benefice during the vicar's illness. There were no retired clergy, non-stipendiary ministers or readers in the deanery. The best that could be provided within the benefice, therefore, during the past nine months has been one service a Sunday. In other words, each church has held one service per month. During a typical month this has meant four services of Holy Communion, at 9.30 a.m. on the first Sunday, 7.00 p.m. on the second Sunday, 2.30 p.m. on the third Sunday and 9.30 a.m. on the fourth Sunday. Occasionally, other services have been arranged at short notice if a spare priest should be available.

The diocesan officer responsible for two small parishes holds one service in each church every Sunday. One of the churches, where there is a resident population of ninety-seven and an electoral roll of twenty, has a service every Sunday morning at 10.45 a.m. On the first Sunday in the month the service is matins, on the second Sunday a family service, and on the third and fourth Sundays Holy Communion. The pattern in the other church, where there is a resident population of 172 and an electoral role of twenty-one, consists of an afternoon service of Holy Communion and healing at 2.30 p.m. on the first Sunday in the month, an evening service of Holy Communion at 7.15 p.m. on the second Sunday, an afternoon family service at 2.30 p.m. on the third Sunday and an evensong at 7.15 p.m. on the fourth Sunday in the month.

The benefice of three parishes and five churches works a different pattern of services for each of the churches. In the largest parish in the benefice, where the vicar lives, the services alternate between 9.45 a.m. Holy Communion on the first and third Sundays and 6.30 p.m. evensong on the second and fourth Sundays in the month. In the second largest parish in the benefice the service times alternate between 11.00 a.m. on the first and third Sundays in the month and 2.30 p.m. on the second and fourth Sundays in the month. Service content in this parish, however, is more varied: on the first Sunday in the month it is Holy Communion, on the second Sunday evensong, on the third Sunday morning prayer and on the fourth Sunday either evensong or family service. The third largest parish in the benefice has four different service times as well as four different types of service during the month. On the first Sunday evensong is held at 2.30 p.m.; on the second Sunday youth church at 10.15 a.m.; on the third Sunday evensong and Holy Communion at 7.00 p.m.; on the fourth Sunday Holy Communion at 9.00 a.m. The other two places of worship in the benefice are both mission churches. One mission church is used twice a month for Holy Communion at 11.15 a.m. on the second Sunday and for morning prayer at 10.00 a.m. on the fourth Sunday; the other mission church is used once a month for a family service and Holy Communion at 11.00 a.m. on the fourth Sunday.

Looked at from another perspective, this pattern means that the vicar is responsible for three services on the first and third Sundays in the month, four on the second Sunday in the month and five on the fourth Sunday of the month. During the course of four Sundays there are seven celebrations of Holy Communion in the benefice and eight non-eucharistic services.

The rural dean, who has responsibility for five churches, believes that he cannot conduct more than two services well on a Sunday morning and that Sunday afternoon is an unsuccessful time for services. His regular Sunday pattern, therefore, includes two morning services and one evening service. During a typical month, one church has an 11.00 a.m. Holy Communion service on the first Sunday and a 7.00 p.m. evensong on the third Sunday; another church has an 11.00 a.m. family service on the second Sunday and a 9.30 a.m. Holy Communion service on the fourth Sunday; a third church has a 6.30 p.m. evensong on the second Sunday and 11.00 a.m. Holy Communion service on the fourth Sunday; a fourth church has a 9.30 a.m. Holy Communion on the first Sunday and an 11.00 a.m. Holy Communion on the fourth; a fifth church has a 6.30 p.m. Holy Communion service on the first Sunday, a 9.30 a.m. Holy Communion on the third Sunday and a 7.00 p.m. evensong on the fourth Sunday. This pattern means that during a typical month there are seven services of Holy Communion in the benefice, three evensongs and one family service.

Although the two churches furthest apart in the rural dean's benefice are only six miles from each other as the crow flies, the distance is considerably longer by the narrow, winding lanes with their steep gradients climbing up and down the valley contours. If a local farmer is moving cows from one field to another along the lane on a Sunday morning, or if the milk lorry arrives late, the rural dean can experience considerable delays in driving from one church to the next. In winter weather the lanes are often neither gritted nor cleared. The rural dean tells of the Christmas morning when a local farm tractor was needed to haul his car up the steep lane between one Christmas communion service and the next.

In summary, only one church in the deanery holds a Sunday service at the same time every week. This is the smallest parish in the deanery where one fifth of the population are on the electoral roll. This regular pattern is possible simply because the parish is part of the small two-parish benefice within the care of a priest who is not in full-time parochial ministry.

Although the area attracts a number of holiday-makers to the camping sites, bed and breakfast establishments and holiday cottages, and although the pattern of services is complex, the Anglican churches in marginal deanery do not make much effort to communicate what is taking place. Only one of the sixteen churches has a notice-board outside giving details of the Sunday services. Ten of the other churches have information about services in the church porch and five say nothing at all about Sunday services. On closer analysis, however, the situation is even less promising. Four of the churches are still advertising a monthly pattern of services which has not been operative for the past nine months due to the vicar's illness.

The vicar's name and telephone number is publicly displayed in nine of the sixteen churches, often as part of the parish newsletter pinned in the porch. On six occasions his address is given as well. Just one of the churches also displays the church-wardens' names, addresses and telephone numbers. The statutory table of fees for weddings and funerals was displayed prominently in six of the churches, four of these being for the current year and two being two years out of date.

Often the most prominent notice in these churches was an appeal for money for fabric restoration; seven churches drew attention to the need for urgent repairs, up to the value of £20,000. One church tactfully combined a welcome to visitors alongside the appeal for money; none of the other churches displayed a notice of welcome.

Generally, the range of notices on the church notice-boards

was very restricted. At the time of the survey, the one poster most frequently displayed throughout the deanery advertised a local narrow gauge steam railway. Next in priority came acknowledgement of diocesan quota payments, sometimes for several past years in succession. Several churches also displayed rotas for flower arranging, sidespersons and, in one case, for the local whist drive. Another church displayed the notice, 'Any person wishing to help with the mowing of the churchyard on a regular basis please sign below.' This rota was particularly noteworthy in view of the lack of signatures and the overgrown condition of the churchyard. Another church used its notice-board mainly to display an assortment of poems, some yellowed with age.

Although many of the churches in marginal deanery are in isolated situations, eleven of the sixteen were kept unlocked. The other five, however, were kept locked without indicating where the key could be obtained.

The upkeep of the churches in marginal deanery is an obvious strain on the small communities. The high standard of the quinquennial inspections means that none of the buildings is actually unsafe. Nevertheless, some of them looked relatively sad and neglected. Many of the churches underwent major restoration or complete rebuilding between the 1840s and the 1870s and they will soon need further major attention. Peeling plaster and damp decay are evident in some.

Inside, most of the churches in marginal deanery were kept clean and tidy; only one of the sixteen churches looked dusty and neglected. The churchyards, however, present a different picture. Only three of the sixteen churchyards looked cared for; eight of them were completely overgrown and unkempt.

Many of the churches in marginal deanery are of considerable historical interest. One contains splendid examples of Jacobean woodwork, including a two-decker pulpit and a complete set of box pews, while another houses an early nineteenth-century memorial chapel built to the glory of the local landowner. One is a fine example of early sixteenth-century Perpendicular architecture, while another is an equally fine example of early Victorian neo-Gothic. Although many of the churches are of such fine historic and architectural interest, only five of them have produced a local guidebook and even fewer offer postcards.

In fact, the churches of marginal deanery seem almost totally unaware of their potential ministry to the countless holiday-makers and the many walkers who pass through them. None of the churches provides literature about the Christian gospel or aids to help visitors spend time in prayer or meditation. Just two of the churches have Christian books on sale; one of these bookstalls is uninspiring but the other carries quite a range of material both for children and adults. This same church has developed a ministry to tourists through prayer cards. Blank cards are left in a side chapel for visitors to write thanksgivings or requests for intercessions. The church is near a youth hostel and a young people's centre. A surprising number of young people respond to these prayer cards.

One redundant church in the deanery has been converted for domestic use. The other redundant church stands in the grounds of a magnificent Georgian mansion. The estate has taken over responsibility for maintenance and upkeep of this church. The church is kept open so that visitors who are brave enough to ignore the 'Private, no right of way' notices on the drive leading to the hall are freely able to go into the church. There are no notices in this church porch, but immediately inside the church itself there is one large notice, written by hand in impressive Gothic script. This text explains the history of the family who built the hall and who still live there. It draws attention to the family memorials in the church. At the bottom of this text a less impressive hand adds the more recent information that the church was closed for public use in 1978. There is no information about arrangements for pastoral oversight of the parish.

Outside, the fabric of the redundant church was in very good condition and the churchyard was kept immaculately. Inside, the building looked very neglected. A thick coat of dust covered the pews. A bare table stood in the sanctuary without covering or cross.

On the fourth Sunday in June, when the church watch survey took place, there were thirteen Anglican services advertised in marginal deanery. In the event, one of the afternoon services did not happen, although it was advertised in the church porch, and one of the morning services actually began half an hour earlier than advertised on the notice-board so that the visitor missed the opening part of the service. The twelve services attended in the course of the day consisted of six from the Book of Common Prayer, including two Holy Communion services, one matins and three evensongs, five from *The Alternative Service Book 1980*, including one Rite B communion and four Rite A communions, and one *Alternative Services Second Series* Holy Communion service.

Some of the Anglican congregations in marginal deanery are very small. Four people attended a communion service from the *Alternative Services Second Series*, five attended a matins from the Book of Common Prayer, six attended an evensong from the Book of Common Prayer, six attended a Rite B communion service, seven attended a Holy Communion service from the Book of Common Prayer. The four Rite A communion services were attended by congregations of ten, eleven, thirteen and fifteen. An afternoon evensong from the Book of Common Prayer had a congregation of thirteen, and a late morning Holy Communion service from the Book of Common Prayer had a congregation of twenty-seven. The best attended service in the deanery that Sunday was a special patronal festival evensong to which the archdeacon had been invited as preacher. The silver band was in attendance from the neighbouring village and the whole local community was caught up in celebration. Here there was a congregation of fifty-four; usually the congregation at the monthly evensong in this church can be counted on the fingers of two hands.

Given the specially large attendance of the Petertide patronal festival, on the fourth Sunday in June 171 people attended Anglican services in marginal deanery, representing 4.3% of the population. Two-thirds (67%) of the worshippers were female; one third (33%) were male. The age group which predominated in the congregations was the forty- and fifty-year-olds, who accounted for 46% of the total worshippers; 25% of the worshippers were over the age of sixty and another 21% were in their twenties and thirties. This leaves a handful of the congregation (8%) under the age of twenty-two. Without the patronal festival, a more realistic measure of Anglican church attendance in marginal deanery is about 3.2% of the population.

The patronal festival lasted for seventy-one minutes, but the general trend in the deanery is for shorter services, the average being forty-eight minutes. All told, sermons were preached at eight of the twelve Anglican services in marginal deanery. Understandably, the same sermon tended to follow the clergyman from church to church. At the patronal festival the archdeacon preached for twenty-eight minutes, but the general trend in the deanery was for shorter sermons, the average lasting for thirteen minutes.

The vision of teams of active lay people sharing in the liturgical ministry of the rural church does not yet seem fully realized in marginal deanery. Indeed, even the lessons were read by the clergy in all but two of the twelve services. The greatest opportunity for lay participation involved taking the collection; by leaving a plate at the back of the church after the service, one church managed to operate without even this central act of lay ministry. Eleven of the twelve services included hymns and involved a lay person as organist. Maintaining the organs and finding someone competent to play are obvious problems in marginal deanery. For at least two of the services the singing seems to have been hindered rather than helped by the organist.

Generally speaking, the Anglican congregations in marginal deanery were not accustomed to making visitors feel at home. At only four of the twelve services were lay people prepared to hand the visitor a service-book, while at two others the minister did so himself. At one service the persistent visitor had to go hunting to find a book in a cardboard box stored behind a curtain at the back of the church. After most of the services, however, both the minister and some of the congregations spoke with the visitors.

Free Churches

Alongside the eighteen Anglican church buildings in marginal deanery there are also twenty remaining Free Church buildings. Other Free Church buildings may, of course, have been demolished and their memory lost. While only two of the eighteen Anglican buildings are no longer used by a congregation, thirteen of the remaining Free Church buildings have ceased to be used by a congregation. The redundant chapel is, therefore, an important symbol in marginal deanery. Just as the building of these chapels spoke clearly during the nineteenth century of the social and religious vitality of non-conformity, so their closure during the twentieth century speaks clearly of the changing social and religious contours of marginal deanery.

Two of these redundant chapels were built as a consequence of the growing prosperity of rural Methodism during the 1870s. Their neo-Gothic architecture stands out in the village landscape as a proud monument to what was once a thriving faith. In both cases, the chapel has been converted into a tasteful country residence, offering bed and breakfast for the passing tourist trade. A ministry to the body now replaces their former ministry to the soul; a ministry to the casual visitor now replaces their former ministry to the local community. In the case of one of these chapels the adjoining schoolroom has become the base for a small village industry in craft design.

Some of the other more substantial chapels have also been converted into private homes. One has been bought by an inner-city school and converted into a rural studies centre; one has been taken over by a small engineering firm.

Other smaller redundant chapels have met a less glorious end. One is used as a garage for a neighbouring house; one is used as a store by an adjoining farm; one stands locked and lonely at a rural crossroads with grass and weeds growing up to the entrance; one was used for a short time as a village garage, but now the garage too has closed and the building is suffering from neglect. Another has been allowed simply to decay. Today the door stands open, all the glass has been smashed in the windows, the pews have been ripped up and the floorboards torn out, slates are slipping from the roof; only the foundation stone, 'built to the glory of God', seems to have escaped desecration. Even in the countryside dereliction encourages vandalism.

Another redundant small chapel, however, tells a completely different tale. This chapel is almost completely inaccessible to motor transport, but stands alongside one of the scenic footpaths up a steeply rising valley. Countless walkers are beginning to feel weary by the time they reach this chapel. To one side of the chapel door a notice-board proclaims that this chapel is no longer used for regular public worship, but gives the times of the services in the nearest market town, some six miles away, and the minister's telephone number. To the other side of the chapel door a notice-board proclaims the message, 'Look around you. Come in and give thanks.' The chapel is maintained and kept open with the sole purpose of a ministry to visitors.

Inside, the chapel is clean and austere, apart from two vases of flowers on the communion table. Also on the communion table is a handwritten card which reads 'Dear Visitor, if you are not replacing flowers in the chapel would you please dispose of dead ones. Thank you.' On the lectern there is a copy of *The New*

English Bible and a visitors' book. The visitors' book alone is evidence of the number of walkers who pause to enter the chapel; many of them have added words of gratitude and praise.

All the surviving Free Churches in marginal deanery are part of a Methodist circuit system; all are served by Methodist ministers who actually live outside marginal deanery in neighbouring market towns. This means that the three full-time and one part-time Anglican clergy are the only professional ministers living in marginal deanery itself. Apart from Methodism, there is no other Free Church presence in marginal deanery.

While the Anglican churches in marginal deanery have generally developed a complex pattern of service times, changing from Sunday to Sunday, the tendency in Methodism has been to stick to a regular pattern week by week. Thus, five of the seven chapels have a service every Sunday at the same time; one has a service every other week at the same time, and the remaining chapel has one service a month. Methodist churches in marginal deanery are more easily able to opt for a regular service time each week because they are less dependent upon the availability of the minister to lead worship. The majority of Methodist services in marginal deanery are conducted by local preachers.

While the rural dean does not feel that afternoon services work well in marginal deanery, five of the seven Methodist chapels have opted for their services at 2.30 p.m., including the two chapels which do not hold a service each week. The other two chapels hold their weekly service at 6.30 p.m. One of the chapels also holds a weekly Sunday school at 11.00 a.m.

If the Anglican churches in marginal deanery seem reluctant to welcome visitors and to make known information about their services and ministry, the Methodist chapels are even more reluctant to do so. All seven chapels are kept locked; none advertises the name or address of the key holder or caretaker. None expects visitors to want to use the chapel for prayer or meditation.

Only three of the seven chapels advertise information about Sunday services, and for one of them the information is totally misleading. While the notice-board at this chapel advertises a service every Sunday at 2.30 p.m., in fact the service now only happens once a month. None of the chapels gives the name and address of a minister or of a local contact person. The most effective means of discovering details of the Methodist Sunday services in marginal deanery seems to be through obtaining the telephone number of the circuit minister from the local Anglican vicar. In some cases random enquiries at neighbouring houses can help to identify the name and address of a chapel member, but this was not found always to be successful.

The surviving chapels in marginal deanery tend to be relatively small and uninspiring buildings. The two architecturally most rewarding chapels in the deanery are among the redundant rather than the active stock. The average accommodation of the remaining chapels is about seventy seats, varying from fifty to 110. This means that collectively the surviving Methodist chapels can provide accommodation for about 490 people, compared with the Anglican accommodation for about 2,580.

Generally, these Methodist chapels appear to be less structurally sound and less well maintained than the Anglican churches in marginal deanery. The outside repair of the buildings clearly reflects the difficulties experienced by small membership chapels in maintaining the fabric. Inside, too, the general impression is of less care and attention. In many cases the interior is shabby, damp and sometimes even dusty. One of the clear advantages these Methodist chapels often have over the Anglican churches is the absence of a churchyard. Some are fortunate in having no grass areas to maintain at all. None of the chapels has a bookstall or inside display screen. None has a local or circuit newsletter available to give to visitors, or a short history of the chapel to share with strangers.

On the fourth Sunday in June, when the church watch survey took place, there were six Methodist services advertised in the deanery, four at 2.30 p.m. and two at 6.30 p.m. All six services were planned to take place without a minister. Four services were taken by fully recognized preachers, a man in his fifties and three women aged around forty, forty-five and sixty. The fifth service was taken by a young woman who was still a local preacher on trial.

The sixth service, however, indicated that the planning of local preachers could sometimes break down. When by 2.30 p.m. no preacher had arrived, the chapel steward began to canvass visitors to the chapel to discover whether any of them felt able to lead the worship. Either by coincidence or by divine providence, one of the young visitors who happened to be camping in the area identified himself as a local preacher from an inner-city circuit. The chapel steward said it had been a long time since the chapel had been blessed with so young a preacher.

The remaining Methodist chapels in marginal deanery attract a slightly larger congregation than the Anglican churches. While the average attendance at the Anglican services is a congregation of eleven, the average attendance at the Methodist services is a congregation of fifteen. The smallest Methodist attendance was a congregation of seven at a 2.30 p.m. service; the largest was a congregation of twenty-four at a 6.30 p.m. service. Three of the other services had congregations of around twenty and the fourth had a congregation of ten.

All told, ninety-two people attended Methodist services in marginal deanery, representing 2.3% of the total population. Just under two-thirds (61%) were women and just over one third (39%) were men. While the forty- and fifty-year-olds predominated in the Anglican congregations, in the Methodist congregations it was the over-sixties who accounted for half (49%) of the worshippers. On the other hand, the Methodist churches also had a higher proportion of children and young people than the Anglican churches. One in six (16%) of the worshippers in the Methodist congregations were under the age of twenty-two. In real terms this meant two children under school age, nine of primary school age, three of secondary school age and a late teenager.

Apart from the one unplanned service, which lasted only thirty-seven minutes, Methodist services in marginal deanery all lasted just under an hour. Preaching played an important part in all the Methodist services in marginal deanery. The average length of the sermons was around twenty minutes. Even the holiday-making lay preacher who found himself suddenly called upon to preach extempore was able to produce a fifteen-minute impromptu address.

While the Methodist services in marginal deanery all depended on lay leadership, this lay leadership did not emerge from within the chapels themselves. The lay preachers came into the chapels to lead the worship and in every case they took total responsibility for everything that happened. Members of the local congregation were never involved in leading worship, even as lesson readers. Even in the case when the local preacher failed to arrive the immediate reaction of the local congregation was not to take responsibility for its own worship but to invite one of the visitors to take charge.

Local lay involvement was always restricted to taking the collection and to playing the organ. The organists in particular gave the impression of being an elderly race. Their standard of playing varied very much from place to place, but generally the standard of music was hampered by the provision of a decaying harmonium.

Generally speaking, the Methodist congregations in marginal deanery were good at making visitors feel welcome. In most cases both the preacher and members of the congregation spoke with the visitors and were keen to appear friendly. There was just one exception to this where the visitor commented, 'The congregation ignored me before, during and after the service. I felt invisible and unwanted.' In a congregation of ten he could have hardly passed unnoticed, but no one extended a welcome.

Roman Catholic

The Catholic presence in marginal deanery is very low-key. A careful survey of the whole area revealed no public information about Catholic services. The grapevine eventually suggested that Mass was celebrated on Saturday evening in the doctor's surgery in one of the villages. A visit to the surgery demonstrated that there was no information displayed there about the Mass; the doctor's receptionist thought the Mass was celebrated each Saturday at 6.00 p.m., but recommended a telephone call to the priest to confirm this.

The priest who serviced this Mass centre was attached to a school some eight miles away. Repeated telephone calls were either not answered or answered by an answerphone. The priest's answerphone seemed unable to elicit a reply to the question about service times. Having begun the process of telephoning early in the week, it was not until Saturday lunch-time that someone ultimately answered at the school. The Saturday Mass was celebrated not at 6.00 p.m. but at 4.45 p.m. It certainly proved to be a test of initiative and perseverance to discover how to attend Mass in marginal deanery.

On Saturday, Mass was attended by a congregation of twelve: three elderly ladies in their late sixties or seventies, a couple in their fifties, a couple in their forties together with a teenage son, and a couple in their thirties together with a young baby and a four-year-old son. The priest was a young man in his early thirties.

The waiting-room to the doctor's surgery provided an informal environment for the Mass. The congregation sat on the chairs round the edge of the room. Towards the centre of the room, a simple table had been covered with a white cloth to act as the altar. Immediately in front of this table, a wider but lower table still contained all the usual magazines found in rural surgeries, including *Home and Country* and *Horse and Hound*.

The children's corner in the waiting-room contained a fascinating set of toys and a large purple teddy bear sitting in a high chair. Looked at from the right angle, teddy appeared to be sitting behind and presiding at the altar. When the four-year-old boy came in with his parents he made directly for the children's corner.

Other aspects of the doctor's waiting-room seemed to fit less congruously with the Catholic teaching. For example, while the young priest was preaching his three-minute sermon, he positioned himself immediately below a poster which read 'Do not be too embarrassed to ask about the pill, coil, cap, sterilization, etc. Family Planning advice is free to all those at risk whatever their age.'

The whole of the service was conducted by the priest, who read all three lessons himself. There was no server to help at the altar. No one was responsible for giving out books at the beginning. No collection was taken. The only opportunity for lay people to take responsibility for anything in the service was when one of the elderly women took a small bell from her handbag and rang it during the prayer of consecration. Hymn-books were not required since there was no singing in the service. Missals were not available, but only the *Redemptorist Mass Leaflet* which contained the propers for the day. These were left out on top of the radiator so that the regular congregation who knew that they were there could pick them up.

Mass began two minutes late at 4.47 p.m. and was over by 5.09 p.m. The small congregation disappeared very quickly and without pausing to speak to visitors. The priest was back in his car before 5.15 p.m., heading off for another Mass centre some eight miles outside the deanery. He, too, had no time to waste talking with visitors.

Summary

When all the denominations present in marginal deanery are viewed together, the 4,023 inhabitants are served by twenty-three churches. In other words, there is one church for every 175 people. Together these churches provide seating for 3,070 people, or three-quarters (76.3%) of the population. On the Sunday of the survey there were 275 attendances at public worship, representing one in fifteen (6.8%) of the population. There are three full-time ministers of religion living in marginal deanery, one for every 1,340 inhabitants.

II
LESS
ACCESSIBLE
COUNTRYSIDE

Church of England

LESS ACCESSIBLE DEANERY is more than an hour's travelling time from the nearest metropolitan centre. It contains forty-nine communities which have had or still maintain their own places of worship. Some of these communities are small hamlets, whose populations are counted as part of neighbouring villages. Of the civil parishes, twenty-five have fewer than 250 inhabitants, five have between 251 and 500 inhabitants, and three have between 501 and 750 inhabitants. Two large villages have now grown to just over 1,000 inhabitants and there are two market towns of around 2,700 inhabitants each. One of these market towns is still served by regional railways. The total population of the deanery stands at 14,954 people.

The deanery is staffed by nine stipendiary Anglican clergy, including one curate based in the more prestigious of the market towns, making an average of one stipendiary post for every 1,660 people. Less accessible deanery is much less attractive for retirement than either urban shadow deanery or accessible deanery. Nonetheless, two Anglican priests have chosen to make their retirement home in the deanery, one in each of the market towns, having served their earlier ministry elsewhere in the diocese. Both are now in their late seventies. Less accessible deanery is also less likely to attract people who wish to train to become licensed readers. There are three readers in the deanery, a male reader in each of the two market towns, and a female reader living in a village of 580 inhabitants.

There are no non-stipendiary clergy in the deanery.

The nine stipendiary clergy staff forty churches. There were eight further Anglican churches in the deanery. One Victorian rebuild has been demolished since Nikolaus Pevsner's architectural survey of the county was published in the mid-1960s. The other seven remain standing.

Each of these redundant churches tells its own particular tale. One is actively supported by a society of friends who arrange a well-attended annual service. One still remains the subject of much anger and controversy. A local appeal is trying to reopen the church, at least for marriages and burials. A handwritten notice is pinned to the locked door, 'Please God can you open this church'. The only official notice left in the porch reads, 'The Archbishops of Canterbury and York: a short guide to church membership'. Its price remains quoted as 2½d in pre-decimalization currency.

The church watch visitor observed about one of these churches: 'A decayed and decaying church with an amazing chancel of Elizabethan funeral monuments.' About another of these churches, the church watch visitor observed: 'Redundant, but in a remarkably fine state of preservation. Flowers indicate someone still cares! Freshly painted outside door. List of past vicars: dead and gone!'

All told, the forty remaining Anglican churches provide seating for about 3,990 people, representing just over a quarter (27%) of the total population. The combined electoral rolls of the churches in the deanery list between 7 and 8% of those resident in the area.

Both market towns maintain a traditional pattern of three services each Sunday. In one town this means 8.00 a.m. Holy Communion, 9.30 a.m. parish communion and 3.00 p.m. evensong. In the other town this means 8.00 a.m. Holy Communion, 10.00 a.m. parish communion and 6.00 p.m. evensong. Both market town benefices also include two small villages each. The market town which supports a curate provides a service in both of its associated villages each Sunday. Morning and evening services alternate between the two villages. The market town which does not support a curate provides a regular 9.00 a.m. communion service which alternates between the two villages. The parish priest commutes to conduct the service between the 8.00 a.m. and 10.00 a.m. services in the town church.

One other large village in the deanery, with 1,300 inhabitants, also maintains the weekly pattern of low Mass at 8.00 a.m., parish Mass at 11.00 a.m., and evensong at 6.00 p.m. There are also two smaller villages combined in this benefice. In one of these villages, parish communion and matins alternate every Sunday at 9.30 a.m. In the other village, parish communion and evensong alternate every Sunday at 3.00 p.m. The parish priest is committed, therefore, to a regular pattern of five services each Sunday.

None of the other thirty-one Anglican churches in the deanery has a service at the same time each Sunday. The pattern varies widely from church to church. One of these churches is used less frequently than once a month. Of the other thirty churches, during a normal four-week month, thirteen are used for one service, nine for two services, four for three services, three for four services, and one for five services.

These thirty-one churches are grouped within five benefices. Again the pattern varies widely from benefice to benefice. Five churches form a benefice of 1,070 people, where the parish priest takes two or three services each Sunday. Six churches form a benefice of 915 people, where the parish priest takes three or four services each Sunday. Another six churches form a benefice of 959 people, where the parish priest takes two or three services each Sunday. Seven churches form a benefice of 1,260 people, where the parish priest takes two or three services each Sunday. Another seven churches form a benefice of 2,555 people, where the parish priest takes four or five services each Sunday.

The proportion of Anglican churches which publicly advertise their services in less accessible deanery is considerably lower than in urban shadow deanery or accessible deanery: twenty-two of the forty churches displayed service times, either on a notice-board outside or in the porch. The vicar's name and telephone number were displayed on the notice-board outside or in the porch at just seven of these forty churches, while six of them provided the vicarage address as well. Churchwardens' names and addresses were displayed by only one church. Information about banns of marriage was displayed at eight of the churches; information about arrangements for baptism was displayed at seven of them. In fact, seventeen of the forty churches displayed no information about themselves at all. One visitor observed that the outside notice-board was smashed and covered with weeds. The last notice on it was nine years out of date.

The two notices most frequently displayed in the churches of this deanery concerned the 'Diocesan churchyard regulations' and the 'Parish quota target'. Other publicly displayed notices included flower rotas, cleaning rotas, treasurer's reports and, in one benefice, notification regarding the sequestration of the living. One church notice-board was displaying a newsletter four years out of date. Another church notice-board welcomed visitors in the following way: 'Every member of the congregation is affectionately entreated to join aloud in the responses, also in each Amen; and, as far as possible, in the singing throughout the service.'

More than two out of every five of the churches in the deanery (seventeen) were kept locked. Five of them made known where the key could be obtained, but the other twelve gave no indication of this. One visitor reported that: 'A key was housed over the road in an outside toilet.' Another visitor reported that: 'Two key holders were given. Tried one address – no reply. I could not find the other house.'

Little provision is made for visitors to churches in less accessible deanery. Only six of the churches made available guidebooks or leaflets on the history and architecture of the building. Only four of the churches made available parish magazines or newsletters. Only the churches in the two market towns provided bookstalls or display screens offering resources to support the Christian faith.

The interior maintenance of the churches in less accessible deanery varied greatly from village to village. For example, nineteen of the forty churches were judged by the church watch visitors to look clean and well cared for. One visitor commented: 'Neat and clean, well looked after, feels alive.' On the other hand, three of the churches were felt to look very neglected. One visitor commented: 'Cobwebs on pews. The dead bumble-bee in front of the altar conveyed the entire feeling of this place – total death – feels neglected.'

A similarly wide variation occurs in the appearance of the churchyards in less accessible deanery, depending on local energy and resources. For example, twenty-two of the churchyards were judged by the church watch visitors to be well maintained, ten were judged to be fair, and the remaining eight were judged to be poor or bad.

With eight churches having been taken out of active service in the deanery, it seems that less accessible deanery may have solved its worst problems with maintaining fabric. Only six of the remaining forty churches had current fabric appeals and only two of the buildings looked in an obviously poor condition.

On the second Sunday in June, when the survey took place, the church watch team's research suggested that twenty-nine services would be conducted in the Anglican churches in less accessible deanery. In the event, three of these services did not take place at all and a fourth happened an hour and a half earlier than advertised.

One visitor who set out to attend a late-morning communion service in a village of 285 people described her experience as follows.

I arrived at 10.50 a.m. for an 11.00 a.m. communion service. There was no notice-board, no notice on the church door, which was firmly locked. Seeing a Methodist chapel in the distance I went there, only to discover it was now a private house. I went back to the church and encountered two elderly ladies who lived in the village. This church is scheduled to have a communion on the second Sunday of the month, but in the summer some services are held at the next village instead and there is no way of knowing this without having a current magazine. The magazine had been late going out this month, so few people would know of the change. The two ladies, having already walked a considerable distance, set off to walk to the next village. I joined them and after twenty minutes we could see the church we were headed for in the distance. We were obviously not going to arrive there before the end of the service and my arthritic hip was beginning to give me trouble so I gave up and made the long walk back. The two old ladies continued on, though one was doubtful if she could make it. They insisted I should call in for coffee in the future – a very pleasant experience of Christian charity in the two old ladies, but a frustrating experience of the rural church.

Fortunately, another member of the church watch team had been planned to attend the service in this neighbouring church, so it was included in the survey.

A second visitor had set out to attend a 9.30 a.m. service of matins in a village of 90 people. He describes what happened in the following way.

> The church was open so I went in when I arrived at 9.20 a.m. and sat down. I got up to leave at 9.30 a.m. since it was obvious that something was wrong, and met the treasurer at the door. He was obviously irritated by the situation and proceeded to have an animated discussion with me. The service had been cancelled. Cancellation was normally carried out by the use of a telephone call – people contacting each other – about twelve of them. He said that the church there felt isolated – their vicar came once a week – and the bishop and other figures of the church seldom or never came. The community at large felt the church was not sympathetic or caring towards the people outside the church, the other villagers who did not attend church but nevertheless regarded the church as their heritage and thus part of their life.

A third visitor had set out to attend an 11.00 a.m. communion service in a village of 140 people. This church, too, was open, but there were no signs of preparation for a service. The altar remained covered with a blue plastic sheet. There was no notice-board outside this church and no notices displayed in the porch. Inside, the parish newsletter from the previous month confirmed the expectation of an 11.00 a.m. communion service on the second Sunday of the month, but there was no newsletter for the current month.

A fourth visitor was spared the disappointment of arriving for a 6.00 p.m. evensong by talking with the vicar earlier in the day. She explains the situation as follows.

> The vicar who took this service was the same one who had taken the 3.00 p.m. service I attended and it had only been by asking if he was taking the 6.00 p.m. service as we left that we found that the time had been changed to 4.30 p.m. The reason given was that it was moved to an earlier time during the winter because of the cold weather and dark nights and people preferred to keep it at that time. The notice-board outside continued to advertise the service as 6.00 p.m.

The twenty-six services which took place in Anglican churches in less accessible deanery on the second Sunday in June included twelve services from the Book of Common Prayer or the 1928 Prayer Book, ten from *The Alternative Service Book 1980*, one *Alternative Services Series 1 & 2 Revised* communion service and three non-liturgical services. From the Book of Common Prayer there were six services of Holy Communion, one matins and five evensongs. From *The Alternative Service Book 1980* there were five communion services following Rite A and five following Rite B. The non-liturgical services comprised one united songs of praise with the local Methodist church, one informal family service, and one family service using the Church Pastoral Aid Society (CPAS) booklet. Thus, on this Sunday there were seventeen communion services, one matins, five evensongs and three non-liturgical services.

Overall, the twenty-six services were attended by 601 people. This represents 4.0% of the population of the deanery as a whole and averages 67 church attenders for each full-time stipendiary minister. Just over two thirds (68%) of the worshippers were female; just under one third (32%) were male. The age group which predominated in the congregations was the over-sixty year olds, who accounted for 34% of the worshippers. Another 27% were in their forties or fifties. This leaves 18% of the worshippers in their twenties or thirties and 21% under the age of twenty-one.

During the course of the day, 368 people attended communion services, eleven attended matins, seventy attended evensong and 152 attended non-liturgical services. This means that the average congregations were twenty-two at communion, fourteen at evensong, eleven at matins and fifty-one at non-liturgical services. Looked at from another perspective, 61% of the Sunday worshippers attended communion services, 25% attended non-liturgical services, 12% attended evensong and 2% attended matins.

The two best-attended Anglican services in less accessible deanery were the mid-morning communions in the two market towns. One of these services was attended by ninety-five people and the other by sixty-three people. The next best-attended service in the deanery was a mid-afternoon family service, following the CPAS pattern, with a congregation of seventy. At the other end of the scale, there were three services in the deanery for congregations of seven and one service for a congregation of two.

Two of the clergy in the deanery have responsibility for seven churches each. One of these priests took four services on the church watch Sunday in four different churches. He began the day with an 8.30 a.m. communion service from the Book of Common Prayer, in a village of 230 inhabitants, for a congregation of ten people in their fifties and sixties. At 10.00 a.m. he led a service of matins from the Book of Common Prayer, in a large village of 1,415 inhabitants, for a congregation of eleven people in their fifties and sixties. Then at 11.15 a.m. he led a non-liturgical family service, in a village of 540 inhabitants, for a congregation of fifty-two people covering the whole age range. At 6.00 p.m. he took a service of evensong from the Book of Common Prayer, in a village of fifty-five inhabitants, for a congregation of twelve, including two people under the age of forty. Overall, the four services made contact with just over 3% of the 2,555 inhabitants of the benefice.

The other priest with responsibility for five churches took two services on the church watch Sunday in two different churches. He began the day with a 9.30 a.m. communion service, using Rite A from *The Alternative Service Book 1980*, in a village of 615 inhabitants, for a congregation of seventeen, including seven children and six adults in their twenties or thirties. Then at 11.00 a.m. he took a communion service from the Book of Common Prayer, in a small hamlet, for a congregation of seven, including two teenagers. Overall, the two services made contact with 2% of the 1,260 inhabitants of the whole benefice.

All but four services in the deanery started within three minutes of the advertised time. Four services lasted for more than an hour: two evensongs, one mid-morning communion and the mid-afternoon united songs of praise with the Methodist chapel. Only one early morning communion service was over in less than half an hour. The average time for Anglican services in less accessible deanery was forty-eight minutes.

Almost three-quarters of the twenty-six services included a sermon. The seven services which did not include a sermon comprised the five early morning communions, a short family service, and the mid-afternoon united songs of praise. A third of the nineteen sermons preached (seven) lasted ten minutes or less, with the shortest lasting only five minutes. The longest sermon was delivered by the rector at evensong in one of the market towns, where he preached for twenty-five minutes. The average morning sermon lasted for eleven minutes, compared with the average afternoon and evening sermon of fourteen minutes.

Three-quarters of the twenty-six services included some hymn singing. The six services which did not comprised the five early morning communions, and a mid-afternoon communion service. One of the market towns was fortunate to have a young and very competent organist. In the other market town the organ was played less competently by a man in his eighties. Some of the village churches appeared to be struggling with very inadequate musicians. In one village the vicar tried to lead the hymns unaccompanied. In two villages pre-recorded tapes were used to lead the singing.

All the services in less accessible deanery were conducted by clergy. The three licensed readers resident in the deanery were not seen to function at any of the services. Although there was an interregnum in one benefice, the services here were conducted by retired clergy. The visitor explained her perception of the situation as follows.

The last vicar retired with a stroke after only three years. The church is again in an interregnum and has been served by three elderly priests all in their seventies, until last week when one of them died on the Monday after he had taken the Sunday services. The one who was there today had travelled nearly twenty miles. For a good part of the service the congregation were completely at sea. The priest went so fast they did not know where they were and he did not give them time to kneel for prayers so there was much indecision. He was part way through the words of the creed while descending the pulpit steps. There was a sense of there still being life among the congregation, but this was almost totally stifled by the priest.

The active involvement of lay people in many of the services was restricted to taking the collection. Lay people read the lessons in less than half of the services (twelve) and led the intercessions in only three services. Lay people were involved in administering the chalice at two communion services.

Overall, the visitors felt themselves made welcome at the Anglican services in less accessible deanery; fourteen of the twenty-six congregations were described as being friendly to visitors and only three were described as being positively unfriendly to visitors. At seventeen services a lay person welcomed worshippers as they arrived, and at a further three services the clergyman was doing so. Books were personally handed to the visitors at seventeen services and ready waiting in the pews at two other services. At the other seven services the books were left out in a prominent place for worshippers to pick up for themselves. At none of the services did the visitors experience difficulty in finding the right books.

After twenty-four of the twenty-six services the clergy were available at the door to speak with members of the congregation. At only three services were the visitors not spoken to by the minister; at only five were they not spoken to by a lay person. The visitors came away from nineteen services feeling that the minister had made friendly enquiries and from seventeen services feeling that a lay person had made friendly enquiries. After twelve services, however, the visitor felt that the clergyman had gone beyond the initial friendly enquiries to begin to interrogate them.

Children's work was not greatly in evidence in Anglican churches in less accessible deanery. Both market town churches held a Sunday school separate from the Sunday services and at a different time. Only four of the village churches made it known that there was a Sunday school available. In one village of 285 inhabitants the Sunday school takes place at 10.00 a.m. every week and on the second Sunday of the month leads into the communion service at 11.00 a.m. The church watch visitor arrived while the Sunday school was still in full swing. She described her experience as follows.

I managed to gatecrash the end of the Sunday school, which contained about twenty girls, aged between seven and thirteen. The minister was taking it – an emergency for him – the Sunday school teacher was ill. He was leading a religious song – guitar in hand, played with vigour, with joy. The children loved it. A really welcome beginning to my brief stay in the village. A pearl! The girls left before the communion service, which was sad.

Free Churches

The decline of the Free Churches in less accessible deanery is illustrated very clearly by the number of closed, redundant, decaying and converted chapels. The church watch team identified and visited thirty-one former chapels in this deanery. Others may well have been demolished and have disappeared from sight and memory. In one of the market towns the former Congregational chapel has been converted into a library, and a former Methodist chapel has been converted into a youth centre. In the other market town three former chapels now serve as a warehouse, a tyre depot and a masonic hall. Just two of the other closed chapels were in communities of over 1,000 inhabitants. The remaining twenty-four former chapels were in smaller rural communities. Two of them had served communities which had never possessed an Anglican church. Three of them were in communities where the Anglican church had also ceased to function. The closure of the other nineteen chapels had left the parish church as a surviving place of worship in the community.

Many of the disused chapels outside the two market towns (seventeen) had been left standing and were now empty and decaying. Of the other nine chapels, five had been converted into homes; two were used as garages; one had been converted into a theatre and one had been demolished and the site partially cleared.

The only denomination currently active in less accessible deanery alongside the Church of England and the Roman Catholic church is the Methodist church. There are twelve Methodist chapels still functioning in the area covered by this deanery. Each of the market towns has retained one Methodist chapel, alongside the Anglican and Catholic churches. Of the other ten chapels, two are to be found in small hamlets where there is now no active Anglican church, two are in villages of less than 150 inhabitants where they stand alongside an Anglican church, and the other six are in larger communities alongside an Anglican church. Collectively, the twelve Methodist chapels provide seating for 1,925 people, representing one in eight (12.9%) of the total population of the deanery.

The Methodist circuit is larger than the Anglican deanery and includes five chapels outside the deanery as well as the twelve within it. The circuit is served by two stipendiary ministers, one resident in each of the market towns. Three supernumeraries (retired ministers) are also resident in one of the market towns. The circuit preaching plan also lists ten active local preachers and one on trial, eight local preachers not currently preaching, and twenty visiting preachers. The total membership of the circuit is listed as 400 names.

The three Methodist chapels in the two market towns and in a village of over 1,000 inhabitants all advertise a regular pattern of two services each Sunday, at 10.45 a.m. and 6.00 p.m. The chapels in the market towns also advertise a weekly Women's Fellowship meeting, in one chapel on Tuesday afternoon and in the other on Wednesday afternoon. Two of the village chapels also advertise on their notice-board two services every Sunday, at 10.45 a.m. and 6.00 p.m. In practice, however, neither of these chapels has maintained this pattern for some years. In one village the service alternates between 10.45 a.m. and 6.00 p.m. In the other village the service alternates between 10.45 a.m. and 2.30 p.m., except when joint services are held with the Anglican church. Another village chapel clearly advertises a pattern alternating between 10.45 a.m. and 6.00 p.m. Of the remaining six chapels, four hold a weekly service at 6.00 p.m., one holds a weekly service at 10.00 a.m., and one holds a weekly service at 2.30 p.m.

Sunday schools are maintained in parallel with the morning service by the chapels in the two market towns and in the village of over 1,000 inhabitants. In three of the smaller villages a weekly Sunday school is maintained on Sunday morning independently of the Sunday service. In one of these chapels, the Sunday school meets before the morning service, while in the other two chapels the services take place during the afternoon or evening.

Both of the market town chapels and four of the ten village chapels display the minister's name and address on the outside notice-board. Only two of the village chapels failed to advertise Sunday service times, although two of the village chapels were continuing to advertise a pattern of services which no longer had currency. All the chapels in less accessible deanery are kept locked and only two of them identified the caretaker or key holder.

One of the market town chapels has been an impressive building with Ionic portico and pediment, built to seat over 800 people. The façade is now crumbling. The chapel in the other market town is much less pretentious and in an even sadder state of repair. Some of the village chapels have been well maintained, while others show signs of neglect. One small chapel with a membership of seven is facing an urgent question about the long-term future of its building.

On the church watch weekend, initial research indicated that three of the chapels were conducting two services, eight were conducting one service, and one chapel was advertising a united service in the local Anglican church. The church watch team, therefore, prepared to attend fourteen Methodist services. In the event three of the expected services did not take place and the visitors waited outside locked chapels.

Both the morning and evening services in one of the market towns were conducted by an ordained minister, the morning service by a supernumerary in his early eighties and the evening service by the stipendiary resident minister in his late fifties. In the other market town the morning service was conducted by a male local preacher in his early thirties, who was said to be training for the ordained ministry. Mysteriously, the advertised evening service did not take place. Five of the services in the village chapels were taken by local preachers, one by a Salvation Army officer and two by a circuit minister. All the local preachers were men, ranging in age from early forties to early eighties. The sacrament of Holy Communion was administered at the evening service in one of the market towns and at the morning service in one of the villages.

A sermon was preached at all the eleven Methodist services. These sermons varied in length from ten to thirty minutes and averaged eighteen minutes. The average length of the Methodist services was fifty-three minutes, five minutes longer than the average length of the Anglican services in the deanery.

The overall attendance at these eleven services was 261 people. This represents 1.7% of the population, compared with 4.0% of the population who attended Anglican services in the deanery. Nearly three-fifths (58%) of the worshippers were female and just over two-fifths (42%) were male. In the Methodist congregations, the age group which predominated was clearly the over-sixties. Almost half (46%) the people who attended Methodist services in less accessible deanery were over the age of sixty, and a further quarter (27%) were in their forties or fifties. This leaves 14% of the worshippers in their twenties or thirties and 13% under the age of twenty-one. In absolute terms there were twenty-nine children under the age of eleven and seven young people between the ages of eleven and twenty. These attendances, of course, do not include the children who attended Sunday schools in the village chapels at times when no adult service was taking place.

The two best-attended Methodist services in the deanery were the morning services in the two market towns. The baptism in one of the market towns attracted an attendance of fifty-eight, including ten children or teenagers, sixteen adults in their thirties or forties and twenty-six adults in their fifties or sixties. A congregation of this size felt quite comfortable in a chapel built to seat 150 people. The service in the other market town attracted an attendance of fifty-nine, including twelve children from the Sunday school and thirty-five people over the age of sixty. Especially after the children had been taken out of the service, this congregation looked quite lost in a chapel built to seat 800 people. At two of the village chapels the congregation consisted of six and seven people.

All the Methodist services included hymn singing accompanied by organ, harmonium or piano. Six women and five men were involved playing these instruments, but only one of them was under the age of sixty. Five of them were described as good musicians, four as fair, and two as poor. The church watch visitor attending an evening congregation of eighteen commented that 'the organist played the electronic organ well and the singing was good'. The visitor attending an evening congregation of seven (including himself and the preacher's wife) commented that the preacher and his wife sang a duet during most of the hymns. The visitor attending an afternoon congregation of eleven commented that 'the organist played at a funereal pace and the congregation found it difficult to sing'.

All the services involved lay people taking the collection. In two services women took the collection; at the other nine services men did so. In three services people in their forties or fifties took the collection; at the other eight services people over the age of sixty did so. At only two services was someone from the congregation involved in reading the lesson. At the other nine services the lessons were read by the minister or the local preacher conducting the service.

All but one of the Methodist congregations in less accessible deanery were described as friendly to visitors. At all eleven services a lay person welcomed the visitors on arrival and in three cases the person leading the service was there to welcome worshippers as well. At ten services the minister or local preacher spoke with the visitors afterwards. On just one occasion the visitor felt interrogated by the local preacher and on three occasions visitors felt interrogated by a member of the congregation. After attending an evening service with six other people, the visitor commented that: 'The very small congregation was most friendly and all were *delighted* to see me. But it felt very sad.' After attending an afternoon service with eleven other people, the church watch visitor commented that: 'The people were very friendly and welcoming.' After attending an evening service with twenty-one other people, the visitor was invited home for coffee by a member of the congregation.

Roman Catholic

There are three Catholic churches in less accessible deanery. All three had been completed by the late 1830s in Gothic brick. Two of these churches are situated in the two market towns at either end of the deanery. The third is situated in the grounds of a large and remote Georgian hall. All three seem to have been built originally to seat a congregation of 100 people. The church in one of the market towns was extended during the 1860s to bring the seating capacity up to 150 people. Collectively, therefore, these three churches provide seating for about 350 people, representing one in forty-three (2.3%) of the total population. For a number of years, the Catholic community also held a regular Sunday Mass in another small village in a private chapel. At the time of the church watch survey the gated driveway to this chapel displayed a planning notice for demolition of part of the building and erection of a garage.

All three Catholic churches clearly displayed information about weekday and weekend Masses. Only one of them, however, gave any information about the parish priest and this was limited to his telephone number. All three churches are served by the same presbytery in one of the market towns. All three Catholic churches in less accessible deanery are kept unlocked, although in one case access is restricted to a small chapel of private prayer. The fabric appears to be in a good condition and both the inside and the grounds are well maintained. Plans are displayed for a proposed extension to the church in the market town where the priest is not resident.

Mass is celebrated at the same time in the same place every

weekend in less accessible deanery. At the church next to the presbytery Mass is celebrated at 11.00 a.m. on Sunday. In the other market town Mass is celebrated at 9.30 a.m. on Sunday. In the church adjoining the Georgian hall, Mass is celebrated on Saturday evening at 7.00 p.m. The priest is also responsible for a Mass at 4.00 p.m. on Sunday afternoon at a nearby RAF base.

On the church watch weekend these three Masses were attended by 234 people. This represents 1.6% of the population of the deanery as a whole. The 9.30 a.m. Mass attracted a congregation of 111, while the 10.00 a.m. mass attracted a congregation of ninety-two. The Saturday evening Mass was attended by thirty-one people. Three-fifths (60%) of the worshippers were female; two-fifths (40%) were male.

The Saturday evening congregation was heavily weighted towards the over-sixties, with over half the worshippers in that category. Nevertheless, there were some younger families present, including two preschoolers, three children of primary school age and one teenager. Young people were very well represented at the two Sunday Masses. Between one third and two fifths of the worshippers (37%) at these services were under the age of twenty-one, nearly a fifth (18%) were in their twenties or thirties, over a quarter (28%) were in their forties or fifties, and one sixth (17%) were over the age of sixty.

Each of the Sunday Masses took about 55 minutes. The Saturday evening Mass was somewhat shorter, lasting forty-two minutes. Each service had a full set of hymns, and each included 'Love divine'. Basically, the same homily was given at all three services. It was described by one of the church watch visitors as 'very rambling and difficult to follow'. Another visitor summed up its message as 'keep to the straight and narrow and remember our eternal destiny'.

The priest made no personal contact with the visitors at all. The visitors agreed that a complete stranger to Catholic services would have been totally lost. At the evening service there were neither missals nor printed service sheets. At the 11.00 a.m. Mass the visitor did not find out about the service leaflet until after the service had finished. In conversation one of the parishioners described the parish priest as a 'very shy monk who had been sent to the parish when the previous priest had suddenly left'.

Lay people were involved in all the services, reading lessons, taking collections and serving at the altar. Women were involved only as lesson readers. Children were involved only as servers. One of the visitors observed that: 'The service had its funny moment when at the gospel the boy holding the Bible was so small that the priest rested the book on top of the boy's head.'

The general feel was that there was hardly any contact between members of the congregation at these three services. The peace was shared, but without people moving from their own pew. The visitors went away from two of the services without being spoken to by any of the worshippers. None of the visitors felt that he or she had attended a friendly church.

Summary

When the Anglican, Methodist and Catholic churches are considered together, the 14,954 inhabitants of less accessible deanery are served by fifty-five churches. In other words, there is one church for every 270 people. Together these churches provide seating for about 6,245 people, or two in five (42%) of the population. On a typical Sunday there were 1,096 attendances at public worship, representing one in fourteen (7%) of the population. There are twelve full-time ministers of religion living in less accessible deanery, one for every 1,250 inhabitants.

12
ACCESSIBLE
COUNTRYSIDE

Church of England

IN ACCESSIBLE DEANERY there are thirty Anglican parishes and thirty-six Anglican churches, all in regular use. There are no redundant Anglican churches in the deanery, although one of the villages contains the remains of the medieval church next to the large estate house. This old church was abandoned when a new church was built nearer to the main centre of population in the 1860s. Today these thirty-six churches serve a total population of 43,315 people, an average of 1,203 each. Collectively, the thirty-six churches provide seating for about 4,830 people, representing one in nine (11.2%) of the inhabitants. The electoral rolls of the thirty parishes contain 2,433 names, representing one in eighteen (5.6%) of the inhabitants.

The thirty parishes and thirty-six churches are now staffed by fourteen full-time stipendiary clergy and a full-time stipendiary Church Army captain. One of the full-time clergymen also holds responsibility for the Anglican chaplaincy of a local psychiatric hospital. Overall, throughout the deanery this produces a ratio of one stipendiary post for 2,888 inhabitants. At the same time, the stipendiary ministry in accessible deanery is significantly augmented by ten readers, eleven retired clergy, a non-stipendiary priest and a non-stipendiary woman deacon. The geographical advantages of accessible deanery favour the development of these kinds of supplementary ministry. Proximity to centres of employment attract middle-class commuters, while lower property prices attract the retired.

At present the stipendiary clergy in accessible deanery are responsible for a range of very different benefices. The four parishes nearest to the cathedral city and mainline rail station have continued to expand in recent years. The largest of these communities has now merged with the suburban sprawl from the city itself and totals a population of over 10,000. In the late 1960s, a second church was built in the parish and a curate appointed to share the work. More recently a small village has been added to the benefice. The main parish church maintains the regular Sunday pattern of 8.00 a.m. Holy Communion, 9.30 a.m. parish communion and 6.30 p.m. evensong. The new church also has a regular Sunday pattern of an early morning communion at 8.30 a.m. and a mid-morning parish communion at 9.45 a.m., but without an evening service. Worship in the small village church is arranged to fit round the pattern established in the two larger churches. The Sunday service alternates between late morning communion at 11.15 a.m. and afternoon evensong at 3.00 p.m. The electoral roll of the benefice includes 3.9% of the inhabitants.

The other expanding communities have remained more clearly separated from the city. One is a single parish benefice of 5,780 inhabitants, served by a full-time parish priest and a non-stipendiary woman deacon. The regular Sunday pattern of services involves Holy Communion at 8.30 a.m. and parish communion at 10.00 am, but no evening service. The second consists of two parishes which have physically merged into one, with a total population of 5,600, served by a full-time parish priest and a reader. In the smaller of the churches the vicar takes an 8.30 a.m. Holy Communion service on the second and fourth Sundays in the month, while the reader has responsibility for the 10.00 a.m. service every Sunday. On the third Sunday of the month this is a family service; on the other Sundays matins. In the larger of the churches the vicar takes an 8.30 a.m. Holy Communion on the first Sunday of the month, followed by a family service at 10.00 a.m. On the other Sundays there is a communion service at 10.00 a.m. There is an evensong every week at 6.00 p.m.

The third expanding parish now totals a population of around 3,200. Recently the incumbent has also taken on responsibility for a small village of 310 inhabitants. He is assisted in his ministry by a full-time Church Army captain, a retired priest and three readers. The benefice has developed a strong charismatic identity and attracts a number of worshippers from the neighbouring city. The main mid-morning service alternates between communion and a non-eucharistic family service. Worshippers are invited to arrive for prayer at 9.50 a.m., praise at 10.15 a.m. and the service itself at 10.30 a.m. The evening service also alternates between communion and evensong. Worshippers are invited to arrive for prayer at 5.50 p.m. and for the service itself at 6.15 p.m. On the first Sunday in the month Holy Communion is also celebrated at 8.00 a.m. In the small village church the retired priest conducts a mid-morning communion service at 10.30 a.m. on alternate Sundays. The electoral roll of the benefice represents 4.6% of the inhabitants.

Two other parishes in the deanery, further away from the city, have also attracted new development. One, with a population of 3,350, is a single-parish benefice, run in an evangelical tradition. The main 10.30 a.m. service is matins on the second and fourth Sundays, a family service on the third Sunday and Holy Communion on the first Sunday in the month. Holy Communion is also said on the second, third and fourth Sundays at 8.00 a.m. and evensong is sung every Sunday at 6.00 p.m. The other, with a population of 3,140, is held in plurality with a small village of 285 inhabitants and run in a Catholic tradition. The main 9.30 a.m. service is family communion, except on the first Sunday in the month when a non-eucharistic family service is preceded by the monthly 8.00 a.m. Holy Communion service. Again, evensong is sung every Sunday at 6.00 p.m. The small village church has two services a month, Holy Communion on the first Sunday and a family service on the third Sunday, both at 11.15 a.m.

The other seven full-time clergy in the deanery have care of much smaller parishes. The chaplain to the psychiatric hospital, in addition to his chaplaincy, takes care of two churches and 1,065 souls. The service in the hospital chapel takes place every Sunday at 11.15 a.m. Each of the churches has an 8.00 a.m. Holy Communion service once a month. One church has two 10.00 a.m. parish communion services each month and the other church has one 10.30 a.m. family service each month. Evensong alternates between the two churches at 6.00 p.m. Another priest has care of three parishes and 1,695 souls. On the third Sunday in the month he holds just one service for the whole benefice,

Holy Communion at 10.00 a.m. On the other Sundays, Holy Communion is celebrated in all three churches at 8.00 a.m., 9.00 a.m. and 10.00 a.m. Each church sticks to its own service time. Evensong is said twice a month at 6.00 p.m., once in each of the larger churches.

Three of the clergy have care of four churches each, with combined populations of 1,665, 1,810 and 2,510. Throughout these twelve churches the pattern of services is very complex. One priest tries to celebrate Holy Communion in each of his four churches every Sunday, and does so at 8.00 a.m., 9.15 a.m., 10.30 a.m. and 6.30 p.m. Another provides just two services a Sunday throughout his benefice, but in different places and at different times from one Sunday to the next.

Another of the clergy has care of six churches and 1,835 souls. His pattern is to operate a single group service at 10.00 a.m. on the second Sunday in the month and to hold this service in turn throughout the six churches. On the first Sunday in the month he celebrates Holy Communion at 9.00 a.m., 10.15 a.m. and 11.30 a.m. and says evensong at 6.00 p.m. in four different churches. On the third Sunday he celebrates Holy Communion at 8.45 a.m. and 10.15 a.m. and says evensong at 6.00 p.m. in three different churches. On the fourth Sunday he celebrates Holy Communion at 9.30 a.m. and 3.00 p.m. and says evensong at 6.00 p.m. in three different churches.

The remaining full-time clergyman in the deanery has just one small parish with a population of 400 and an electoral roll of thirty-five. He is one of the longer-serving clergy in the deanery and has missed out on the process of pastoral reorganization. Like his colleagues with multiple parish cures, he has decided against a stable pattern of services each Sunday. On the first Sunday in the month there is Holy Communion at 8.00 a.m. and a family service at 11.00 a.m. On the second Sunday there is Holy Communion at 9.30 a.m. and evensong at 6.00 p.m. On the other Sundays there is just one service of Holy Communion at 9.30 a.m. These twenty-four small churches, within the care of seven full-time clergy, have combined electoral rolls of 1,043 names, representing 9.5% of the local inhabitants.

By way of summary, in a typical month of four Sundays, 157 services will take place in the Anglican churches in the deanery. Of these, 64% are communion services, 24% are evensongs, 5% are matins and 7% are non-eucharistic family services. All the thirty-six churches are holding at least one communion service a month, twenty-three of them are holding at least one evensong and eight are holding at least one matins. Ten of the churches are holding at least one non-eucharistic family service in an attempt to broaden their outreach to the community.

The general rule throughout the deanery seems to be that the more complex the Sunday pattern of services, the less likely the church is to display the times of Sunday worship. While all seven churches serving large parishes in the deanery display the times of Sunday services outside or in the porch, the proportion falls to 60% of the churches serving smaller parishes and those where the pattern of services generally varies from Sunday to Sunday.

The vicar's name was publicly displayed outside or in the porch of twenty-four of the thirty-six churches; all but three of these churches also included his address and telephone number. The churchwardens' names were displayed by eleven of the churches, their addresses by ten and their telephone numbers by seven. Information about baptism was displayed in eleven of the churches and information about banns of marriage in ten. Ten of the churches displayed various editions of the statutory table of fees, some as much as ten years out of date. Six of the churches in the deanery displayed a notice of welcome to visitors and only three publicly advertised an appeal for money.

Generally speaking, the churches in accessible deanery were not making particularly good use of notice-boards and other media for communicating their work. Twenty-five of the churches had some kind of notice-board outside, but only seven of these were in really good shape. Twenty-five of the churches used their porches to display notices, but only five or six of these were used to good effect. Inside, ten of the churches had some sort of display screen, but only four were attractively and informatively set out. The most frequently found notices in the deanery concerned rotas for flower arranging and the annual greeting sent from the cathedral to mark the patronal festival of the church. A few notice-boards displayed a recent police warning about vandalism in churches; a few others displayed a large and attractive poster advertising a local craft fair, which had taken place a few weeks earlier. One church displayed one pattern of service times on the notice-board outside and a different pattern in the church.

Only fourteen of the thirty-six churches in accessible deanery were kept unlocked and a further four indicated where the key could be obtained. The other eighteen churches were locked without naming a key holder. One of these locked churches perhaps displayed the most poignant notice in the deanery. On an otherwise empty notice-board the following message had been pinned by the electricity meter reader: 'We called today to read the meter. On this occasion it is essential that we obtain our own meter reading. Please indicate when it would be convenient to call back.'

Almost all the churches in accessible deanery looked in a reasonable state of repair from the outside. Only one building looked sadly neglected and another five were obviously in need of some attention. Generally a good deal of effort was expended on the churchyards, 25% of which were kept in a smart condition. Inside, the majority of the churches were clean and tidy, while half of them contained rather fine displays of flowers. Generally the churches possessed a good supply of hymn-books and service-books, although noticeably in some of the smaller village churches the hymn-books and copies of the Book of Common Prayer were looking the worse for wear. Parish magazines were available in fourteen of the thirty-six churches and guidebooks in nine of them. Just five of the churches had some kind of bookstall, while one of these was restricted to a few British and Foreign Bible Society pamphlets which had clearly seen better days.

Sunday school or similar weekday provision for children is offered by thirteen of the thirty-six churches in accessible deanery. The seven largest parishes in the deanery, the smallest of which has a population of 1,715, all support some form of children's work. When these larger parishes have been amalgamated with a small neighbouring village, these villages do not support their own children's work. This leaves six village churches with a Sunday school and twenty-three without. In theory, however, two of the village Sunday schools are operated for the benefit of the whole benefice, which in one case includes three churches and in the other case six churches. In another case the church Sunday school meets every other Sunday alternating with the Methodists.

On the third Sunday in October, when the church watch survey took place, there were thirty-five Anglican services advertised in accessible deanery. In the event, one of the morning services did not take place, although it was clearly advertised in the church porch. The thirty-four services attended in the course of the day consisted of seventeen from the Book of Common Prayer, or the 1928 Prayer Book, fourteen from *The Alternative Service Book 1980*, one *Alternative Services Series 3* morning prayer, one CPAS family service and one non-liturgical family service. From the Book of Common Prayer there were eight services of Holy Communion, one matins and eight evensongs. From *The Alternative Service Book 1980* there were ten communion services following Rite A and four following Rite B. Thus, on this Sunday there were twenty-two communion services, eight evensongs, two matins and two family services. The most popular time for services in the deanery is mid-morning; sixteen services started between 9.30 a.m. and 10.30 a.m. There were also seven early morning services and two late morning services. No services took place during the afternoon, and seven began at 6.00 p.m., 6.15 p.m. or 6.30 p.m.

Overall, the thirty-four services were attended by 1,266 people. This represents 2.9% of the population of the deanery and averages eighty-four church attenders for each full-time stipendiary minister. Two-thirds (67%) of the worshippers were female; one third (33%) were male. The age groups which predominated in the congregation were the forty- to sixty-year-olds and the over-sixties; 32% of the worshippers were in their forties or fifties and another 34% were over sixty. This left 14% of the worshippers in their twenties and thirties and 20% under the age of 21.

The best-attended service in the deanery was the harvest festival evensong, to which the archdeacon had been invited as guest preacher, in a community of 2,855. There were 130 worshippers in this congregation or 4.6% of the population. This service was taken from the Book of Common Prayer. The other evensongs in the deanery attracted congregations of ten from a community of 3,880 (0.3%), forty from a community of 10,000 (0.4%), eighteen from a community of 3,350 (0.5%), fourteen from a community of 725 (1.9%), fifteen from a community of 635 (2.4%), sixteen from a community of 395 (4.0%) and twenty-seven from a community of 220 (12.3%). The Book of Common Prayer service of matins was attended by sixteen people from a community of 287 (5.6%), while the *Alternative Services Series 3* service of morning prayer was attended by forty-three people from a community of 2,715 (2.5%).

The best-attended Sunday morning service was the 9.30 a.m. Rite B Eucharist in the largest parish in the deanery, with a congregation of 125. The smallest congregation of the day met for the 11.15 a.m. Book of Common Prayer Eucharist in the small village church in the same benefice, with a congregation of five. Overall, there was an average congregation of sixteen for the Book of Common Prayer Communion services, forty-one for the Rite A and fifty-six for the Rite B services. The two family services, both in communities of a little over 3,000 inhabitants, attracted congregations of around one hundred people and were particularly strong on six- to ten-year-olds.

The longest services in the deanery were both in the charismatic parish where the morning family services lasted eighty minutes and the evening Holy Communion service lasted eighty-five minutes, in addition to the periods of prayer and praise preparing for the services. The general trend in the deanery is for shorter services, the average being fifty-five minutes.

Only four of the thirty-four services did not include some form of sermon or address, all early morning communion services. The two longest sermons were given at the charismatic church, thirty-three minutes for the morning family service and twenty-eight minutes for the evening eucharist. The average length of the sermons, however, worked out at thirteen minutes, with fifteen of them lasting ten minutes or less.

Five of the early morning services and one late morning service did not include hymn singing, but the other twenty-eight did. Ten services used the old *Hymns Ancient and Modern: Standard Edition*; nine used the *Hymns Ancient and Modern Revised* and five of these supplemented the repertoire with *100 Hymns for Today*; one used the *Hymns Ancient and Modern: New Standard Edition*; four used *The English Hymnal*; three used *Songs of Fellowship* and one used *Hymns of Faith*. In some cases the singing was made more difficult rather than helped by the organist. In only four of the churches did the music seem to be of a satisfactory standard, including the charismatic church where the organist was joined by a pianist and a group of instrumentalists, including guitar, cello, flute and drums.

Thirty-one of the thirty-four services were led by a priest. In five of these services the priest was assisted by a second priest and in one by a reader. The other three services were conducted by readers, one reader taking two services. Both readers were men in their sixties or seventies. In over half the services (56%) the officiating ministers took complete responsibility, including reading the lessons. Members of the congregation were involved in reading lessons in fifteen services, administering the chalice at eight services, giving out notices in five services and leading the intercessions in three services. In all but two of the services lay people were involved in taking the collection. Although fourteen of the communion services used *The Alternative Service Book 1980*, only four of them included a physical exchange of the peace. All of these four services took place in the larger parishes.

Generally speaking, it was the larger parishes in the deanery which were better equipped for making visitors feel at home. At all but one of the services in the larger parishes, lay people were ready at the door to greet the worshippers as they came in and to hand out books. By way of contrast, this happened in only three of the small parishes. In some cases the visitors experienced considerable difficulty in finding where the service-books were stored. In both the small and large parishes the clergy generally made a point of trying to speak to the congregation as they left after the service, even when the clergy needed to move on to take a service in another church. At only three of the thirty-four services did the visitor feel completely ignored by the minister. At more than half the services the visitors reported that a lay person had made friendly enquiries and had welcomed them to the service.

Free Churches

Alongside the thirty-six Anglican churches in accessible deanery, there are also thirty-three Free Church buildings. While all the Anglican churches remain in active service, nine of the remaining chapels have now closed. In addition to these closures, other chapels may also have been demolished, leaving no signs of their former existence. One of the closed Methodist chapels still has a notice-board outside displaying a regular pattern of Sunday services. Another of the chapels, attached to a remote farmhouse, is now used just once a year for the harvest festival service. This leaves twenty-three chapels in accessible deanery in regular use; twenty-two belong to the Methodist church and one to the Elim

Pentecostal church. Just one stipendiary Methodist minister actually *lived* in the area designated accessible deanery, since much of the deanery belonged to the same circuit as the neighbouring cathedral city.

All but one of the surviving Methodist chapels are within a third of a mile of an Anglican parish church, built at the heart of a rural settlement to serve a rival religious community. Some are almost next door to the parish church. The one exception is a chapel built just before the First World War in a small settlement some three miles from the parish church. All of the seven largest parishes in accessible deanery, with populations over 1,700, are served by a Methodist chapel. The average population of the communities in which the other chapels are situated is 580 inhabitants. Collectively, the twenty-two Methodist chapels provide seating for about 2,360 people, representing one in eighteen (5.4%) of the inhabitants of the total deanery, and about half the provision made by the Anglican churches.

The Methodist chapels maintain a more regular pattern of services in accessible deanery than do the Anglican churches. This contrast is especially noticeable in the smaller villages. Just two of the small village chapels had opted to hold only one service a month, a monthly evening service at 6.00 p.m. in each case. All the other chapels were in regular use every Sunday.

In four of the larger communities, the chapels maintain the traditional pattern of a morning service at 10.30 a.m., 11.00 a.m. or 11.45 a.m. and an evening service at 6.00 p.m. In another of the larger communities, the regular evening service is augmented by a 10.30 a.m. family service on the first Sunday in the month. In the two other larger parishes in the deanery, the chapel provides a regular morning service at 10.30 a.m. or 10.45 a.m. In the smaller villages, three chapels hold their weekly service at 10.30 a.m. or 10.45 a.m., three at 11.00 a.m., three at 2.30 p.m. or 2.45 p.m. and three at 6.00 p.m. One of the chapels which holds a weekly evening service augments its provision with a monthly 10.30 a.m. family service. The final chapel in the deanery holds its weekly service on alternate Sundays at 10.00 a.m. and 11.00 a.m. All told, four of the chapels are providing a special form of service once a month which they describe as 'family worship'.

In addition to the Sunday services, Sunday school work is maintained by ten of the twenty-two chapels. Six of these

Sunday schools are held in the larger communities where the Anglican church is also making similar provision for children. The other four Sunday schools are held in communities of 845, 745, 615 and 465 inhabitants. One of these Sunday schools operates on alternate Sundays in conjunction with the Anglican church, while the others make provision for children in communities where the parish church does not.

Four of the twenty-two chapels in accessible deanery gave away no information about themselves at all. The other eighteen all displayed Sunday service times on a notice-board outside. The problem for the visitor, however, is that four of these chapels had in fact changed their pattern of services, but left the notice-board unchanged. Two displayed morning and evening services long after the morning service had been abandoned. One advertised services at 11.00 a.m. and 6.00 p.m., when the only Sunday service takes place at 10.30 a.m. The fourth advertises its service for 10.00 a.m., but actually holds the service at 10.45 a.m. Local regular attenders, of course, know all this and visitors are clearly not expected. Only ten of the chapels display the name of the circuit minister, nine his telephone number and two his address. None provides the name of a local contact person. All the chapels are kept locked, with just three of them naming a caretaker or key holder.

Although little care has been taken to advertise services in the surviving Methodist chapels in accessible deanery, considerably more care is taken to maintain their upkeep. Two-thirds of the chapels convey the impression of good structural repair and regular expenditure on the fabric. Inside, three-quarters of them appear well kept, clean and tidy. Another similar sign of care and ongoing financial investment is that sixteen of the twenty-two chapels have been equipped with sets of *Hymns and Psalms*. Two of the chapels have a rudimentary bookstall and one produces its own newsletter.

On the third Sunday in October, when the church watch survey took place, there were twenty-seven Methodist services thought to be taking place in accessible deanery. However, three of the services advertised outside the chapel as happening every Sunday had long since been abandoned and two others were found not to take place when the visitors arrived to attend them. This left a total of 22 services which actually took place, twelve in the morning, starting at 10.30 a.m., 10.45 a.m. or 11.00 a.m., three in the afternoon at 2.30 p.m. or 2.45 p.m. and seven in the evening at 6.00 p.m.

The availability of stipendiary and supernumerary ministers based in the neighbouring cathedral city means that ten of the twenty-two services were led by ordained ministers, while the leadership of one service was shared by two ministers, one in his mid-forties and the other in his mid-seventies. The ministers were much more likely to be found leading services in the larger communities. Of the ten services in communities of over 1,700 inhabitants, six were led by ordained ministers and four by local preachers. Of the twelve services in small village communities, eight were led by local preachers and four by ordained ministers. Three of the four village services led by ordained ministers were communion services. Two of the local preachers were women in their forties or fifties, one was a young man in his twenties, two were men in their forties, two were men in their fifties and the other five were men in their sixties or seventies.

All but one of the Methodist services included a sermon. These varied in length from thirteen to thirty-one minutes and averaged twenty minutes. The other service was an afternoon songs of praise, when the congregation chose their favourite hymns and hoped that the organist could play them. This was the shortest service of the Sunday, lasting only thirty-two minutes, compared with the longest service of seventy-five minutes. The average length of service was fifty-eight minutes, just three minutes longer than the Anglican services in the deanery.

The overall attendance at these twenty-two services was 530 people. This represents 1.2% of the population, compared with 2.9% who attended Anglican services in the deanery. Two-thirds (66%) of the worshippers were female and one third (34%) were male, exactly the same ratio as in the Anglican services. The major difference with the Methodist congregations, however, concerns the age profile. Half the Methodists (49%) in chapel that Sunday were over the age of sixty, compared with a third (34%) of the Anglicans. At the other end of the age continuum the Methodist chapels are attracting more children, in proportion to their adult worshippers, primarily because six chapels run Sunday school withdrawal classes during part of the morning service. This, however, leaves the Methodist chapels very weak in the sixteen-to-sixty age category, the very age group which is essential to ensure the continuity of chapel life. This trend is evident even in the large communities.

All the Methodist services were accompanied by organ, harmonium or piano. In all but three of the services the musician was over the age of fifty and quite often the standard of playing was poor. Apart from providing the music, the major point for lay involvement in the services was taking the collection. Generally, this responsibility was entrusted to a senior member of the church, although in two services it was undertaken by children. At thirteen of the twenty-two services lay people gave out the books at the beginning of the service and at eleven services the steward gave out the notices. Passages from Scripture were read by members of the congregation at five services. At three of the same services members of the congregation led some of the prayers. At one family service children presented a play and announced two hymns.

Generally speaking, the Methodist congregations in accessible deanery were good at making visitors feel welcome. At eighteen of the twenty-two services the visitors were welcomed at the door as they arrived and at three services they were shown to a seat. At every service the visitors were spoken to by a member of the congregation and at all but three services the visitor was spoken to by the minister or local preacher. At two services, however, the visitors felt that the minister was interrogating them a little too much. Afterwards one of the visitors commented that he had been among an 'exceptionally welcoming congregation', while another felt that the congregation was 'doing its best to proclaim the gospel in the twentieth century'. On the other hand, the visitor to one small chapel came away saying that 'the whole set-up felt a bit exclusive' and no one had bothered to make her feel at home.

Apart from Methodism, the only other Free Church presence in the deanery was the Elim Pentecostal church, situated in a community of nearly 3,000 inhabitants, where there were also Anglican and Methodist churches. This Elim church is a very small building with seating for twenty-five people. The noticeboard outside displays the Sunday and weekday meetings, but gives no information about the local pastor or leader. The regular Sunday pattern includes breaking of bread at 10.45 a.m., Sunday school at 2.30 p.m. and gospel service at 6.00 p.m. The regular weekday pattern includes prayer and Bible study at 7.30

p.m. on Thursdays and youth fellowship at 7.00 p.m. on Fridays. From the outside the building looks quite run down. It is locked and neither key holder nor caretaker is named.

On the church watch weekend the morning service was attended by two children, three teenagers, five adults in their twenties or thirties, four in their forties or fifties and four in their sixties or seventies. The evening service was attended by three teenagers, nine adults in their forties and fifties and four in their sixties or seventies. All told, there were nineteen male and fifteen female worshippers. The morning service lasted for an hour and a half and the evening service for an hour and three-quarters. Both morning and evening services made extensive use of hymns from *Redemption Hymnal* and choruses projected from an overhead projector. In the morning the sermon lasted twenty-one minutes; in the evening it was somewhat longer, thirty-five minutes. At both services many of the congregation participated in ministries of intercession and exhortation. On both occasions the pastor and congregation tried very hard to welcome the visitors, so hard in fact that the visitor to the evening service felt quite intimidated by it all.

Roman Catholic

There are three Catholic churches in accessible deanery. The oldest was built in a quasi-Romanesque style as the private chapel to a large country house in a village of 620 inhabitants. The second was a more recent building, also in a community of about 620 inhabitants. Both these communities were served by Anglican and Methodist churches as well as the Catholic church. The third Catholic church was built on an airfield, and although the airfield has been disused for many years the chapel has been kept for local services. All three churches displayed information about Sunday Masses and gave the parish priest's telephone number; two of them also gave his name. All three churches were kept locked and only one of them gave the name and address of the key holder. Collectively the three churches provided seating for 210 people.

One Mass was celebrated in each of the churches every Sunday at the same time, namely 9.00 a.m., 9.30 a.m. and 11.15 a.m., so that regular worshippers could be quite clear about service times. The church on the disused airfield also advertised a regular Thursday evening catechetical group for children. All three churches are served by priests who live outside the area and commute from the neighbouring city.

On the church watch weekend the three Masses were attended by congregations of thirteen, thirty-two and forty-five, a total of ninety people. The age group which predominated was the forty- and fifty-year-olds who account for 44% of the congregation. All told, there were four children under the age of six, five six- to ten-year-olds, four eleven- to fifteen-year-olds, six sixteen-to twenty-year-olds, seventeen adults in their twenties or thirties, forty in their forties or fifties and fourteen over the age of fifty. A little less than half (46%) the worshippers were male, a little over half (54%) were female. The presence of young children in the congregation gave opportunities which were not always fully grasped by the priest. At one Mass the priest had chosen for the theme of his message the need for childlike trust in prayer. Throughout the short sermon a toddler walked about the church causing interest and a certain amount of chaos. In one sense she was a wonderful visual aid, but the priest ignored her. She did not quite fit what he wanted to say about the trusting child in parents' arms.

The three Masses lasted for forty, forty-six and forty-nine minutes. At the two shorter services the priest preached for six and seven minutes. At the longer service the sermon lasted for eighteen minutes. Three or four hymns were sung at each service, all from *Celebration Hymnal*. In all three cases the congregation seemed extremely unenthusiastic about joining in the singing, although in two of the churches the hymns were supported by very competent organists.

All three services involved lay people taking collections, serving, reading lessons and leading intercessions. The peace was exchanged among the congregation at all three Masses, although at two of them the congregation appeared quite reluctant to participate.

None of the three Catholic services seemed to expect to be joined by visitors, and very little effort was made to make the newcomer feel welcome. No one welcomed the worshippers at the door. They were left to find their own books and in one case in particular this was quite difficult. At one of the services the visitor arrived and left without anybody speaking to her. At the other two churches the priest stood by the door after the service and tried to speak to most people as they went out. At only one service was the visitor spoken to by a member of the congregation.

Summary

When all the denominations present in accessible deanery are viewed together, the 43,315 inhabitants are served by sixty-two churches. In other words, there is one church for every 700 people. Together these churches provide seating for 7,425 people, or one in six (17.1%) of the population. On a typical Sunday there are 1,920 attendances at public worship, representing one in twenty-three (4.4%) of the population. There are sixteen full-time ministers of religion living in accessible deanery, one for every 2,700 inhabitants.

13
URBAN
SHADOW
COUNTRYSIDE

Church of England

URBAN SHADOW DEANERY occupies a beautiful tract of country-side stretching away from a major centre of industrial conurbation. The motorway passes through one end of the deanery, while both ends are served by major rail stations. The population of the deanery stands at around 39,500 inhabitants.

The deanery is staffed by fifteen stipendiary Anglican ministers, including three curates and a Church Army captain, making an average of one stipendiary post for about 2,700 people. Urban shadow countryside is a relatively popular location for retired clergy because of the accessibility of major services and facilities, although somewhat less popular than the accessible countryside, where housing is cheaper. In addition to the fifteen stipendiary clergy, the deanery also includes eight retired clergy, ranging in age from sixty-eight to seventy-nine years. At present there are no non-stipendiary ministers in the deanery, but there are five licensed readers.

The deanery maintains twenty-eight parish churches and a mission church. Anglican services are also held on a regular basis in a community centre. There are two redundant Anglican churches in the deanery and the ruins of a medieval church which was replaced in the late 1830s by a new building closer to the centre of the village it was intended to serve. A further Anglican church was closed in the deanery in the mid-1960s and has been subsequently demolished, leaving no trace of its former presence.

All told, the twenty-nine remaining Anglican churches provide seating for about 6,075 people, representing one in seven (15.4%) of the total population. The electoral rolls of the parishes contain 2,398 names, representing one in seventeen (6.1%) of the population.

The population of urban shadow deanery is by no means evenly divided throughout the twenty-eight parishes. In fact more than half, around 24,000, live within just three of the ecclesiastical parishes. The historic market town at one end of the deanery, which is served by a mainline rail station and is close to the motorway, has continued to expand throughout the twentieth century to encroach on two of the neighbouring ecclesiastical parishes. In one case, the former village has been thoroughly enveloped by the new development. In the other case, the old established village continues to preserve its own identity and is separated from the new development by a clear tract of open land. Now a team ministry has been formed in the market town to include one of the satellite villages, but not the other.

The team ministry is staffed by a team rector, a team vicar, a Church Army captain and a curate. The team rector and curate share responsibility for the large parish church in the market town, ministering to a population of around 10,000, and for a small village of 230 inhabitants. For all practical purposes, however, this small village is cared for by a retired priest. The other medieval church in the market town is now redundant, while the Victorian parish church has been demolished without trace. The town church has a regular pattern of three Sunday services: Holy Communion at 8.00 a.m., parish communion at 10.30 a.m. and sung evensong at 6.00 p.m. Once a month this pattern is augmented by a family communion service at 9.30 a.m. The village church has one service each Sunday, Holy Communion at 9.30 a.m. on the first and third Sundays in the month, and evensong at 3.00 p.m. on the second and fourth Sundays in the month.

The team vicar has responsibility for the expanded satellite community around the former village church, now totalling over 9,000 inhabitants. The regular Sunday pattern here involves Holy Communion at 8.00 a.m., family communion at 9.30 a.m., parish eucharist at 10.30 a.m. and evensong at 6.30 p.m. On the fourth Sunday in the month evensong is followed by another service of Holy Communion. The Church Army captain concentrates much of his work on a large new housing estate, where the Anglican and Methodist churches hold a fortnightly family service in a community centre at 3.00 p.m. on a Sunday afternoon. All told, the electoral roll of the team ministry includes 4.9% of the inhabitants.

The other ecclesiastical parish into which the market town has expanded has successfully resisted all attempts to become part of the team ministry. Its rector serves the old village church at one end of the parish and a small corrugated-iron mission church at the other end. While the village church serves directly fewer than 1,000 inhabitants, it maintains the traditional pattern of three Sunday services: Holy Communion at 8.00 a.m., parish eucharist at 10.30 a.m. and evensong at 6.30 p.m. The small mission church which directly serves nearly four times as many inhabitants has one service each Sunday: Holy Communion at 9.00 a.m. The electoral roll of this parish includes 5.7% of the inhabitants.

There is one other parish in the deanery with a population of more than 5,000 people. This is now joined to a neighbouring small village of fewer than one hundred inhabitants. Together they are served by a vicar and a curate. The larger parish has three services every Sunday, Holy Communion at 8.00 a.m. and again at 10.15 a.m. and evensong at 6.30 p.m. The smaller parish has evensong at 3.00 p.m. on the first Sunday, Holy Communion at 9.00 a.m. on the second and fourth Sundays and matins at 9.00 a.m. on the third Sunday in the month. Here the electoral roll includes 3.2% of the inhabitants.

Just two other benefices in the deanery include parishes with more than 1,000 inhabitants. The first is a village of 1,700 held in plurality with two small villages of 225 and 120 inhabitants. In the largest village, Holy Communion is celebrated at 8.00 a.m. on the first, second and fourth Sundays and at 10.00 a.m. on the third Sunday in the month. Evensong is said at 6.00 p.m. on the second and fourth Sundays and the family service is conducted at 11.00 a.m. on the first Sunday by a reader. In the village of 225 inhabitants there is a service every Sunday at 11.00 a.m., alternating between Holy Communion and matins. On the third Sunday there is also an early morning service of Holy Communion at 8.00 a.m. In the village of 120 inhabitants there is a celebration of Holy Communion at 9.45 a.m. on the second and fourth Sundays and evensong is said at 5.45 p.m. on the first and third Sundays in the month.

The other parish in the deanery with more than 1,000 inhabitants is a small town of 1,500 people, held in plurality with a small village of 150 inhabitants. In the small town, Holy Communion is celebrated at 8.30 a.m. on the first, second and fourth Sundays and at 11.00 a.m. on the third Sunday in the month. Matins is held on the second Sunday at 11.15 a.m. and on the fourth Sunday at 11.00 a.m. On the first Sunday in the month there is a family service at 11.00 a.m. Each week there is an evening service at 6.00 p.m., evensong on the first, second and third Sundays and a service of praise on the fourth Sunday in the month. In the village of 150 inhabitants, Holy Communion is celebrated at 9.30 a.m. on the first and third Sunday, matins is said at 9.30 a.m. on the fourth Sunday and a family service is held at 10.00 a.m. on the second Sunday in the month. All told, the electoral rolls of these two benefices include 9.2% of the inhabitants.

The other benefices in the deanery are all composed of relatively small parishes, giving six full-time clergy pastoral care over 6,180 parishioners, scattered over eighteen communities. These communities are currently organized within five benefices, one of which has been allocated a curate specifically to provide training opportunities within a rural area. The five benefices all operate on rather different lines. All told, their electoral rolls include 11.2% of the inhabitants.

Two of these benefices are comprised of three parishes. In one, where there is a total population of around 1,100, one of the churches is temporarily out of use because of major structural problems and is awaiting a redundancy order. Holy Communion is celebrated in the other two churches every Sunday. The two churches take it in turns to hold their services at 9.00 a.m. and at 10.30 a.m. On the first Sunday in the month, evensong is said at 6.00 p.m. in the smaller of the two parishes.

In the other benefice of three parishes, where there is a total population of around 970, the rector is assisted by a retired priest. In the main parish of 570 inhabitants, where the rector lives, there is a family communion service on the first and third Sundays at 11.00 a.m. and evensong every Sunday at 6.30 p.m. On the second and fourth Sundays in the month the 11.00 a.m. service takes place in the neighbouring village of 200 inhabitants.

On the second Sunday this is a straightforward service of matins and on the fourth Sunday a hybrid service of matins and Holy Communion. On the other two Sundays of the month the small village is served by an early Holy Communion service at 8.30 a.m. The rector visits his third parish, also a village of 200 inhabitants, only on the first Sunday in the month for a family communion at 9.30 a.m. The retired priest, however, takes responsibility for a service here every Sunday, including the first Sunday of the month when the rector also visits the parish. His pattern involves evensong at 6.00 p.m. on the first Sunday, matins at 11.00 a.m. on the second and fourth Sundays and Holy Communion at 11.00 a.m. on the third Sunday in the month.

The three benefices of four parishes are also run on very different patterns. In one, where there is a total population of around 1,500, the morning services are all concentrated in the two larger parishes. Evensong rotates round all four churches, at 6.30 p.m. in three of them and 6.00 p.m. in the fourth. The morning services are always Holy Communions. In one church, Holy Communion is celebrated at 8.30 a.m. on the first Sunday in the month and at 10.15 a.m. on the other Sundays. In the other church, Holy Communion is celebrated at 9.30 a.m. on the first Sunday, 9.00 a.m. on the second and third Sundays and 11.30 a.m. on the fourth Sunday in the month.

In the second benefice of four parishes, where there is a total population of around 990 people, Holy Communion is celebrated in one church every Sunday at 8.30 a.m. and in another at 9.30 a.m. In the other two parishes the Sunday service alternates between evensong at 3.30 p.m. and a morning service at 11.00 a.m. Once a month the morning service is matins and on the other occasion Holy Communion. Here the parish priest emphasizes the need for continuity and anticipates the reluctance of rural congregations to move from church to church.

In the third benefice of four parishes, where there is a total population of around 1,600 people and where there is both a curate and a reader, the parish priest emphasizes the importance of each church being treated the same way, whether in a parish of 790 or 90 inhabitants, and expects the rural congregation to move from church to church to attend the service of their choice. Every Sunday there are four services, Holy Communion at 8.30 a.m., matins at 9.30 a.m., family eucharist at 10.30 a.m.

and evensong at 6.00 p.m. These services rotate in strict pattern around the four churches.

By way of summary, in a typical month of four Sundays, 166 services will take place in the Anglican churches in the deanery. Of these 60% are communion services, 27% are evensongs, 10% are matins and 4% are non-eucharistic family services or non-liturgical services of praise.

The proportion of Anglican churches which publicly advertise their services in urban shadow deanery is higher than in other rural areas: twenty-four of the twenty-nine churches displayed information about Sunday services, either in the porch or outside, and a further three of the churches had this information clearly available inside. The vicar's name was publicly displayed outside or in the porch of twenty of the twenty-nine churches; sixteen also included his telephone number and thirteen gave his address. Churchwardens' names were displayed by twelve of the churches, their addresses by eight and their telephone numbers by six of the churches. Information about baptisms and about banns of marriage was displayed in eleven of the churches, while eighteen displayed the statutory table of fees, usually an up-to-date edition.

Architecturally, the churches in the deanery present a wide range of styles, from medieval and Victorian masterpieces to the corrugated-iron mission church. Comparatively little attempt, however, has been made to market these buildings to the many tourists who visit them. Only five of the twenty-nine churches have a guidebook for sale and ten a copy of the parish magazine. Only four have a bookstall. Over half (seventeen) of the churches are kept unlocked during the day, but only two of the remaining twelve indicate how a key may be obtained to gain entry.

Generally speaking, the churches in urban shadow deanery were not making particularly good use of notice-boards and other media to communicate their work; nineteen of the churches had some kind of notice-board outside, but only six or seven of these were in really good shape. In addition to the usual rotas concerned with church cleaning, flower arranging and sidespersons' duties, the main message conveyed by the church notices concerned fund-raising and cultural events. A number of churches displayed a glossy leaflet about the diocesan budget and information about giving under covenant. The main cultural events advertised included a charity antique fair, a patchwork and needlework exhibition, a flower festival and a concert in aid of guide-dogs for the blind.

Many of the churches are beginning to show signs of structural decay, and nine of them are appealing for money for urgent repairs. The market town of 10,000 inhabitants is appealing for £75,000. One of the villages of 260 inhabitants is appealing for £200,000. Many of the small village churches are struggling quite hard to keep their churchyards under control, with voluntary labour from the parish. The awards for the best-kept churchyards have consistently gone to the church which stands in the grounds of and is maintained by a country club.

The six largest parishes in the deanery, the smallest of which has a population of 1,500, all support some form of children's work. Only two of the smaller parishes undertake children's work, one with a population of 200 and the other of 230 inhabitants. The third parish, with a population of 260 inhabitants, had until recently maintained a Sunday school and there is still evidence of some imaginative children's work displayed in the church. However, when the family responsible for running this group moved away, no one else was willing to carry on with the work.

On the fourth Sunday in April, when the church watch survey took place, there were forty-one Anglican services advertised in urban shadow deanery. All the advertised services took place. They included twenty-four services from the Book of Common Prayer or the 1928 Prayer Book, thirteen from *The Alternative Service Book 1980*, one *Alternative Services Second Series* communion service, one *Alternative Services Series 1 & 2 Revised* communion service and two non-liturgical services. From the Book of Common Prayer there were eight services of Holy Communion, four matins, two Holy Communion and matins combined, and ten evensongs. From *The Alternative Service Book 1980* there were eleven communion services following Rite A and two following Rite B. Thus, on this Sunday there were twenty-five communion services, two of which also included matins, four matins without communion, ten evensongs, one family service and one non-liturgical evening service of praise.

Overall, the forty-one services were attended by 1,385 people. This represents 3.5% of the population of the deanery as a whole and averages ninety-two church attenders for each full-time stipendiary minister. In the main area of conurbation served by the team ministry 2.9% of the population attended an Anglican service, averaging 140 worshippers for each full-time minister, while throughout the rest of the deanery 4.1% of the population attended an Anglican service, averaging seventy-five worshippers per full-time minister. Just under two thirds (63%) of the worshippers were female; just over one third (37%) were male. The age group which predominated in the congregations was the forty- to sixty-year-olds, who accounted for 37% of the worshippers. Another 28% were over the age of sixty. This leaves 18% of the worshippers in their twenties or thirties and 17% under the age of twenty-one.

During the course of the day, 67% of the Sunday worshippers attended communion services, 23% attended evensong, 7% attended matins without communion and the remaining 3% attended non-liturgical services.

The best-attended service in the deanery was the 10.30 a.m. Rite A parish communion at the town centre church within the team ministry, where there was a congregation of 190. This church also had a congregation of fifty-seven for the early morning Holy Communion service and seventy-one for even- song. The next best-attended service in the deanery was the 11.15 a.m. Rite A Holy Communion service in the small town of 5,500 inhabitants with a congregation of about one hundred. This church also had a congregation of twenty-six for early morning Holy Communion service and thirty-six for evensong. At the other end of the scale, there were eight services in the deanery with fewer than ten people in the congregation.

Two of the clergy in the deanery are each responsible for four services each Sunday in four different churches. One of them began his Sunday at 8.30 a.m. with Rite A Holy Communion for a congregation of sixteen in a community of 200 people. He arrived five minutes late for the 9.30 a.m. Rite A Holy Commu- nion in a community of 260, where there was a congregation of thirty people. He then arrived eight minutes late for the 11.00 a.m. Book of Common Prayer Holy Communion in a community of 220, where there was a congregation of nine. The Book of Common Prayer evensong at 3.30 p.m. in the fourth parish, where there is a population of 310, attracted a congregation of ten. Overall, the four services made contact with 7% of the inhabitants of the benefice.

The other priest in the deanery who is responsible for four

services each Sunday began at 8.30 a.m. with a Rite A Holy Communion, this time in a community of 790 inhabitants for a congregation of nine. The second service of the day, matins from the Book of Common Prayer at 9.30 a.m. in a community of 500 inhabitants, was left in the hands of a reader. Here there was a congregation of twenty people. The third service, Rite A family eucharist at 10.30 a.m., acts as the main service for the benefice. Held this week in a community of ninety inhabitants, it attracted a congregation of thirty-six. The Book of Common Prayer service of evensong at 6.30 p.m. in the fourth parish, where there is a population of 230, attracted a congregation of seventeen people. Overall, the four services made contact with 5% of the inhabitants of the benefice.

The longest service in the deanery was the combined service of matins and Holy Communion in a parish of 850 inhabitants with a congregation of fifteen. This service lasted for seventy-three minutes. The average time for services in the deanery is fifty-one minutes. Over three-quarters of the forty-one services included a sermon. Half of the sermons (sixteen) lasted ten minutes or less, with the shortest lasting only two minutes. The longest sermon was delivered by a visiting missionary who preached for forty minutes at a village evensong. The average morning sermon lasted for nine minutes, compared with the average evening sermon of seventeen minutes.

Over three-quarters of the forty-one services included some hymn singing. A range of hymn-books was used in the deanery: seven services used the old *Hymns Ancient and Modern: Standard Edition*; sixteen used the *Hymns Ancient and Modern Revised*; one used the *Hymns Ancient and Modern: New Standard Edition*; three used *Mission Praise*; two used the *Anglican Hymn-book*; one used *Hymns for Today*; one used *Sing Praise*; one used the BBC hymn-book for schools, *Come and Praise*.

The parish church at the centre of the team ministry has a very fine musical tradition, with a high quality choir and organist. Some of the other parishes in the deanery also enjoy the benefit of good musicians to play the organ. The family service in the community centre was accompanied by piano and guitar. A guitar was also used to accompany some of the singing in one of the family eucharists. Other parishes in the deanery have difficulty in finding musicians to accompany the singing. In a couple of cases the hymns were sung unaccompanied and in a third the vicar played the organ himself, still robed in stole and chasuble.

The presence of retired clergy, curates, readers and a Church Army captain in the deanery meant that fourteen of the forty-one services were conducted by more than one minister. The ministry resources were not, however, evenly distributed throughout the deanery. In one area services were being conducted by two clergymen and a reader, or by two readers and a clergyman. In other parts of the deanery one priest was to be found conducting four services in four different churches without any form of assistance. Just two services were conducted by readers without the presence of a priest.

Generally, there seemed to be more lay involvement in lesson reading in urban shadow deanery than in other parts of the countryside. Lay people read lessons at three-quarters (thirty) of the services and led some of the prayers at a fifth (eight) of the services. At all but three of the services lay people were involved in taking the collection.

Overall, Anglican churches in urban shadow deanery were better equipped to welcome visitors and to make them feel at home in the service than in other parts of the countryside. At thirty of the forty-one services conducted in the deanery, a lay person welcomed the visitors as they arrived before the service and at three other services this function was being fulfilled by the minister. Service-books and hymn-books were personally handed to the visitors at twenty-eight of the services and were ready waiting in the pews at seven other services. At the remaining six services the books were left out in a prominent place for worshippers to pick up for themselves as they came into church. At none of the services did the visitors experience difficulty in finding the right books.

After thirty-eight of the services the ministers were available to speak with members of the congregation. At only five of the services were the visitors not spoken to by the ministers; at only six were they not spoken to by a lay person. The visitors came away from twenty-eight of the services feeling that the minister had made friendly enquiries and welcomed them, and from twenty-four of the services feeling that a lay person had made friendly enquiries and welcomed them.

Free Churches

Next to Anglicanism, the denomination with the largest number of buildings in the countryside is Methodism. In urban shadow deanery there are today six active Methodist churches, compared with twenty-nine active Anglican churches. There are also eleven closed Methodist chapels which have either been converted to other uses or left to stand empty, compared with two redundant Anglican churches. In addition to these closures, other chapels may also have been closed and demolished, leaving no sign of their former existence.

Three of the surviving Methodist chapels are in the three historic towns in the deanery, currently with populations of 10,000, 5,500 and 1,500 people. In each of these centres the Methodist church has retained a manse and continues to employ a full-time stipendiary minister. Two of the surviving Methodist chapels are in villages of 900 and 260 inhabitants and stand quite close to the Anglican churches. The sixth chapel is in a small hamlet, nearly a couple of miles from the nearest Anglican church. Collectively, the six Methodist chapels provide seating for about 640 people, representing one in sixty-one (1.6%) of the total population.

The eleven closed chapels are scattered widely throughout the deanery. Some have been closed for many years, as congregations representing various branches of Methodism have gradually united. Others have closed much more recently as dwindling membership has found it increasingly difficult to maintain the fellowship. Methodist policy in urban shadow deanery has tended to favour concentrating resources on the larger chapels and accepting the closure of the smaller chapels in more rural communities. In one quite small village in the deanery the closed Wesleyan chapel and the closed Primitive chapel stand in the same street. One closed when the congregations joined in the 1930s and the other closed quite recently when the membership could no longer afford the upkeep of the ageing building.

All of the six surviving Methodist chapels maintain a regular pattern of Sunday worship. Each of the three chapels in the towns hold two services every Sunday, at 11.00 a.m. and 6.30 p.m. The chapels in the little hamlet and the smaller of the two villages hold their services at 2.30 p.m., and the other chapel at 10.30 a.m.

In addition to the regular pattern of Sunday services, all six chapels maintain weekly Sunday schools. The four chapels which hold a Sunday morning service operate their Sunday schools concurrently with this service. The children attend the first part of the service and then withdraw for their own class. One of the smaller chapels runs its Sunday school on Sunday morning, although it has no service at this time, while the other holds a Friday club between 6.00 p.m. and 7.00 p.m. for five- to seven-year-olds.

The three town chapels in urban shadow deanery have professional notice-boards and provide all the key information about Sunday and weekday activities, and about the minister. The three smaller chapels make quite a contrast, since none of them provides any information about ministry or pastoral care and only one displays a notice about Sunday service times. All six chapels are kept locked and only the one in the largest town gives the caretaker's name and address.

The three town chapels are all well cared for and in good state of repair. One had a new building opened in the mid-1960s, while another, built originally sixty years ago, was significantly enlarged and modernized in the 1980s. The three village chapels were built between 1811 and 1837 and all of them are now in need of significant restoration.

On the church watch weekend all nine of the regular Sunday Methodist services took place, one at 10.30 a.m., three at 11.00 a.m., two at 2.30 p.m. and three at 6.30 p.m. All three of the Methodist ministers who live in the deanery conducted one of the services in the town in which they lived, the other service in these three chapels being conducted by local preachers. Two of the services in the village chapels were conducted by local preachers and one by a minister who lives outside the deanery. Four of the local preachers placed in the deanery this Sunday were men in their fifties, while the fifth was a woman in her thirties. One of the Methodist services included Holy Communion.

A sermon was preached at all the nine Methodist services. These varied in length from fifteen to thirty minutes and averaged twenty-three minutes. Overall, the average length of the Methodist services in the deanery was sixty-two minutes, eleven minutes longer than the average length of the Anglican services in the deanery.

The overall attendance at these nine services was 364 people. This represents 0.9% of the population, compared with 3.5% who attended Anglican services in the deanery. Two-thirds (66%) of the worshippers were female and one third (34%) were male, making very similar proportions to those found in the Anglican churches in the deanery. While the age group which predominated in the Anglican congregations was the forty- to sixty-year-olds, in the Methodist congregation it was the over-sixty year olds. In the Methodist congregation nearly two out of every five worshippers (37%) were over sixty and a further quarter (25%) were in their forties or fifties. This leaves 7% of the worshippers in their twenties or thirties and 30% under the age of twenty-one. In comparison with the number of adult worshippers, the Methodist churches are attracting a considerably larger number of children than the Anglican churches in the deanery, primarily because all six chapels provide a specialist ministry for children. It is mainly the under-eleven year olds who are attracted by this ministry. The real weakness in these chapels occurs in the absence of sixteen- to forty-year-olds.

Another way of assessing the strength of Methodism in urban shadow deanery is to examine the number of adult worshippers attending the services. The best-attended morning service in the deanery attracted 112 adult worshippers in the main market town. The evening service in the same chapel attracted fifty-one adult worshippers. In the second town there were twenty-eight adults in the morning congregation and fourteen in the evening congregation. In the third town there were twenty adults in the morning congregation and ten in the evening congregation. The three village chapels attracted nine, eight and three adult worshippers.

All the Methodist services were accompanied by organ or harmonium. Generally, the standard of playing in the deanery was good. In one of the village chapels the young female organist did double duty as Sunday school teacher. After the children were withdrawn halfway through the service into their own class, the remaining hymns were sung unaccompanied. All the services involved lay people in taking the collection. This task was performed either by senior adults or by children under the age of ten. At five of the nine services lay people gave hymn-books to the worshippers as they came in. At only one of the nine services was someone from the congregation involved in reading a lesson. At the other eight services the lessons were read by the minister or the local preacher conducting the service.

All the Methodist congregations in urban shadow deanery helped the visitors to feel welcome. At eight of the nine services the visitors were welcomed by a lay person as they arrived and at two of the services they were shown to a seat. At six of the services the minister or local preacher leading the worship made a point of speaking to the visitor after the service and four of them found time to make friendly enquiries. One of the ministers went as far as inviting the visitor back to the manse for coffee after the service, saying how delighted he was to find a young visitor joining his usual evening congregation of ten people.

In addition to Methodism, the urban shadow countryside is able to support a much wider range of denominations than are the accessible, less accessible and marginal countryside. In the urban shadow countryside it is not the villages, but the expanded market town and its satellite communities which provide the context for the other churches, chapels and centres of worship. Within less than three miles in this part of the deanery, the Anglican, Methodist and Catholic churches are joined by nine other places of worship, including Baptist, Christadelphian, Christian Fellowship, Christian Science, Elim Pentecostal, Salvation Army, Society of Friends, the United Reformed church and the Jehovah's Witnesses. Members of these denominations who live in the smaller towns and villages in urban shadow deanery are often able to commute into the expanded market town to attend their preferred type of service, with much greater ease than people who live in the accessible, less accessible or marginal countryside.

The Baptist chapel is a sturdy Victorian building, complete with adjoining schoolroom. The notice-board outside indicates that there are two services every Sunday at 11.00 a.m. and 6.30 p.m. and that Junior Church is held concurrently with the morning service. The only other information available on the notice-board is the minister's name, but neither his address nor telephone number is provided. The chapel is kept locked. Inside there is seating for about 160 people.

During the week the chapel offers a range of activities for its members. The Girls' Brigade meets on Tuesday. The company section of the Boys' Brigade meets on Thursday and the junior section on Friday. The prayer and Bible study group meets on Wednesday and the choir practice happens on Thursday. There is a prayer meeting on Saturday morning and a youth club after the evening service on Sunday. Various house groups meet on Tuesday and Wednesday evenings. The chapel supports a full-time minister who lives in the town.

On the church watch weekend the morning congregation contained just over 180 worshippers who filled every available pew. The whole age range was present in church, but the emphasis was clearly on the under-tens and the over-sixties. The evening congregation contained thirty-four worshippers, with the emphasis on the forty-to-sixty age group. No one under the age of thirty attended the evening service, in spite of the advertised youth group happening after the service. The morning service was conducted by the minister, while the evening service was conducted by a lay leader.

The Christadelphian meeting room is in a new building near the market square. Outside, the notice-board draws attention to the 'memorial meeting' on Sunday morning at 10.45 a.m., the 'public lecture' on Sunday evening at 6.30 p.m. and the Bible class on Tuesday evening at 8.00 p.m. The meeting room is kept locked and no other information is available from the notice-board. Inside there is seating for about fifty people. Christadelphians do not employ full-time ministers.

On the church watch weekend the morning congregation contained thirty-one people, including two children of primary school age, a sole secondary school student, three adults in their thirties, six adults in their forties or fifties and nineteen people over the age of sixty. The evening congregation contained thirty people, including a single teenager, eight adults in their twenties or thirties, eleven adults in their forties or fifties and ten over the age of sixty.

While the evening service is advertised as a public lecture, the tightly knit congregation seemed somewhat surprised to receive a visitor, especially someone who is not a member of another Christadelphian meeting. The morning memorial meeting is clearly not intended for non-members. The visitor was made to feel an outsider and was actually told that she did not need to contribute to the two collections, because she was not a member.

The Christian Fellowship is based on the local youth centre, where the notice-board displays the fact that the fellowship meets every Sunday at 10.30 a.m. During the week a network or prayer-and-study group takes place in individual members' homes. The Christian Fellowship would like to be able to set aside one of its members for full-time ministry, but the fellowship is not yet sufficiently well established in the town to be able to afford to do this. At present its effective leader is a former Baptist minister who supports himself and his family through a part-time job.

On the church watch weekend the congregation contained forty-three people, including two preschoolers, nine primary aged children, four secondary aged children, twenty adults in their twenties or thirties and eight adults in their forties of fifties. There was no one in the fellowship over the age of sixty.

The Christian Science reading room is housed in a delightful eighteenth-century private house, set back from the market square in its own grounds. A new meeting room has been built on to the side of this old house to provide seating for about sixty people. The notice-board outside advertises the morning and evening services at 11.00 a.m. and 6.30 p.m. and sets out the times when the reading room is open during the week. The church has no full-time minister.

On the church watch weekend there was a morning congregation of seventeen and an evening congregation of nine, making a total of twenty-six worshippers, of whom seventeen were over the age of sixty. One teenager attended the evening service with her grandmother. Before and after both services the steward welcomed the visitors most warmly and invited them to return when the reading room was open to the public.

The Elim Pentecostal chapel is a small Victorian building tucked away in the old part of the village which has now become absorbed by the expanding town. The notice-board indicates that on the first Sunday in the month there is a family service at 11.00 a.m. and communion at 6.30 p.m. On the other Sundays at 11.00 a.m. there is a communion service and at 6.30 p.m. a gospel service. On Wednesday evenings there is the Good News club for children at 6.15 p.m. and a Bible study or discussion group for adults at 7.30 p.m. The notice-board also displays the pastor's name and telephone number. The pastor lives in another large town some thirty miles away.

On the church watch weekend there was a morning congregation of twenty-three and an evening congregation of fifteen, making a total of thirty-eight worshippers. A high proportion (42%) of the attenders were over the age of sixty and the majority (82%) were female. The morning congregation included a single preschooler and three primary aged children; the evening congregation included a sole young teenager attending with her parents.

The Salvation Army citadel is a slightly scruffy turn-of-the-century hall in a side street not far from the market square. The notice-board advertises two Sunday services: the 'holiness meeting' at 11.00 a.m. and the 'salvation meeting' at 6.30 p.m. On Tuesday there is a ladies' meeting at 3.00 p.m. and on Thursday a prayer and Bible fellowship at 7.30 p.m. No information is displayed about the local minister, although a full-time commanding officer occupies the house adjoining the citadel.

On the church watch weekend there was a morning congregation of twenty-nine and an evening congregation of seventeen. Half of the morning worshippers were over the age of sixty, but there was also a significant group of young people in their late teens or twenties. Two-thirds of the evening worshippers were over the age of sixty and there was no one present under the age of thirty.

The Society of Friends meets in the private house of one of its members, at 11.00 a.m. every Sunday. On the church watch weekend twelve members attended, four men and eight women. Three of their members were in their late forties or fifties and the other nine were over the age of sixty. An elderly lady opened the meeting and during the next hour two of the members made a brief contribution. The members were anxious to welcome the visitor.

The United Reformed church occupies a prominent site on the market square. It is a Victorian Gothic building, complete with small tower and spire, built to seat about 250 people. Currently the building is in need of major structural repair. The notice-board outside indicates that the minister lives in another town some ten miles away. It still advertises a regular pattern of morning and evening worship, although in practice dwindling congregations have encouraged the church to abandon its evening service and to concentrate entirely on a pattern of morning worship. The minister comes twice a month, once to conduct 'morning worship and communion' and once to conduct 'morning worship and family church'. On the other Sundays morning worship is often conducted by visiting ministers or preachers.

On the church watch weekend the morning service was attended by a total of sixty-five people, an evenly balanced mixture of men and women. This included ten children of primary school age, who were withdrawn during the second hymn for the Sunday school, a teenager, twenty adults under the age of sixty and thirty-six adults over the age of sixty.

The Jehovah's Witnesses have recently built a new kingdom hall on the edge of the old market town. The kingdom hall has no notice-board outside and displays no information about times of meetings. For those in the know, every Sunday there is the 'Bible educational talk', a different vital topic on current needs each week, at 10.00 a.m. and the 'watchtower study', a question-and-answer meeting on selected Bible subjects, at 10.50 a.m. On Tuesday evening at 7.30 p.m. there is the 'congregation book study', a systematic discussion of religion's role in life. On Thursday evening there is the 'theocratic ministry school', a speaking course featuring the teachings of the Bible, at 7.00 p.m., followed at 7.50 p.m. by the 'service meeting', talks and demonstrations on practical use of Bible knowledge.

On the church watch weekend the Sunday service was attended by about one hundred people, with three times as many women as men. The predominant age group was the forty- to sixty-year-olds who accounted for 45% of those present. There were three preschoolers, six children of primary school age, six teenagers, thirty adults under the age of forty and ten adults over the age of sixty. The Sunday service lasted for 125 minutes.

By way of summary, the Baptists, Christadelphians, Christian Fellowship, Christian Scientists, Elim Pentecostalists, Salvation Army, Society of Friends, United Reformed church and Jehovah's Witnesses provide seating for about 760 people, representing one in fifty-two (1.9%) of the total population. On the church watch weekend these denominations attracted a total of 605 worshippers, representing one in sixty-five (1.5%) of the total population.

Roman Catholic

There are five Catholic churches in urban shadow deanery. The oldest was built in the 1850s in the small village where the Anglican church is now temporarily closed. The largest was built in the 1860s in the major market town in the deanery. As the market town expanded to absorb the two neighbouring villages, two new Catholic churches were opened to serve the growing needs of the Catholic community. Another new Catholic church has been recently built in a village of 1,500 inhabitants. Collectively, these five churches provide seating for about 760 people, representing one in fifty-two (1.9%) of the total population. The Catholic community also holds a weekly Mass in the Anglican parish church in the town of 5,500 people.

All five Catholic churches clearly displayed information about Sunday Masses and weekday Masses and gave the parish priest's telephone number; one also gave the parish priest's name. Three Catholic priests live within the area of urban shadow deanery. Three of the churches are kept unlocked during the day. The other two are kept locked without indicating where the key may be obtained. The oldest of the churches, in a very small village, is appealing for £2,000 towards urgent repairs on the roof. The other four buildings appear to be in good structural repair.

Mass is celebrated at the same time in the same place every week in urban shadow deanery. In the main church in the town there are four 'Sunday Masses', at 5.30 p.m. on Saturdays and at 8.30 a.m., 11.00 a.m. and 6.30 p.m. on Sundays. In the two satellite villages around the town, Mass is celebrated on Sunday at 9.30 a.m. and 10.00 a.m. In the other two village churches Mass is celebrated at 10.00 a.m. and 11.00 a.m. and in the Anglican parish church at 5.00 p.m. on Saturday evenings.

On the church watch weekend these nine Masses were attended by 1,111 people. This represents 2.8% of the population of the deanery as a whole and averages 370 church attenders for each priest. The best-attended mass was the Saturday evening service in the town, with a congregation of 220, while the Saturday evening Mass held in the Anglican parish church in the market town of 5,500 attracted the smallest congregation of thirty-one people.

The proportions of male and female worshippers attending

the Catholic services were almost exactly the same as those attending the Anglican services. Just under two-thirds (64%) of the worshippers were female; just over one third (36%) were male.

Overall, the Catholic services attracted a more even spread of ages than the Anglican services. At the Catholic services a quarter (25%) of the worshippers were under the age of twenty-one, a little over a quarter (27%) were in their twenties or thirties, a little over a quarter (28%) were in their forties or fifties and a little under a quarter (21%) were over the age of sixty. Different Masses were particularly strong on different age groups. The 10.00 a.m. Mass in one of the satellite villages attracted a number of young families with children. At this Mass the hymns were accompanied by a children's music group and the offertory procession was conducted by six- to twelve-year-olds. The Sunday evening Mass in the main parish church attracted a number of teenagers. At this service the music was provided by young guitarists, while the lessons, intercessions and offertory were all in the hands of teenagers.

The Masses varied in length from thirty to sixty-three minutes and averaged forty-six minutes. The preaching at these Masses was variable. One priest seemed to have taken a great deal of trouble to prepare his message and adapt it to the different styles of congregation, while another priest simply read a homily prepared by the Catholic Missionary Society and made that homily sound dull. The sermons ranged in length between three and eleven minutes and averaged seven and a half minutes. Two of the services, the Saturday evening service in the Anglican church and the early morning Sunday service in the main town, involved no singing. At two services the hymns were accompanied by young musicians and at four by quite competent organists. At the Saturday evening Mass in the main town the singing was unaccompanied and unenthusiastic. Six of the services used *Celebration Hymnal*, augmented in some cases by printed sheets; the other service used the *Catholic Hymn-book*. At four of the Masses a layman took a significant role in leading the ministry of the word. At all but one of the services lay people were involved in reading lessons, including a preadolescent boy and three teenagers. The peace was celebrated at all but one of the services.

The Catholic services in urban shadow deanery very clearly gave the impression that they were not expecting non-Catholics in the congregation, and little attempt was made to welcome visitors or to help them feel at home. At none of the services was the visitor welcomed by the priest or by a lay person. At eight of the services hymn-books and missalettes were left in a pile near the door or left ready in the pews. For the Catholic service in the Anglican parish church no Catholic books or missalettes were available. The regular worshippers brought their own and the visitor felt excluded. After four of the nine services the priest was available near the door to speak with members of the congregation, but only after one service did he try to greet everyone on departure. Only three of the nine visitors were spoken to by the priest or by other members of the congregation. The other six came away without having made any personal contact with the people among whom they had worshipped. Only a single visitor felt that she had been to a friendly church.

Summary

When all the denominations present in urban shadow deanery are viewed together, the 39,500 inhabitants are served by forty-nine churches. In other words, there is one church for every 800 people. Together these churches provide seating for 8,235 people, or one in five (20.8%) of the population. On a typical Sunday there are 3,464 attendances at public worship, representing nearly one in eleven (8.8%) of the population. There are twenty-three full-time ministers of religion living in urban shadow deanery, one for every 1,700 inhabitants.

POSTSCRIPT

WHEN EACH CHURCH watch weekend draws to a close, it is inevitable that those who have been involved in the exercise of participant observation will want to stand back from the objective recording of what they have seen, heard and experienced, in order to reflect on the significance and meaning of their newly organized data. This, after all, is part of the learning process.

Listening to the personal reflection and interpretation of data by those who have painstakingly organized them may involve at least three dangers. The first danger is to assume that the skill needed to collect the data may confer a particular authority on the interpretation. This is clearly not the case. Very different skills are involved in conducting church-related research, from the skills involved in drawing out the practical implications for ministry and mission. The second danger is to dismiss the research out of hand, if we disagree with the researchers' interpretations and conclusions. Clearly, the evidence must be allowed to stand or fall on the criteria according to which it was assembled, independently of the interpretation placed on it. The third danger is to accept uncritically the interpretation offered by the researchers, if we happen to respect the underlying methods of research. Clearly, data may be open to multiple interpretations.

In the case of interpreting research data about the rural church, there is also a fourth danger. It is very easy to misunderstand and to misrepresent the dynamics of rural religion, especially for people brought up in the atmosphere of urban or suburban churches.

In spite of these limitations, I have listened with respect to the insights generated in the minds of ordinands from the church watch experience. Their discussions have raised in my mind seven crucial questions. I believe that these questions have to be faced and resolved, if rural churches are to be given the chance of a secure future into the twenty-first century.

The first question is the fundamental one as to whether there is still a natural link between rural churches and rural society. Many commentators still draw the distinction between the *associational* church, which characterizes towns, cities and suburbia, and the *community* church, which characterizes the countryside. This distinction argues that in towns, cities and suburbia people identify with churches because they attend them. In the countryside they identify with churches because they live alongside them. In the countryside, it is argued, the threshold between church and society is much lower and easier to cross.

Our experience, gained from the church watch programme, causes us to question the long-term validity of this distinction. Talking with people in villages, we have been surprised how little many of them know about the local churches or how little many of them care about the local churches. It seems to us that, where the community model of the rural church still operates, it operates best among an ageing population who have their roots firmly fixed in the countryside. It has not transferred so well to incomers; nor has it been communicated so successfully to a younger generation.

The second question concerns the capability of rural churches to attract and to nurture a new generation of churchgoers. The community model of the rural church argues that it is inappropriate for rural churches to attempt to emulate the suburban model of house groups, children's classes, and so on. The nurturing process into the Christian community is sustained in other less obvious ways.

Our experience, gained from the church watch programme, causes us to wonder whether there are now sufficient opportunities in some rural churches properly to secure the Christian future. We simply wonder whether small and elderly congregations are capable of attracting, involving and nurturing children and young families into the Christian heritage, against the background of an increasingly secular society which is not cooperating with the churches in their mission.

The third question concerns the preservation of the historic distinctions between the denominations in the countryside. In some small communities we have seen chapel and church continue to struggle side by side, each maintaining a strenuous commitment to buildings and to traditions.

Our experience, gained from the church watch programme, causes us to recognize the intractable nature of this problem in so many areas. From talking with committed churchgoers and committed chapelgoers in these situations, we know that historic divisions die hard. In so many places, the solution seems only to come when those religious groups, less well subsidized than the Church of England, age, die and close, and when yet another chapel is converted into an attractive country cottage or left to decay.

The fourth question concerns the patterns of services provided by rural Anglican churches. Three main models exist. Some clergy operate the system of holding one major service and inviting churchgoers from several communities to join together. Some clergy try to hold a service at the same time in the same church each week. Some clergy try to offer each church a varied pattern, with a different form of service at a different time each week. It seems strange to some of us that there was no consensus about the respective merits of these different models, and no clear research to assess their respective effectiveness.

Our experience, gained from the church watch programme, highlights problems with all three models. In some places the theory that churchgoers will travel to one central act of worship is clearly contradicted by their practice. The model of different services at different times each week was clearly confusing to some worshippers and left some of our visitors waiting for services which never happened. The model of a single priest conducting four services on a Sunday morning in four different churches can often lead to rushed services and to exhausted clergy.

The fifth question concerns the development of local lay ministry, in whose hands the future of the rural churches can be safely left. The current generation of ordinands is clearly impressed by the theory of all-member ministry, and by the theology that baptism equips for ministry. Shared ministry and ministry teams offer much promise for the future of rural religion.

Our experience, gained from the church watch programme, however, fails to find much of this vision as yet in practice. More disturbingly, when the church watch visitors looked round many of the congregations, they failed to identify easily the potential for this form of ministry waiting there to be developed. When we talked with some rural churchwardens, we recognized how stretched some busy lay people were already in maintaining their commitment to the rural church and how they shrank from having further expectations placed upon their shoulders.

The sixth question concerns the deployment of training professional ministers in the countryside. One school of thought argues that only those churches which can generate sufficient income to support a minister should justify receiving one. According to this school of thought, the time has come for larger suburban churches to stop subsidizing failing rural churches. A different argument sees the rural church as an area of mission, which deserves support and financial subsidy.

Our experience, gained from the church watch programme, highlights the poverty of areas of the rural church in comparison with the suburban church. Some small congregations are clearly not in a position to take responsibility for their own future and necessarily remain dependent on the provision of a subsidized ministry. It seemed to us that to reduce ministry any further in some rural areas would be to pronounce the demise for rural religion in those communities. Unfortunately, the church watch team had not been able to visit the Borchester deanery and to observe the experience of church life at St Stephen's in Ambridge, during the period of time when pastoral care was in the hands of the Revd Robin Stokes. Mr Stokes was licensed as non-stipendiary priest-in-charge of Ambridge and installed in the vicarage, while earning his living as the local vet. For some of us, however, it seems eminently sensible to develop *The Archers'* model of rural ministry, deploying a fully professional non-stipendiary priest, resident within the vicarage.

The seventh question concerns the potential ministry of rural churches and chapels to tourists, holiday-makers and occasional residents. It is often when people are away from their place of work that they have time to reflect on life and to face the deeper questions of meaning, purpose, values and religion. An enormous resource exists in the buildings, services and ministry of the rural churches to respond to the needs and questings of people who turn to the countryside for their personal recreation.

Our experience, gained from the church watch programme, underlines a repeated story of missed opportunity at this level. So many rural churches now seem to exist as tightly knit inward-looking communities. They see no need to open their building to visitors. They see no need to provide Christian literature or aids to prayer to help visitors on their spiritual pilgrimage. They see no need to identify who it is within the community who can proclaim the gospel of salvation and meet with those in need. They see no need to advertise their services. They feel able to change the times of services or to cancel services, simply by telephoning round the faithful few.

In sharing these reflections, I am not wishing to inflict yet another 'doom-laden' report on the rural church. I acknowledge and welcome all the signs of life and vitality which we have discovered on our visits. I rejoice in those places which have extended to us a warm welcome and furthered our pilgrimage. At the same time, however, I recognize that it is of crucial importance for the churches to be *realistic* about the challenges facing them in rural ministry.

Personally, I can only see a promising future for rural religion, if the various denominations still concerned with churches and chapels in the countryside agree on a coherent and coordinated strategy. This strategy needs to plan ecumenically for the provision of buildings (including churches, chapels, halls, manses and parsonages), for the deployment of trained professional personnel (including both stipendiary and non-stipendiary ministers), and for the training and support of local ministry teams. Such planning could revitalize the future of rural religion.

NOTES

Chapter 1

1. Carroll, Lewis, *Through the Looking Glass* (London: Puffin, 1962), p. 274.
2. Russell, Anthony, *The Country Parish* (London: SPCK, 1986), p. 4.
3. Russell, Anthony, 'The Changing Rural Community', in *A Second Workbook on Rural Evangelism* (Dorchester: Partners, 1984), p. 3.
4. Russell, *The Country Parish*, p. 3.
5. Russell, Anthony, *Christian Unity in the Village* (London: British Council of Churches, 1987), p. 8.
6. *A Rural Strategy for the Church of England: A Proposal for an Archbishops' Commission on Rural Areas* (London: General Synod, GS Misc 247, 1986), p. 2.
7. Lewis, Richard and Talbot-Ponsonby, Andrew (eds.), *The People, the Land and the Church* (Hereford: Hereford Diocesan Board of Finance, 1987), p. 24.
8. Bowden, Andrew, *Ministry in the Countryside: A Model for the Future* (London: Mowbray, 1994), p. 67.
9. Francis, Leslie J., *Rural Anglicanism* (London: Collins Liturgical Publications, 1985), ch. 8.
10. Francis, *Rural Anglicanism*, p. 87.

Chapter 2

1. See Leech, Joseph, *Rural Rides of the Bristol Churchgoer* (Gloucester: Alan Sutton, 1982).
2. Moore, Charles, Wilson, A. N. and Stamp, Gavin, *The Church in Crisis* (London: Hodder and Stoughton, 1986).

BIBLIOGRAPHY

Archbishop of Canterbury's Commission On Urban Priority Areas (1985), *Faith in the City*. London: Church House Publishing.

Archbishops' Commission on Rural Areas (1990), *Faith in the Countryside*. Worthing: Churchman Publishing.

Bailey, E. (ed.) (1986), *A Workbook in Popular Religion*. Dorchester: Partners Publications.

Beasley-Murray, P. and Wilkinson, A. (1981), *Turning the Tide*. London: Bible Society.

Blunden, J. and Curry, N. (1988), *A Future for Our Countryside*. Oxford: Basil Blackwell.

Bowden, A. (1994), *Ministry in the Countryside*. London: Mowbray.

Brierley, P. (ed.) (1980), *Prospect for the Eighties: From a Census of the Churches in 1979*. London: Bible Society.

Brierley, P. (1983), *Prospect for the Eighties,* Volume Two. London: MARC Europe.

Brierley, P. (1991), *'Christian' England*. London: MARC Europe.

British Council of Churches (1945), *The Land, the People and the Churches*. London: SCM.

Calvert, I. (ed.) (1977), *A Workbook on Rural Evangelism*. Guildford: The Archbishop's Council on Evangelism.

Calvert, I. (ed.) (1984), *A Second Workbook on Rural Evangelism*. Dorchester: Partners Publications.

Carr, W. (1981), *Organising the Ministry of the Church of England in a Rural Context*. Chelmsford: Cathedral Centre for Research and Training.

Church in Wales (1992), *The Church in the Welsh Countryside*. Penarth: Church in Wales Board of Mission.

Clarke, J.E. (1978), *Mission in Rural Communities*. London: Methodist Church Home Mission Division.

Clarke, J.N. and Anderson, C.L. (1986), *Methodism in the Countryside*. Horncastle: Clarke and Anderson.

Cloke, P. and Edwards, G. (1986), 'Rurality in England and Wales 1981: A Replication of the 1971 Index', *Regional Studies*, 20, 289–306.

Cutts, D. (1989), *Worship in Small Congregations*. Nottingham: Grove Books.

Davies, D., Pack, C., Seymour, S., Short, C., Watkins, C. and Winter, M. (1990), *Staff and Buildings: Rural Church Project*, Volume One. Cirencester: Centre for Rural Studies, Royal Agricultural College.

Davies, D., Pack, C., Seymour, S., Short, C., Watkins, C. and Winter,

M. (1990), *The Clergy Life: Rural Church Project*, Volume Two. Cirencester: Centre for Rural Studies, Royal Agricultural College.

Davies, D., Pack, C., Seymour, S., Short, C., Watkins, C. and Winter, M. (1990), *Parish Life and Rural Religion: Rural Church Project*, Volume Three. Cirencester: Centre for Rural Studies, Royal Agricultural College.

Davies, D., Pack, C., Seymour, S., Short, C., Watkins, C. and Winter, M. (1990), *The View of Rural Parishioners: Rural Church Project*, Volume Four. Cirencester: Centre for Rural Studies, Royal Agricultural College.

Davies, D., Watkins, C. and Winter, M. (1991), *Church and Religion in Rural England*. Edinburgh: T and T Clark.

Diocese of Chelmsford (1993), *Sharing Faith in the Countryside*. Chelmsford: Council for Mission and Unity.

Diocese of Ely (1988), *Ministry: A Report to the Bishop from the Ministry Advisory Group*. Ely: Diocesan Office.

Dorey, T. (1979), *Rural Ministry*. Oxford: Oxford Institute for Church and Society.

Dow, G., Ashton, P., Gillett, D. and Prior, D. (1983), *Whose Hand on the Tiller?* Nottingham: Grove Books.

Down, M. (1984), 'The Shape of the Rural Church', *Theology*, 87, 164–172.

Dudley, C.S. (1978), *Making the Small Church Effective*. Nashville, Tennessee: Abingdon.

Eaton, D. (1984), 'Ministry in Surrey Villages', *New Fire*, 8, 203–8.

Ecclestone, G. (ed.) (1988), *The Parish Church?* London: Mowbray.

Edmondson, C. (1989), *Strategies for Rural Evangelism*. Nottingham: Grove Books.

Edwards, G. (1980), *Rural Mission*. London: Baptist Church House, Mission Department.

Francis, L.J. (1985), *Rural Anglicanism: A Future for Young Christians?* London: Collins Liturgical Publications.

Francis, L.J. (1989), *The Country Parson*. Leominster: Gracewing.

Francis L.J. (1994), 'Priority Given to Rural and Urban Ministry in Initial Clergy Training in the Church of England', *Crucible*, 33, 186–9.

Francis, L.J. and Lankshear, D.W. (1990), 'The Impact of Church Schools on Village Church Life', *Educational Studies*, 16, 117–29.

Francis, L.J. and Lankshear, D.W. (1991), 'Do Small Churches Hold a Future for Children and Young People?' *Modern Churchman*, 33, 15–19.

Francis, L.J. and Lankshear, D.W. (1991), 'Faith in the Isle of Wight: A Profile of Rural Anglicanism', *Contact*, 105, 28–33.

Francis, L.J. and Lankshear, D.W. (1992), 'The Rural Factor: A

Comparative Survey of Village Churches and the Liturgical Work of Rural Clergy', *Modern Churchman*, 34, 1–9.

Francis, L.J. and Lankshear, D.W. (1992), 'The Rural Rectory: The Impact of a Resident Priest on Local Church Life', *Journal of Rural Studies*, 8, 97–103.

Francis, L.J. and Lankshear, D.W. (1992), 'The Impact of Children's Work on Church Life in Hamlets and Small Villages', *Journal of Christian Education*, 35, 57–63.

Francis, L.J. and Lankshear, D.W. (1992), 'The Impact of Children's Work on Village Church Life', *Spectrum*, 21, 35–45.

Francis, L.J. and Lankshear, D.W. (1993), 'Ageing Anglican Clergy and Performance Indicators in the Rural Church, Compared with the Suburban Church', *Ageing and Society*, 13, 339–63.

Francis, L.J. and Lankshear, D.W. (1993), 'The Implications of Changing Trends in Anglican Confirmation for Local Church Life', *Journal of Empirical Theology*, 6, 1, 64–76.

Francis L.J. and Lankshear, D.W. (1994), 'The Deployment of Ageing Clergy within the Church of England', *Psychological Reports*, 75, 366.

Francis, L.J. and Williams, K. (1991), *Churches in Fellowship: Local Councils of Churches in England*. London: BCC/CCBI.

Gill, R. (1977), 'Theology of the Non-Stipendiary Ministry', *Theology*, 80, 410–13.

Gill, R. (1988), *Beyond Decline: A Challenge to the Churches*. London: SCM.

Gill, R. (1989), *Competing Convictions*. London: SCM.

Gill, R. (1993), *The Myth of the Empty Church*. London: SPCK.

Hodge, M. (1983), *Non-Stipendiary Ministry in the Church of England*. London: Church Information Office Publishing.

Hopkins, S. (1970), *The Rural Ministry*. London: SPCK.

Jewiss, O.R. (Chairman) (1981), *The Rural Face of the Diocese*. Oxford: Diocesan Board for Social Responsibility.

Lathe, A. (1986), *The Group: The Story of Eight Country Churches*. Norwich: The Hempnell Group Council.

Lewis, R. and Talbot-Ponsonby, A. (1987), *The People, the Land and the Church*. Hereford: Hereford Diocesan Board of Finance.

Luke, R.H. (1982), *The Commission of the Church in the Countryside*. London: Chester House Publications.

Martineau, J. (ed.) (1995), *Turning the Sod: A Workbook on the Multi-Parish Benefice*. Stoneleigh: Acora Publishing.

Morgan, E.R. (Chairman) (1940), *The Church in Country Parishes*. London: SPCK.

Mullen, P. (1984), *Rural Rites*. London: Triangle/SPCK.

Musselwhite, M. (Chairman) (1975), *Youth and the Rural Church*. London: Methodist Home Mission Department.

Newton, C. (1981), *Life and Death in the Country Church*. London: Church of England Board of Mission and Unity.

Nott, P. (1978), 'Teams and Groups and their Problems', *Theology*, 81, 14–17.

Obelkewitch, J. (1976), *Religion and Society in South Lindsay*. Oxford: Clarendon Press.

Osborn, B. (1992), *The Key to Effective Rural Evangelism*. Hastings: Sunrise Ministries.

Paul, L. (1964), *The Deployment and Payment of the Clergy*. London: Church Information Office.

Paul, L., Russell, A. and Reading, L. (eds) (1977), *Rural Society and the Church*. Hereford: Diocesan Board of Finance.

Poulton, J. (1985), *Fresh Air: A Vision for the Future of the Rural Church*. Basingstoke: Marshall.

Ranson, S., Bryman, A. and Hinings, B. (1977), *Clergy, Ministers and Priests*. London: Routledge and Kegan Paul.

Richardson, J. (ed.) (1988), *Ten Rural Churches*. Eastbourne: MARC.

Rural Theology Association (1989), *The Rural Church: Towards 2000*. Bulwick: Rural Theology Association.

Russell, A. (ed.) (1975), *Groups and Teams in the Countryside*. London: SPCK.

Russell, A. (1975), *Village in Myth and Reality*. London: Chester House.

Russell, A. (1980), *The Clerical Profession*. London: SPCK.

Russell, A. (1986), *The Country Parish*. London: SPCK.

Russell, A. (1987), *Christian Unity in the Village*. London: BCC.

Russell, A. (1993), *The Country Parson*. London: SPCK.

Sedgewick, P. (ed.) (1984), *A Rural Life Reader*. Satley: Northern Institute for Rural Life.

Sim, R.A. (1990), *The Plight of the Rural Church*. Toronto: United Church Publishing House.

Smethurst, D. (1986), *Extended Communion: An Experiment in Cumbria*. Nottingham: Grove Books.

Smith, A.C. (1960), *The South Ormsby Experiment: An Adventure in Friendship*. London: SPCK.

Stuart, J. (ed.) (1992), *Rural Realities, Creation or Chaos: Report of the Third Australasian Rural Ministry Conference*. Christchurch: University of Canterbury.

Thomas, W.J. (1969), 'Is the Vicar Dead?', *Theology*, 72, 264–7.

Tiller, J. (1983), *A Strategy for the Church's Ministry*. London: Church Information Office Publishing.

Toon, P. (1984), 'Preserving Medieval Churches', *Theology*, 87, 110–13.

Towler, R. and Coxon, A.P.M. (1979), *The Fate of the Anglican Clergy*. London: Macmillan.

United Reformed Church (1986), *Stepping Forward: A Scheme for Youth Work in Rural Areas*. London: United Reformed Church.

van de Weyer, R. (1986), *Wickwyn: A Vision for the Future*. London: SPCK.

van de Weyer, R. (1991), *The Country Church: A Guide for the Renewal of Rural Christianity*. London: Dartman, Longman and Todd.

West, F. (1960), *The Country Parish To-day and To-morrow*. London: SPCK.

Wignall, P. (1982), *Taking Custody of the Future*. Oxford: Oxford Institute for Church and Society.

Winter, M. and Short, C. (1993), 'Believing and Belonging: Religion in Rural England', *British Journal of Sociology*, 44, 635–51.